SILENT COUP

Confronting the Big Business Takeover of Canada

TONY CLARKE

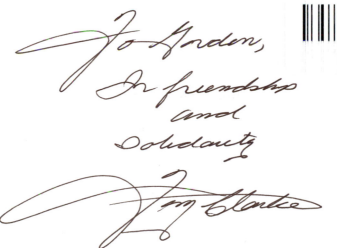

D0219517

co-published by

Canadian Centre for Policy Alternatives, and
James Lorimer & Company Ltd.

1997

Canadian Cataloguing in Publication Data

Clarke, Tony.

Silent Coup

Co-published by: Canadian Centre for Policy Alternatives. Includes bibliographical references.
ISBN 0-88627-923-2

1. International business enterprises -- Canada. 2. International business enterprises -- Political aspects -- Canada. 3. International business enterprises -- Social aspects -- Canada. 4. Big business - Canada. I. Canadian Centre for Policy Alternatives. II. Title.

HD2809.C53 1997   322´.3´ 0971   C97-950105-9

This publication was produced with the assistance of a grant from the Council of Canadians.

Printed and bound in Canada

Co-published by

The Canadian Centre for Policy Alternatives
804-251 Laurier Avenue West
Ottawa, Ontario   K1P 5J6

James Lorimer & Company Ltd., Publishers
35 Britain Street
Toronto, Ontario   M5A 1R7

Contents

ACKNOWLEDGEMENTS

As ALWAYS, MANY PEOPLE have contributed directly or indirectly to making this project possible, some of whom I have thanked personally while others are acknowledged in the chapter notes. In particular, I want to express here a deep sense of gratitude to Maude Barlow for her unflagging inspiration, advice and encouragement in making this book a reality; and to Ed Finn for his steadfast commitment to the basic theme of this project, along with his expert advice and editing skills.

As well, my thanks and appreciation to Jim Turk and Bruce Campbell for their constant encouragement in the development of this project, and their feedback on the manuscript. I want to express my appreciation to the Council of Canadians and the Canadian Centre for Policy Alternatives for providing the resources needed for this project, and to Jim Lorimer for agreeing to co-publish the book. And my thanks here to Diane Touchette for her professional expertise in doing the layout and design for this project.

I also wish to acknowledge several international colleagues who have helped me wrestle with many of the ideas and issues that lie at the heart of this book, including John Cavanagh, Sara Larrain, David Korten, Vandana Shiva, Richard Grossman, Lori Wallach, Martin Khor, Jerry Mander, Ward Morehouse, and Colin Hines.

In addition, there are several other colleagues here in Canada who share a similar vision and who are doing important work on the issues addressed in this book, including David Robinson, Colleen Fuller, David Langille, Diana Ralph, Murray Dobbin, Heather-jane Robertson, James Winter, Joyce Nelson, John Dillon, Kathleen Connors, Hassan Yussef, Mary Boyd, and Jim Grieshaber-Otto.

Finally, a special word of thanks to my family—my wife Carol and our children, Tanya and Chris—who not only continue to stand by me in this life-long struggle but are also finding that their own lives are increasingly affected by the forces and issues addressed in this book. ❧

PREFACE

IN EARLY DECEMBER, 1994, U.S. President Bill Clinton hosted a gala event in the ballroom of the Miami Hilton Hotel to commemorate the first Summit of the Americas on the expansion of free trade throughout the hemisphere. Thirty-two heads of state from throughout North and South America, including Canada's Jean Chrétien, were on hand to celebrate the occasion with Clinton. Also present were the chief executive officers of some of the largest corporations in the U.S., or for that matter, the entire world.

Just as the festivities drew to a close, two colleagues of mine, who happened to be journalists from Mexico, spotted David Rockefeller, the president and CEO of Chase Manhattan Bank in New York, who has had a long track record of personal working relationships with U.S. presidents and other powerful political figures elsewhere in the world. Approaching him, they asked: "Mr. Rockefeller, you were present back in the 1960s during President Kennedy's Alliance for Progress summit with the leaders of Latin America. Can you tell us what, if anything, has changed since then?"

"Well," he replied, "back then business leaders like myself were more or less sitting on the sidelines watching the negotiations unfold. But now we're sitting in the driver's seat and writing many of the documents ourselves."

Rockefeller's calm statement was a startling reminder of what many of us had experienced here in Canada during the prolonged fight over the North American Free Trade Agreement. As the former chair of the Action Canada Network, a national coalition of labour and social organizations which had helped mobilize public opposition to the Mulroney government's free trade deals, I had been asked to go to Miami to monitor what was happening at the Summit of the Americas and to meet with representatives of social movements from other countries.

What struck me most about Rockefeller's remarks at that time was the realization that, in many ways, we had let big business

off the hook in our seven-year struggle against free trade. Between 1987 and 1993, one of the largest social movements ever
assembled in this country came together to fight this battle. We
knew full well that the Business Council on National Issues, composed of the largest domestic and foreign-owned corporations in
Canada, had been the driving force behind the free trade deal
with the U.S. We even labelled it the "corporate agenda" in our
campaigns. But our strategies and tactics did not measure up to
our analysis.

Instead of targeting and unmasking the corporate players
who had developed the free trade agenda, we focused virtually
all of our resources and energies on tackling the Mulroney government alone. While we managed to force a national election on
the issue in 1988, and even turned public opinion around to the
point where the majority of Canadians voted against free trade,
the Mulroney Conservatives still swept back into power.

In the years that followed, the resistance against the Mulroney
government continued to build around a range of issues and struggles related to the free trade battle—the deficit, jobs, social programs, health care, immigration, the constitution, unemployment
insurance—to the point where Mulroney eventually resigned.
Meanwhile, the BCNI and its big business cohorts were working
behind the scenes preparing for the inevitable transition to a
Chrétien-led Liberal government. When the Liberals took over
Parliament Hill by storm in the 1993 election, reducing the mighty
Conservatives to a rump of two in the House of Commons, they
immediately abandoned their long-standing opposition to the
Mulroney free trade agenda by ratifying NAFTA and reneging
on many of the social promises they made in their Red Book
election platform.

In effect, the corporate agenda was alive and well in Ottawa,
with the BCNI still firmly in the driver's seat.

As I reflected on these and related developments, it became
more and more clear that, as a country, we were moving into a
new political era in the twilight years of the 20th century. To be
sure, corporations, both Canadian-based and foreign-owned, have
always played a powerful role in shaping public policy directions in Canada. But in the new global economy, free trade agreements like NAFTA had become nothing less than charters of rights
and freedoms for transnational corporations.

Coupled with the measures adopted over the past 10 years or
so to radically reduce government intervention and regulation of

the economy and to sell off public enterprises, the new free trade regimes have served to greatly enhance the power of transnational corporations over that of governments and nation states. Through these new institutional mechanisms, the power wielded by corporations in determining public policy directions has become much more pervasive, systemic and decisive. In short, we are now living in a new political era of corporate rule. Moreover, these new political realities, in turn, have profound implications for the model and strategies used by citizens' movements to bring about democratic social change.

If this was an accurate reading of the signs of the times, then the question arose as to how citizens' movements could adapt to these hard new realities. It is probably fair to say that there was a higher degree of political literacy in Canada about corporations and the power they wield 25 years ago than there is today. Back then, the press and air waves were filled with lively debates about foreign ownership. Finance Minister Walter Gordon had commissioned Mel Watkins to produce a provocative study on the subject. George Grant had stirred the political mood of the country with his *Lament for a Nation*, and Kari Levitt followed later with her eye-opening portrayal of the *Silent Surrender* of Canada to the multinational corporations. Wallace Clement's work on *The Canadian Corporate Elite* and *Continental Corporate Power* helped to further widen and deepen these debates.

In more recent years. however, there has been surprisingly little analysis done on the political influence of modern corporations, let alone public discussion and debate about what to do about it. In short, there is an urgent need to develop new tools to improve political literacy about the power being exercised by corporations over governments today, and what this has to say about democratic struggles for social change in the new global economy.

This is what *Silent Coup* is meant to do. Part One looks at the *past* to understand how the corporate takeover was accomplished. Chapter 1—**Corporate Canada**—traces the story of how big business developed a game plan and organized a series of campaigns to take strategic control over key areas of public policy-making in Ottawa, while Chapter 2—**Global Managers**—shows how these developments coincide with and are reinforced by the expanding powers of transnational corporations and the new forces of economic globalization.

Part Two looks at the *present* to identify the nature and mechanisms of corporate rule in Canada today. Chapter 3—**National Surrender**—describes how the Chrétien government collaborated with its new corporate masters and abandoned most of its Red Book promises, while Chapter 4—**Corporate Rule**—goes on to outline the nature of the corporate state in Ottawa and how it now operates in governing the country.

Part Three looks at the *future* to develop a new politics for citizen movements. Chapter 5—**Citizens' Agenda**—explores how citizens' movements could develop campaign strategies around key policy struggles by targeting and unmasking the political machinery of corporations on several battlefronts over the next five years. Chapter 6—**Democratic Control**—outlines some components of an alternative political platform for rebuilding our economy and society by re-establishing democratic control over corporations in the long term.

The nature of the coup d'état that is described here differs from the conventional political coup. The corporate takeover of Canada did not occur through a sudden and dramatic series of events. Instead, it was quietly engineered in a gradual, step-by-step fashion over a period of 20 years. Although not carried out by military or openly revolutionary methods, it was nonetheless a hostile takeover. Nor will it be argued that this coup was the product of a conspiracy. While highly calculated plans were certainly made and carried out to capture key policy-making areas of governance, these were not necessarily done in a clandestine manner. Moreover, the moves made by the corporate élite were in keeping with the logic of capitalism itself.

It should also be understood that the story of this corporate takeover is primarily portrayed here in terms of broad strokes and trends. There is no intention of either highlighting one pivotal event, or targeting one individual villain, or disclosing one smoking gun. That is a task for investigative journalists, and there is a whole field here waiting to be tilled. Instead, the intent is to focus on the "big picture," recognizing that more detailed case studies need to follow.

This raises the question of why it is important to **confront** the big business takeover of Canada. The simple fact is that the vast majority of Canadians are living in a state of denial when it comes to the new political realities of corporate rule.

Deep down, most people in this country sense that there is something wrong with our political system and the way it is working—or failing to work. They know that the politicians they send to Ottawa to represent them—especially if they belong to the governing party—change their priorities when they are sworn into office. The voters may even be aware that government actions are heavily influenced these days by corporate interests. But few people go so far as to say that the governments we elect have become, in effect, the puppets of big business. Indeed, most would probably deny such a claim.

This mental block obstructs an appropriate response. To confront a political reality, one must first become conscious of it. This, in turn, requires not only an open mind, but a new way of looking at how this country is now being run—a new set of lenses to focus and sharpen our perceptive abilities. It is the purpose of this book to provide Canadians with the lenses they need to stop denying the new political reality and begin confronting it.

At the same time, there is a need for citizens' movements to develop new capacities, strategies and tools to overturn the political coup that has taken place. In particular, attention is given here to developing both short-term and long-term plans of action aimed at dismantling the mechanisms of corporate rule and instituting new forms of democratic control. To move in this direction, citizens' movements in this country will need to give priority to rebuilding their organizational capacities and retooling their campaign strategies.

In addition to the challenges and proposals outlined in the last two chapters, the appendices contain a set of "corporate research tools" and "campaign strategy tools." These are tools that I hope will be helpful to both individuals and groups who want to curb the corporate power that is now determining (if not dictating) the economic, social and environmental priorities of governments, both in Ottawa and in our provincial capitals.

Although the focus of this work is on the corporate takeover of the federal government and what can be done about it, many of the insights and options can be applied to citizen action campaigns directed to provincial and even municipal governments. Some readers may be inclined to assess what follows as an exercise in indiscriminate "corporation-bashing." After all, they will say, there are "good" as well as "bad" corporations, and big as well as small ones, and it's important to make these distinctions. This is true. But this is not a book about good vs. bad corporate citizenship. Nor is the net being cast here meant to cover all corporations. What this book deals with is the way in which large corporations—most of them transnational—have been able to seize political as well as economic power in this country, and in the process substitute corporate rule for true democracy. In examining the origins, scope and consequences of the big business takeover of Canada, it matters little what size any one corporation may be, or whether its business practices may be considered moral or ethical. What we are addressing here are the new political and economic realities of corporate rule, and the radically different kind of society they are creating in this country.

In the final analysis, the dynamics of corporate rule today demand a new kind of politics. For what is at stake is nothing less than a fight to restore fundamental democratic rights and freedoms in this country. The challenge that lies before us today is to revitalize the democratic left by building a new political movement. I hope this work can make a small contribution by encouraging citizen activists to take up this challenge. ❧

1. CORPORATE CANADA

Hey! Who's really running this country, anyway?

...Well, I don't know about you, but I can't figure out what's coming down on us. I thought we got rid of the Mulroney Conservatives because they were tearing the country apart with their free trade, GST and a whole slew of social cutbacks. But the Chrétien Liberals seem to be doing the same thing, only faster!

...Yeah! And on top of that they got themselves elected to another four years of government in Ottawa.

...Remember all those promises we heard during the 1993 federal election campaign from that Red Book of theirs—about jobs! jobs! jobs! and protecting our social programs, our Medicare and the environment? Whatever happened to all those promises? It's as if we elect politicians to do one thing, only to find out that once in power they do the opposite.

...Hmm. People used to say that Brian Mulroney's government marched to the tune of big business. They called it the "corporate agenda" or something like that. You know, "whatever's good for the big corporations is good for Canada" kind'a thing. Well, as far as I can see, Jean Chrétien and his gang are doing the same thing, only more so.

...Say, maybe you've just put your finger on something here. Maybe the politicians we elect to represent us in Ottawa aren't really in charge, after all. Or not as much as we think they are. Maybe it's really the big banks and corporations who are calling the shots in Ottawa these days.

...I'm beginning to think that's the only way to make any sense out of what's happening in this country. But, if we're right, then when did this all begin? How long has it been going on? And how come we didn't know about it before?

Business Blues

THE STORY OF THE BIG business takeover of Canada does not begin under the political leadership of Jean Chrétien, nor even Brian Mulroney. The origins of this story date back to well over 20 years ago. At that time, it was Corporate Canada that was crying the blues about what was happening to big business and the direction in which the country was heading. In the 1972 federal election, the New Democrats, under the leadership of David Lewis, mobilized widespread public support for their campaign against the "corporate welfare bums." When the votes were counted, the Liberals under Pierre Trudeau were reduced to a minority government, with the NDP holding the balance of power. Thereafter, public confidence in big business slipped even further.

As York University's Jim Laxer once described it, Corporate America was also singing the blues. Whereas opinion polls in the late 1960s showed major U.S. corporations enjoying a high degree (58%) of public confidence, by 1974 public support of business had plummeted to 29%. The main reason for this dramatic slump in public confidence was the behaviour of the giant oil companies during the 1973 energy crisis. As millions of Americans and Canadians braced themselves for a quadrupling of oil prices by the OPEC countries and long line-ups for rationed gasoline, the news media told about oil tankers waiting offshore for the price to go up further before completing their shipments. And then, while the economy slipped further and further into a deep recession, Exxon and the other majors reported rising profits. In short, as most people suffered gas shortages and sharp oil prices in the winter of 1973, the major oil companies were laughing all the way to the bank.

For big business in both the U.S. and Canada, the episode became a political nightmare. Not only were people losing their trust and confidence in corporations, but serious doubts were being cast on profit-making and the free market system itself. To prevent further damage, big business went on the offensive. The business press, including the *Wall Street Journal in the U.S.* and the *Globe & Mail in Canada*, began carrying stories and editorials portraying the oil companies as victims of unfair and ill-informed attacks. Turning up the heat, the petroleum giants decided to bypass the mainline media and take their message directly to the people through advocacy or political advertising.

Millions of dollars were poured into a massive advertising blitz designed to promote the oil giants' side of the story and to safeguard the free market system. In the end, the campaign succeeded in dissipating people's anger and restoring public confidence. But the scenario also showed how powerful corporations can be in dramatically altering public opinion through their own political advertising.

In Canada, big business began to dig itself in for the long haul. For most members of the corporate élite, the post-war experiment of a social welfare state in Canada had gone too far. From the corridors of Bay Street, a growing chorus of complaints surfaced in the mid-1970s over "too-high" corporate taxes, rising public deficits, social spending costs, "bloated" government bureaucracies, and the entanglements of regulatory red tape. The straw that broke the camel's back was the introduction of wage and price controls in 1975 by the Liberal government under Pierre Trudeau, which was seen by business leaders as a massive intrusion by the government into the free market economy.

While explaining his government's actions during a year-end interview with CTV in 1975, Trudeau admitted that the controls amounted to "a massive intervention in the decision-making power of the economic groups, and it's telling Canadians that we haven't been able to make it work, the free market system."

More than any other single event, recalls Laxer, Trudeau's remarks served to undermine public confidence in business leaders and the market system. They were also seen as a threat to resort to even more government intervention in the future as a means of dealing with the failures of the market and the private sector. It is no secret, of course, that relations between Ottawa and big business in Canada deteriorated substantially during the early years of the Trudeau era. The prime minister's aloof and arrogant style often angered corporate executives, almost as much as it did labour leaders. For Trudeau—at least in his first few terms in office—big business was just another special interest group in the dynamic interplay of national forces. But, for the corporate élite, this was an insult. The time had come, they now decided, to launch their own counter-offensive in support of the private sector and the free market system.

At this point, two figures emerged to lead the charge of Corporate Canada. The first was W.O. Twaits, the CEO of Imperial Oil, who had spent most of his career advocating the case of big business to the federal government and the Canadian public. Frequently, Imperial Oil's jet aircraft was sighted at Uplands Airport in Ottawa, signifying Twait's relentless efforts to lobby the country's political leaders on behalf of big business. At the time, Liberal cabinet minister Eric Kierans described Twaits as the most powerful man in Canada.

The second corporate giant was Alfred Powis, the CEO of Noranda Mines, who was considered at the time to be the most persuasive representative of big business. Powis rose through the corporate ranks with mercurial speed, taking over the top job at Noranda at the youthful age of 38. By the mid-1970s, Powis had reached the zenith of his career, wielding an extraordinary range of influence, not only in the business community but in the corridors of Ottawa as well.

The opening salvoes came in early 1975, when Powis called on business leaders to launch a vigorous defence of free enterprise in Canada. In a major address on February 3 of that year before the Canadian Club in Toronto, Powis warned that public attacks on the private sector had gone too far. "The private sector," he declaimed, "is increasingly subject to uninformed, but strident and highly publicized attacks which seem to have a pervasive impact on government policies." He went on to describe, from his perspective, the kinds of constraints that governments had imposed on the operations of the private sector in Canada. As a result, Powis warned, the vitality of the business community "is steadily and insidiously being sapped."

For his part, Twaits tended to be a little more graphic, but no less passionate, in his defence of Canada's free market economy. Speaking at a Tory party conference, Twaits compared the country's economy to that of a cow that had been milked dry. According to this scenario, the private sector was symbolized by a bull who had lost interest in performing his natural duties. The name of the game now, Twaits suggested, was to find all sorts of incentives that would make the cow more attractive so that the bull would be reinvigorated enough to resume the performance of his reproductive duties. Twaits' own list of "foreplay" incentives included a freeze on social spending, restrictions on new government borrowing, reduced unemployment insurance premiums, lower corporate taxes, and the removal of foreign investment reviews.

Shortly after Trudeau ruminated about the failures of the free market system in his 1975 year-end interview, Powis launched another counter-offensive. On February 25, 1976, Powis went after the prime minister in a speech to a general meeting of the Mining Association of Canada. Improvements in the Canadian economy, he charged, "cannot be achieved in the context of self-fulfilling prophecies regarding the free market, in which the private sector is first handcuffed and then subjected to even greater control because its performance is unsatisfactory."

For both Powis and Twaits, the traditional post-war compromise between the public sector and the private sector was no longer working properly. The trend towards greater and greater government intervention in the market system had to be stopped and reversed. Instead, big business and the private sector had to be freed up to create wealth.

Market Theories

The crusade of Powis and Twaits was further fuelled by a resurgence of neo-classical economic theories in defense of the free market system. Since the Great Depression, industrialized countries like Canada had largely followed the theories outlined by the celebrated British economist John Maynard Keynes, in building what we now call the social welfare state. Keynes argued that governments had a key role to play as a balance wheel evening out boom-and-bust cycles in market-based economies. In order to ensure that the market better reflected the public interest, Keynes said that governments had an obligation to intervene and regulate the economy, making use of the techniques of deficit financing to sustain a more even transition between upturns and downturns.

By the 1970s, however, Keynes' theories were being fiercely and constantly attacked by the neo-classical school of economics, led by the newly acclaimed University of Chicago economist, Milton Friedman.

Friedman was a passionate exponent of 19th-century economics, with its undaunted faith in the marketplace and competitive enterprise. During the early 1970s, he emerged as a vocal opponent of both government bureaucracy and of state interference in the economy. Drawing upon libertarian ideals, Friedman argued that it was the marketplace, not government, that had the capacity to respond automatically and sensitively to the tastes and wishes of the people, thereby creating what he called "unanimity without conformity." Governments, he maintained, impose decisions on people from above and therefore represent, at best, a "conformity without unanimity," or, in other words, the tyranny of an uncertain majority. To allow the dynamism of the private sector to flourish, Friedman held that the role of government in the economy should be reduced to being no more than an umpire.

By the 1970s, it was clear that the Keynesian solutions for economic recession were not working, as unemployment, inflation and uncertainty continued to rise. Friedman seized the moment to launch a series of intellectual attacks against government interventionists. From Franklin Roosevelt's New Deal in the 1930s to Lyndon Johnson's Great Society in the 1960s, Friedman put together a hard-hitting critique of big government in America with all its bureaucratic inefficiencies and insensitivities. The only real alternative, Friedman argued, was the restoration of the free market system, with its own smooth functioning, responsive and competitive mechanisms. To allow the free market to work in this way, however, government intervention and red tape had to be substantially restrained, if not eliminated altogether.   At the same time, Friedman also advanced his own package of economic proposals designed to reduce government intervention and regulation in favour of a more free market economy. For example, he called for the elimination of corporate income taxes altogether and proposed that a flat, non-graduated personal income tax be introduced, with no loopholes. Under this system, a negative tax would be adopted to provide lower-income people with a cash payment which, in turn, meant that most other forms of social assistance would be removed.

He urged governments to stop applying the Keynesian strategy of using deficit financing to ease the economy through periods of high unemployment, and to remove artificial mechanisms to maintain price controls for such commodities as oil. He also promoted the movement toward free trade in the global economy, the adoption of trade restraints to weaken the bargaining powers of large unions, and the elimination of minimum wage legislation.

Friedman's vigorous defence of the free market system against government intervention soon took on the status of a new orthodoxy. In Canada, as well as the United States, his theories and doctrines were taken up by most university departments of economics, as well as schools of business. To a somewhat beleaguered business community, Friedman's market theories were clearly seen to be both a blessing and a bonanza. For here was a set of economic theories that put the blame for hard times squarely on big government rather than big business. Here was a set of economic theories that gave big business the intellectual credibility and legitimacy to build public support and confidence for an assault on government intervention and the social welfare state. The task now was to make sure that Friedman's market theories were adopted by government bureaucrats.

In Canada, the economic think tanks and advisory bodies provided the starting place for the infiltration of Friedman's theories in government bureaucracies. When the NDP under Dave Barrett came to power in British Columbia, a small group of powerful B.C. corporate executives led by Pat Doyle of MacMillan Bloedel met in 1975 and discussed the formation of a propaganda think-tank to combat the "socialists." As author Murray Dobbin explains, they brought in Michael Walker, a Newfoundlander working for the Bank of Canada, who told his backers: "If you really want to change the world, you have to change the ideological fabric of the world."

Walker went on from there to establish the Fraser Institute, an agency explicitly based on the free market theories of Milton Friedman. Focusing on the promotion of market values and cultural change, Walker and his associates at the Fraser developed a multi-faceted program that included writing anti-government and free market articles for weekly newspapers, engaging university students in discussions about free market philosophy, and distributing free market studies to legislators across the country.

However, it was the adoption of Friedmanite theories by established mainstream economic advisory bodies like the C.D. Howe Institute and the Economic Council of Canada that began to turn heads in the Ottawa bureaucracy, as well as several of the provincial capitals. During this period, the president of the C.D. Howe Institute, Carl Beigie, emerged as one of the country's chief economic gurus in the fight against increased government intervention in the economy. On almost a daily basis, Beigie made pronouncements in the business press, warning against rising budget deficits and the threats of increasing protectionism, and calling for free trade with the United States and a new role for government.

In effect, the C.D. Howe Institute became the staging ground for the resurgence of free market theories in official circles within Canada. To be sure, the Fraser Institute was known to be Canada's No. 1 cheerleader for Friedmanite doctrines. But it was the

Howe Institute, which had become recognized as Canada's most prestigious economic think-tank under Beigie's direction, that paved the way for legitimizing Friedman's market theories in government circles and the mainstream press. Later, it would come as no surprise to discover that both the Howe and the Fraser Institutes were heavily funded by some of Canada's major corporations and banks.

Ottawa Bureaucracy

In the mid-1970s, the Trudeau government was largely influenced by the work of Canadian-born Harvard economist John Kenneth Galbraith, who was deeply rooted in the Keynesian tradition. According to Galbraith's analysis, the modern market economy has become dominated by large transnational corporations which are able to control costs, prices, labour, and materials through their capacity for long-term planning and minimization of risks. Since these corporate giants are able to generate their own capital internally, they can ignore government efforts to fine-tune the economy through traditional monetary and fiscal policies. As a result, Galbraith argued, attempts to fight inflation and curb the cost-price spiral had become ineffectual. With the market system in the traditional sense no longer operative, Galbraith recommended that governments bring large corporations and unions into line by introducing permanent controls over prices and wages. It was primarily Galbraith's advice that led Trudeau in 1975 to bring in wage and price controls, declaring that the market system no longer works.

Galbraith's prescriptions quickly became the target of the former federal deputy finance minister, Simon Reisman. Described as "a tough-willed, entertaining, and utterly frank individual," Reisman developed a long and colourful career in the civil service. At the height of his career, he became Secretary of the Treasury in the late 1960s and then went on to become deputy minister of finance until 1974. In this last post, he became very close to then Finance Minister John Turner. In 1975, however, Reisman left the Ottawa bureaucracy with great fanfare to become an independent economic consultant. At this point, Reisman was in the ideal position to champion the cause of big business by taking on the Galbraithian mindset in the Trudeau government.

When Trudeau announced his mandatory wage and price

controls in the fall of 1975, the former deputy minister launched a counter-offensive against permanent government intervention in the economy. Reisman chose a conference sponsored by the *Financial Post* in October 1976 as the occasion to deliver his broadsides against Galbraith. He repudiated Galbraith's analysis, declaring that there was no evidence to support his claims that giant corporations now occupy a major segment of the market economy, and that "the degree of corporate power—and hence oligopolistic power—has increased significantly over the past several decades in either the United States or Canada and thereby altered the basic structure of the economy."

Instead, Reisman argued, the market system is alive and well. The real culprit responsible for persistent inflation, he insisted, was not the big corporations, but big government. He went on to identify three factors: the massive increase in government spending in Canada between 1965 and 1975; the 1971 revisions in the unemployment program "which established the most generous and open-handed benefit provisions to be found anywhere in the world;" and the spread of militant unionism among public sector workers which had set the pace for rising wage settlements in Canada.

Yet, curiously enough, Reisman was doing an about-face with his attack on the Trudeau government's wage and price controls. Following his departure from the finance department, Reisman had initially urged the adoption of mandatory wage and price controls. But in his *Financial Post* conference speech, he tried to explain away this contradiction by saying that he had only recommended controls "for a limited time and for a limited purpose." It was now clear that the former deputy finance minister had taken up the cause of big business in his frontal attack against Galbraith.

Adopting a Friedmanite position, Reisman concluded his speech with a ringing defence of the free market system: "... More important than the damage to economic efficiency is the loss of freedom which a control system entails ... Their permanent use would deliver a vital blow to the very innards of our free society. Indeed, the ultimate result would, in my view, be an authoritarian system ruled by force."

Reisman's attack against Galbraith's theories had a significant and lasting impact on the Ottawa bureaucracy. After all, a former deputy minister of finance had not only publicly challenged Galbraith as the Trudeau government's chief economic

guru, but had also given legitimacy to the free market theories of
Milton Friedman. Space was now open for bureaucrats of a
Friedmanite persuasion to gain a toehold on public policy-making in Ottawa. This was essential if big business was going to be
ultimately successful in its campaign against government intervention in the economy and its defence of the free market system.

Meanwhile, Corporate Canada had been wrestling with a related set of problems on how to develop a more effective voice
in Ottawa. It was clear that the traditional business lobbying operations had become ineffective. Neither the Canadian Manufacturers' Association nor the Canadian Federation of Chambers of
Commerce were doing an adequate job of representing the interests of big business. At times they were too rhetorical in pushing
for narrow special interests, and they lacked the capacity to develop clear policy options with which the Ottawa bureaucracy
could interact. Representing an amorphous constituency composed of big, medium and small enterprises, the CMA and the
CCC had become "too diffuse." What's more, the CEOs of the
major corporations no longer played an active role in these associations. As Michael Pitfield, then Secretary of the Cabinet, put
it, there was no organization that could reflect the interests of the
major corporations, let alone the broad range of interests in the business community at large, in the national corridors of government.

As well, the Ottawa bureaucracy itself had undergone a radical overhaul during the Trudeau period. Following the 1968 cabinet reforms, decision-making power became further centralized
in the executive, relegating individual parliamentarians to a less
influential role. Opportunities for directly influencing individual
ministers also diminished as a more collegial system for cabinet
decision-making was adopted. At the same time, the increasing
complexities of government at all levels required that more and
more power be concentrated in the hands of deputy ministers and
their senior civil servants. For all these and related reasons, the
time had come for big business to develop its own association
with the appropriate policy-making apparatus and lobbying machinery.

At the same time, the Trudeau government realized there was
a need for a more coherent business presence in Ottawa's policy-
making circles. Recognizing what it called "the need for a closer
business-government interface," a federal government task force
was set up in 1976 under the chairmanship of Roy MacLaren,
then an advertising agency executive in Toronto (who later be-

came Minister of Trade in the Chrétien government). In its report, the MacLaren task force recommended that a business council be established in order that there would be a more coherent business presence in national affairs and that "a systematic management of the relationship between public and private sectors" could be put in place. The report further emphasized that "an effective forum for business and government" was essential in order "to consider the economic challenges facing the country" and "to provide a better shared perspective on where the economy is going and suitable methods to sustain a dialogue about it."

Corporate Alliance

By the time the MacLaren task force was completing its report, Corporate Canada was putting the finishing touches on a new alliance. Beginning in 1975, the country's top business leaders held a series of meetings behind closed doors to map out their plan of action. Their task was to create a new, streamlined and effective business lobby. In terms of a model to follow, they took their cues from their counterparts in the U.S. who, in 1972, formed the Business Round Table composed of the chief executive officers from the largest corporations and banks in that country. Since the Round Table was made up of CEOs only, it quickly surpassed the older business lobbies in the U.S. as the most effective voice for Corporate America. Similarly, Canada's top business leaders decided that they too wanted a new association comprising the CEOs of the largest corporations and banks in the country. Furthermore, membership would be by invitation only.

The new alliance of big business interests was launched in April, 1977. Called the Business Council on National Issues (BCNI), this new, highly prestigious coalition moved quickly to establish its identity in Ottawa and the country at large. The two founding chairs of the BCNI were none other than W.O. Twaits, who had just retired as CEO of Imperial Oil, and Alf Powis, the venerable and still powerful CEO of Noranda. Within a few months, the BCNI membership encompassed the CEOs of no less than 140 of Canada's major corporations and banks, representing over one-third of all private capital in the country.

Besides Powis and Twaits, the BCNI's active leadership then was made up of several prestigious members of Corporate Canada, including Earle McLaughlin of the Royal Bank, Paul Desmarais of the Power Corporation, Jack Armstrong of Imperial Oil, and Thomas Bell of the Abitibi Paper Company.

With the launch of the BCNI, big business served notice that it was striking out on its own. The brakes had to be put on both government intervention in the economy and the expansion of the social welfare state. As Twaits described it in an interview with the *Toronto Star* later that year, it was high time that both the government and the public "gave up the popular game of beating the hell out of business.

"When David Lewis was conducting his campaign about corporate ripoffs," Powis said in the same interview, "there was no credible, cohesive voice of business." But, with the formation of the BCNI, we have "the voice of big, or bigger, business." For both Powis and Twaits, now was the time to get the message across to politicians and the public that Canada was a free enterprise country. In effect, this new blue ribbon corporate alliance was sending out a signal that the old post-war political accommodations between capital and labour and between the private and public sectors was about to come to an end.

From the outset, the BCNI was designed to be a powerful alliance. Its membership list included the presidents or CEOs of the country's eight leading chartered banks, the 10 top insurance companies, and no less than 18 oil and pipeline corporations. Brand name oil and gas companies like Shell, Imperial Oil, Gulf and Texaco were represented by their CEOs on the BCNI, along with their counterparts from big manufacturing firms such as Ford, Kodak and CIL. Canadian transnational enterprises like Inco, Alcan, Stelco, and Trizec worked side by side with U.S. giants like IBM, Xerox, Bechtel and ITT. Indeed, the BCNI was largely composed of corporations that followed the dictates of international capital. While foreign ownership of business remained high in Canada, there was now the added complication of increasing numbers of Canadian-owned companies becoming transnational enterprises in the emerging global economy. Indeed, the distinction between foreign and domestic corporations became increasingly blurred.

The BCNI net did not pull in all of Canada's blue chip corporate leaders. Family empire figures, for example, like the Reichmans, Bronfmans, Irvings and Thomsons do not sit at the BCNI table themselves. Instead, they were—and still are—indirectly represented on the Council through a network of corporations that are under their control. Nevertheless, the BCNI was carefully constructed so as to maintain a common front within the business community at large. Even though its formation was designed to eclipse the traditional business lobbies, the architects of the Council saw to it that the heads of the Canadian Chambers of Commerce, the Canadian Manufacturers' Association, and the Conseil du patronat were all included in the BCNI's policy-making body. While differences existed between the various corporate conglomerates, the glue that unified the Council's membership was a common political commitment to a free market economy, dominated by a dynamic private sector and very limited (if any) forms of government intervention and regulation.

To develop their platform for building a free market economy and dismantling the social welfare state in Canada, all the CEO members of the BCNI met behind closed doors every six months. Between these biennial plenary sessions, an inner circle of 21 members composed of one CEO representing each of the major economic sectors on the Council (e.g., agriculture, auto industry, financial institutions, petroleum industry, steel manufacturers, food processors, etc.), met to plot detailed strategies. Task forces were set up around a wide range of policy concerns, including national finances, international trade, corporate taxation, energy policy, social programs, natural resources, and foreign policy (to name but a few). Studies were commissioned from business consultant firms like Touche-Ross Associates and business research institutes like the C.D. Howe Institute on a range of economic and social policy issues that were of special interest to big business.

In advocating its platform, the BCNI carefully cultivated what political scientist David Langille describes as a non-adversarial and a non-confrontational style. This allowed the Business Council in its formative stages to clearly distinguish itself from groups like the Canadian Federation of Independent Business, which had developed a reputation for being "blow-hards." Instead, the BCNI started out attempting to work in partnership with Ottawa, adopting a quiet, low-key approach behind the scenes. What's more, the Council developed a strategic approach to policy-making that was deliberately pre-emptive or pro-active. Here, the BCNI's objective was always to "gain the edge" in the policy-making process, not only by defining the issues in their own terms, but upstaging the Ottawa bureaucracy by presenting it with a comprehensive package of analysis and recommendations. Above all, timing was a key factor—the ability to stay several steps ahead of the bureaucracy in developing policies. In adopting this strategic approach, big business would be in a position to establish the over-all framework and direction of economic and social policy-making in Ottawa.

The new corporate alliance also had substantial resources at its disposal when it came to developing its policy options and implementing its strategies. Not only did the BCNI have direct access to the top decision-makers in Canada's largest and most profitable corporations, but it could also draw upon the resources of corporate think-tanks like the C.D. Howe Institute. Indeed, most of the main corporate sponsors of the Howe were also members of the BCNI, including Air Canada, Alcan Aluminum, Bank of Montreal, Bank of Nova Scotia, Canadian Pacific, Great West Life, General Motors, London Life, MacMillan Bloedel, Noranda Mines, Power Corp., Royal Bank, Southam News, Shell Canada, Toronto-Dominion Bank, and George Weston Ltd.

Moreover, the fact that the alliance included news networks like Southam and media corporations like Power Corp., ensured that the message of big business would be communicated to the Canadian public. And while the BCNI was careful not to develop any formal or even informal connections with right-wing movements, it knew that its basic message would soon be echoed by networks like the National Citizens' Coalition.

In virtually no time at all, the BCNI emerged as the single most important and effective voice of Corporate Canada inside Ottawa. Not only did the country's top CEOs make their presence known in meetings with the prime minister's office and the Privy Council office, but also in several provincial capitals and in addresses to numerous business forums across the country. At first, the Council's work was managed by its initial president, William Archibold. But soon the BCNI would take on a higher public profile and a more active presence in Ottawa under the leadership of Thomas d'Aquino. As a former Trudeau advisor and international law specialist, d'Aquino knew the inner workings of the Ottawa bureaucracy, as well as the strategic interests and priorities of big business. With d'Aquino at the helm, it would not be long before the BCNI and its member CEOs would take control of the reins of governance in the nation's capital.

Round One

In the late 1970s, the BCNI began to mount a series of campaigns. The objective of these early campaigns was to create a climate in government policy-making in favour of both the de-regulation of the economy and the privatization of public enter-prises. The testing ground became the newly elected Conserva-tive government of Joe Clark. Under Clark's minority govern-ment of 1978-79, Finance Minister John Crosbie opened the door by introducing a variety of new measures designed to deregulate key sectors of the economy. Treasury Board Minister Sinclair Stevens followed suit by drawing up a target list of 401 Crown corporations and public enterprises to be put up for sale to the private sector.

At the same time, says Langille, the BCNI task force on com-petition policy, assisted by 25 legal counsel, virtually ended up rewriting the Combines Investigation Act and putting it in the hands of the government (complete with statutory amendments) a year before Ottawa planned to issue a discussion paper on the matter. As d'Aquino later commented, this was a sign of how the BCNI would operate in the future.

The re-election of the Trudeau Liberals, however, threw a monkey wrench into the plans of big business. Throughout the 1980 election campaign, the Liberals had campaigned on a plat-form of economic nationalism. Spurred on by the opposition New Democrats, a revitalized Trudeau government proceeded to en-act its new mandate by focusing attention on the task of revers-ing the already high levels of foreign ownership and control of the Canadian economy. The cornerstone of their platform was the controversial National Energy Program (NEP), which was aimed at increasing Canadian ownership of the petroleum indus-try in this country, from 30 per cent to 50 per cent by 1990. The objective here was to give Ottawa the tools it needed, not only to regain control over the vital energy sector which was seen as the centrepiece of the Canadian economy, but also to lay the ground for developing a national industrial strategy. In addition, the Lib-eral government planned new measures to strengthen the man-date and the powers of the Foreign Investment Review Agency (FIRA).

In response, the U.S. petroleum giants, aided by the newly elected administration of Ronald Reagan, organized a campaign of economic retaliation. Suddenly, new investment plans in Al-berta's oil patch were cancelled and steps were taken to prevent the use of U.S. oil rigs and other production equipment in Canada. In short, U.S. petroleum corporations like Exxon, Gulf, Texaco, Mobil, Amoco, and Chevron (to name the most prominent) had launched what amounted to a capital strike against Canada.

The new Reagan administration in Washington, which after all had come to power for the expressed purpose of eliminating obstacles to the free flow of investment and trade, trained its guns on both the NEP and FIRA. In no uncertain terms, the Reaganites soon made it clear that they wanted the NEP "buried" and FIRA "declawed." And when the NEP buy-out measures started to go into effect, Congress demanded more aggressive U.S. reaction before another Canadian government-controlled firm "picks the bones of a U.S. corporation."

The BCNI found itself in a Catch-22 situation. While the Business Council viewed Ottawa's NEP and FIRA plans as anathema to its free market agenda, some of its member corporations, including several independent petroleum companies and banks like the CIBC, stood to gain windfall profits from the NEP's buy-out measures. Compromised, the BCNI became somewhat sidelined in the early stages of the battle. But when Finance Minister Allan MacEachen signalled that the government was bowing to the massive U.S. pressure that had been mobilized, by announcing in his August budget of 1981 that the NEP would not be used as a model for the Canadianization of other industries, as originally planned, and that legislative action would not be taken to expand the mandate and powers of FIRA, the Business Council began to plan for a much more active role in the follow-up.

Anticipating a renewed battle when the federal pricing agreement with the Alberta government expired in 1985, Langille reports, the BCNI set up a task force on energy policy chaired by the then CEO of Imperial Oil, Donald McIvor. D'Aquino was sent out to hold one-on-one meetings with the key government players: Alberta Premier Peter Lougheed, Ontario Premier Bill Davis, and federal Energy Minister Jean Chretien. This was followed by a two-day summit meeting behind closed door at the Niagara Institute in Ontario in November 1983.

After another round of consultations, a second summit was held in June 1984, co-chaired by d'Aquino and McIvor. While government officials participated in this second summit, it was on an ex-officio basis. In effect, the final details of the new energy policy for Canada were mainly hammered out by the CEOs. The deal called for the virtual scrapping of the NEP, adoption of world prices, and an overhaul of corporate taxation.

Meanwhile, the Trudeau government had already signalled its desire for a truce with big business. After the 1982 cabinet shuffle which sent an embattled Marc Lalonde from Energy to replace MacEachen at Finance, tensions began to subside. Shortly after taking over the finance portfolio, Lalonde went to meet with BCNI leaders at d'Aquino's home in Rockliffe, where he allegedly made a peace pact with business leaders and promised them the government's cooperation and support in the future.

By this time, the Trudeau government was beleaguered by two fundamental problems with the economy: inflation (which had risen to a high of 12% before falling back to 6.6%), and unemployment (which had stalled at an official rate of 13% with an estimated two million jobless). Along with the C.D. Howe Institute, the BCNI had waged a vigorous campaign to keep the government's focus on fighting inflation rather than unemployment, arguing that keeping input costs and wage gains down was essential for big business to be competitive on world markets. Lalonde agreed and brought forward his 6-and-5 wage restraint program for "wrestling inflation to the ground." Not only was Lalonde's 6-and-5 program largely drafted on the basis of recommendations made to him by the BCNI, but he also appointed the CEO of Canadian Pacific, Ian Sinclair, along with Senator Keith Davey, to co-chair the program.

Round Two

Brian Mulroney's landslide victory at the polls in 1984 opened up new doors for Corporate Canada. A former American branch plant manager (with the Iron Ore Co. of Canada, a subsidiary of Hanna Mining of Cleveland, Ohio) had now become the chief executive officer of the Canadian state. Taking full advantage of the fact that the public had grown tired of the Trudeau Liberals, the Mulroney Conservatives swept into power with a strong mandate for economic renewal in Canada. The problem for the Mulroney team, once in office, was that they lacked the program needed to carry out their mandate. At this point, the BCNI was only too happy to oblige.

Shortly after being sworn into office, the new Tory cabinet was invited by the BCNI to an extensive briefing at a secluded retreat in the Gatineau hills. Highly distrustful of the Ottawa bureaucracy after decades of Liberal rule, Mulroney was only too happy to have the various BCNI policy task forces assist him in guiding his ship of state. At this point, the CEOs chairing the Council's task forces included Darcy McKeough of Union Gas on finance policy, Alf Powis of Noranda on trade policy, and Charles Baird of Inco and Sidney Jackson of Manulife on social policy.

One of the policy fronts for the BCNI in the early stages of the Mulroney government was tax reform. Ever since the Reagan administration had lowered corporate taxes in the U.S., big business had been calling on Ottawa to take similar action. With Michael Wilson, a trusted ally of Bay Street, as minister of finance, the BCNI seized the opportunity to put forward its own blueprint for overhauling the country's tax system. In exchange for a substantial lowering of the corporate tax rate, big business was prepared to forgo various tax concessions (including, if necessary, half the $500,000 capital gains exemption) and business subsidies (which cost the federal government an estimated $11 billion annually). But capital cost allowances, which allow corporations to write off the depreciation on their equipment and buildings, must be retained. The tax rate for high-income earners should also be reduced.

To make up for the shortfall in public revenues, the Council recommended that the tax rate be broadened by introducing a national sales tax, which became known as the GST. Wilson bought the entire BCNI tax package, made a few minor modifications, then implemented them piece by piece over the next few years.

As far as big business was concerned, however, the No. 1 priority on the national agenda during the Mulroney government's first term in office was to secure a bilateral free trade agreement with the United States. After all, 200 Canadian corporations, most of them members of the BCNI, accounted for 90 per cent of all trade between Canada and the U.S., and more than 95 per cent of all foreign direct investment in the two countries. But, while Corporate Canada had become heavily dependent on the U.S. market, their U.S. interests became less secure, with American producers launching "unfair" trade actions against Canadian exports and Washington threatening to take tougher trade and investment actions against Canada.

In order to secure guaranteed access to the U.S. market, the BCNI and its member corporations began to map out a plan for a comprehensive free trade agreement between the two countries. A free trade treaty would also compel Canadian governments to adhere to a formal set of economic rules. Canada's economy would become more harmonized with the business-friendly U.S.

economy, limiting forms of government intervention and regulation while curbing social program costs and workers' wage demands.

First, however, big business needed to sell free trade to the new Mulroney government. During the 1983 Tory leadership race, Mulroney had declared emphatically: "Don't talk to me about free trade... Free trade is a threat to Canadian sovereignty." Nevertheless, the BCNI began working behind the scenes as early as 1982 to convince economic and political élites on both sides of the border to start free trade negotiations. In 1983, d'Aquino went to Washington to actively promote the idea with the U.S. Business Round Table and the Reagan administration, which had already made noises about creating a North American free market. That same year, the BCNI joined with the Chambers of Commerce in a common effort to sway the business community away from its traditional protectionism in favour of a free trade pact with the U.S. Shortly after the 1984 federal election, a 45-member business task force was set up by the BCNI "to coordinate a responsible Canadian business approach to the Canada-U.S. trade issue at a time when the policy and the options were far from clearly decided on the part of the Canadian government."

By 1985, Brian Mulroney was singing a different tune, this time arm-in-arm with Ronald Reagan at the Shamrock Summit in Quebec City, where the two committed their countries to begin negotiations on the first comprehensive free trade pact in the world. Mulroney's commitment to free trade negotiations was further fortified by the release of the report of the Macdonald Commission, the Royal Commission that had been set up by Trudeau to study Canada's future economic development prospects. Under the chairmanship of Donald Macdonald (former Liberal finance minister and later Bay Street lawyer), the Commission had made free trade with the U.S. the centrepiece of its three-volume report on Canada's economic future.

With no guarantees as to its outcome, Macdonald himself called free trade "a leap of faith." As it turned out, the Macdonald Commission's recipe was not much more than a carbon copy of the presentation that the BCNI had made to the Commission's cross-country hearings. By 1986, Mulroney had appointed none other than Simon Reisman himself to lead the negotiations for a continental free trade deal.

The battle for free trade quickly became a full-time preoccupation for d'Aquino and the Business Council. To generate more widespread public support and to offset growing Canadian opposition to a free trade deal with the U.S., the BCNI established what was called the Alliance for Trade and Job Opportunities in April 1987. The new Alliance was co-chaired by both Peter Lougheed and Donald Macdonald himself. Not surprisingly, the Alliance's membership turned out to be corporations and banks which were also members of the Business Council. The economic weight they mustered behind the Alliance was considerable. Alcan, Noranda and the Royal Bank put up $400,000 each, while another $3 million was raised by dozens of other companies, including 19 that were foreign-owned.

The Alliance also worked closely with its counterpart in the U.S., the American Coalition for Trade Expansion with Canada, representing some 600 corporations and business associations. Through their Canadian subsidiaries, a significant number of U.S. corporations also became directly involved in the Canadian Alliance.

As Canadians braced themselves for what turned out to be the Great Free Trade Election of 1988, big business made certain that the pro-free-trade political forces were well-heeled. With the Liberals under John Turner, as well as the New Democrats under Ed Broadbent, opposed to the free trade deal, the Mulroney Conservatives were the only game in town for Corporate Canada. Both the Alliance and the Conservatives were bankrolled by the country's major corporations. In the lead-up to the '88 election, for example, Imperial Oil gave $200,000 to the Alliance and $46,000 to the Tories, while Bombardier gave $69,000 to the Alliance and another $30,000 to the Conservatives.

Foreign-based corporations also contributed heavily to the pro-free-trade forces, with Shell giving a reported $250,000 and Texaco another $100,000. The Alliance itself spent well over $5 million on a slick advertising campaign leading up to the election. And when it looked like the Mulroney Conservatives were in trouble after the nationally televised leadership debate, millions more from the coffers of big business were poured into a last-minute pro-free-trade advertising blitz. A four-page tabloid, for example, called "Straight Talk" from Canada's corporate leaders, assuring Canadians that free trade would bring more jobs and preserve social programs, was inserted in every major newspaper throughout the country just two weeks before election day.

Round Three

The 1988 election proved to be a watershed event for Corporate Canada. Not only had the pro-business Tories squeezed out a crucial victory at the polls, but the destiny of the country in terms of continental free trade had been signed and sealed. Within 24 hours after the polls closed, d'Aquino declared that, with the free trade deal now in hand, the BCNI would be turning its attention to the task of making the deficit the No. 1 national priority. There was, of course, nothing new here. Slashing government spending had been a major and growing objective of big business since the mid-1970s. But, during the months leading up to Michael Wilson's 1989 federal budget, the BCNI, along with the Canadian Chambers of Commerce and the Canadian Manufacturers' Association, launched a vigorous and relentless lobbying campaign in Ottawa to move deficit reduction to the top of the national agenda.

At the core of their message was the claim that rampant government spending, especially social program spending, was the principal cause of spiralling public deficits.

Tackling the deficit, however, was not some sort of magnaminous gesture by the business community to improve the nation's economic health. On the contrary, fighting the deficit involves deeply-rooted financial interests. The BCNI, for example, represents powerful financial institutions, including the big five national banks—Royal, CIBC, Scotia, Montreal and Toronto Dominion—plus a complex network of related investment houses, including RBC Dominion Securities, Scotia Mcleod, Ernst and Young, Nesbitt Burns, and Midland Walwyn Capital. These are the financial institutions that are in the business of managing money and investment deals in financial markets. They are the institutions that stand to gain most when it comes to the buying and selling of bonds by governments in financial markets to reduce deficits. Add to this the vested interests of banks and investment houses on Wall Street, coupled with credit rating agencies like Moody's and Standard & Poor, and the BCNI was in a pivotal position to effectively demand that Ottawa give top priority to reducing the deficit.

Canada's major banks and investment houses wanted to secure greater control over the country's fiscal and monetary policy. Historically, the federal government was responsible for managing monetary policy through its agency, the Bank of Canada. But, throughout the 1980s, both the BCNI and the Howe Institute called for substantial changes in the central bank's mandate and greater independence from the cabinet and elected officials. At the same time, they urged Ottawa to depend more on private financial markets. In the past, when the government needed extra funds to finance its debt load, it traditionally relied on interest-free loans from the Bank of Canada. In 1977, for example, the Bank of Canada held 21 per cent of the federal debt. When the Mulroney government took office in 1984, the Bank held only 10.5 percent of the federal debt, and this portion dwindled to 6 per cent by 1993. Moreover, Ottawa not only agreed to borrow more from private banks at much higher interest rates, but it also abolished the requirement that private banks hold non-interest-paying cash reserves with the Bank of Canada, thereby allowing them to pile up many millions more in interest and profits. In turn, these new monetary policies served to multiply Ottawa's mounting debts.

To counter public charges of serving vested interests, both the BCNI and the Howe put the blame for rising deficits squarely on "excessive" government spending, especially on social programs. In 1989, the Howe commissioned a study on "Social Policy in the 1990s" by Tom Courchene of Queen's University in which he argued that the unemployment insurance program was a major cause of the deficit and unemployment (because it allegedly contained disincentives to work). The Institute went on to call for a major overhaul of Canada's social programs, including UI, Family Allowance, Social Assistance, Old Age Security and Child Benefits. It advocated a new approach to fiscal federalism in which federal/provincial transfer payments would be replaced with a transfer of tax points to the provinces for both health care and social assistance. The Howe also promoted more privatization of health care and a replacement of post-secondary education assistance with direct transfers to students. Meanwhile, the business press covered numerous speeches by bank presidents calling on Ottawa to slash the deficit through massive cutbacks in social spending.

Starting with his 1989 federal budget, Michael Wilson moved ahead with the social reform agenda promoted by big business. The first target was UI, with the federal government announcing in the wake of the free trade deal that it was withdrawing as a major funding partner in the program. Within months, Family Allowance and Old Age Security were put on the chopping block. The federal-provincial cost-sharing agreement for the Canada

Assistance Program, which provides social assistance for people living in poverty, was broken when transfer payments to the three wealthier provinces (Ontario, Alberta, and British Columbia) were unilaterally frozen. Legislation was passed which, in effect, mapped out a schedule for the gradual withdrawal of Ottawa from making transfer payments to the provinces for health care and post-secondary education. Instead, as the Howe Institute had advocated, the provinces would be given tax points to raise public revenues for these programs. As a result, Ottawa would effectively be out of the health care business by the year 2003.

Meanwhile, other policy changes pushed by the BCNI and the Howe on behalf of big business contributed to rising government deficits during this period. Together, they solidly backed Bank of Canada governor John Crow in 1988 when he escalated interest rates to wrestle the last digits of inflation to the ground. Over the next two years, Crow raised the nominal bank rate of interest from 8.8 to 14 per cent, more than double what it was in the U.S. By 1990, the rate of inflation remained the same at 4 per cent, but the country's economy was in the throes of another full-blown recession. During the next three years, unemployment and bankruptcies soared, resulting in a depletion of tax revenues for both Ottawa and the provinces.

In 1993, the loss of tax revenue from high unemployment, together with the rising cost of higher welfare and UI payments, resulted in an estimated net loss of $47 billion in public revenues for governments at all levels. Add to this the dramatic drop in corporate tax rates (from 15 per cent in the mid-1980s to around 7.5 per cent by 1993), which resulted from Michael Wilson's adoption of the BCNI's tax reform initiatives, and it is little wonder that Ottawa felt it was on the brink of bankruptcy.

But this is only half the story. Most of the big member corporations of the BCNI, which had promised in 1988 to create "more and better jobs" if the U.S.-Canada free trade deal was ratified, ended up chopping well over 200,000 jobs instead. In 1988, 37 BCNI companies, employing a total of 765,338 workers, had "downsized" to a combined total of 549,924 employees by 1994, for a total loss of 215,414 jobs. Topping the list of BCNI member "downsizers" during this six-year period were Canadian Pacific with 49,200 and Imasco with 26,553 jobs eliminated. Ford Motor Co. and Noranda followed with approximately 13,000 job cuts each. Then came Sears Canada and Abitibi-Price with close to 10,000 job losses each, followed by General Motors, Domtar,

Alcan, and Dofasco averaging around 6,500 job cuts apiece. At
the same time, the 37 BCNI member corporations increased their
combined annual revenues by $32.1 billion (from $141.9 billion
in 1988 to $174.0 billion in 1994). Since the signing of the FTA,
11 BCNI companies did create more jobs, but only a relatively
modest 11,993 of them.

Nor did the situation, as promised, improve much as a result
of increased foreign investment. Shortly after coming to power,
the Mulroney government killed FIRA and replaced it with Investment Canada which was mandated to actively promote foreign investment. In the decade that followed, notes economist
David Robinson, Investment Canada approved the sale of more
than 6,000 Canadian companies worth more than $64 billion to
foreign corporations. In almost every case, these foreign takeovers resulted in job losses and shifts in production. When Con-
solidated-Bathurst of Montreal was taken over by Chicago-based
Stone Container, for instance, the number of employees at its
head office fell from 400 to 150.

Given the fact that foreign-based corporations exert considerable control over their Canadian subsidiaries, says Robinson,
parent companies have been busy buying up minority shares in
their Canadian branch plant operations since the Free Trade
Agreement came into effect and restructuring their continental
operations. In 1991, for example, Union Carbide bought back its
Canadian shares, laid off more than 4,000 employees, and shifted
its production back to the U.S. As a result, Union Carbide was
reduced to little more than a sales office in Canada.

To make matters worse, the Mulroney government had
moved into the final stages of negotiating the North American
Free Trade Agreement (NAFTA). While the core of NAFTA was
to be the original U.S.-Canada FTA, the new agreement involving Mexico would include some additional elements. Trade law
expert Barry Appleton, for instance, argues that negotiations
around NAFTA emphasized a much more limited role for governments. In effect, the role and authority of future governments
for all three countries was being redefined in terms of the U.S.
model of minimal government. Under NAFTA, corporations
would be given a virtual veto over any future government decisions to set up new public enterprises or programs to provide
public goods or services to Canadians. Any attempts by Ottawa,
in other words, to rebuild Canada's public sector or social security system in the future could be thwarted by corporations or

our partner countries under NAFTA.

The new free trade regime would also include rules designed to protect the rights of corporations on their intellectual property. For Canadians, this would have an immediate impact on health care costs through rising drug prices for patented pharmaceuticals. Monopoly protection for corporate drug patents had already been extended by the Mulroney Conservatives in 1992 (Bill C-91) from 10 to 20 years, thereby preventing Canada's generic drug manufacturers from providing patented drugs at much lower prices. With the intellectual property rights protection entrenched in NAFTA, this legislation could not be reversed.

By this point, however, it was clear that the BCNI and its allies had already won the public relations battle. In 1993, the polls were showing that Canadians were coming around to seeing the "logic" of making deficit reduction the No. 1 priority. Corporate downsizing, along with government downsizing, had become a necessary (or unavoidable) fact of life. Public opposition to free trade had also simmered down to the point where NAFTA would not become a major issue in the 1993 federal election as its forerunner, the FTA, had been in 1988.

Recognizing that public confidence in the Mulroney Conservatives had been severely damaged, the BCNI had already begun to switch horses. Behind the scenes, consultations and briefings had already begun with Jean Chrétien and the Liberal party.

Shadow Cabinet

When Brian Mulroney got around to announcing his resignation and election fever began to spread in the spring of 1993, it had become clear that a fundamental shift in power had taken place in the country. The BCNI had emerged as the powerful political arm of Corporate Canada in Ottawa. Representing 150 of the largest corporations and banks in the country, with assets totalling over $1.5 trillion, the BCNI had established itself as a permanent and formidable political force. According to Langille, it functioned as "a virtual shadow cabinet." The BCNI's 28-member policy council was made up of some of the most powerful CEOs in the country. By this time, the Council had six policy task forces in operation, covering the national economy, social policy, political reform, environmental policy, international economy, and foreign affairs. All of these task forces (including previous ones which could still be reactivated, if needed) were chaired by CEOs of member corporations, backed up by advisory committees and a battery of policy research personnel from institutes like the C.D. Howe and other corporate think-tanks.

This description, however, still does not fully convey the degree of corporate power that drives the agenda of economic and social policy-making in Ottawa. No less than 18 out of the 25 most powerful CEOs in Corporate Canada, ranked by the *Globe & Mail Report on Business* in terms of their annual multi-billion dollar operations, were (and are) members of the BCNI (see Appendix III). Twelve of these were members of the BCNI's Policy Council: Maureen Darkes, General Motors Canada; Lynton R. Wilson, BCE Inc.; John Cleghorn, Royal Bank of Canada; Al Flood, Canadian Imperial Bank of Commerce; Matthew Barrett, Bank of Montreal; Jean Monty, Northern Telecom; John D. McNeil, Sun Life Assurance; Robert B. Peterson, Imperial Oil Ltd.; Jacques Bougle, Alcan Aluminum Co.; Brian Levitt, Imasco Ltd.; David Kerr, Noranda Inc.; and David O'Brian, Canadian Pacific. Of these, three became members of the BCNI's five-person executive: Flood, Monty, and O'Brian. Surprisingly, the Top 25 does not include some of the better known corporate leaders, such as Conrad Black of Hollinger Inc., Paul Desmarais of Power Corporation, or Peter Munk of Barrick Gold Co.

Indeed, few of these Top 25 CEOs would be considered household names in Canada today. They have nowhere near the kind of name recognition enjoyed by Jean Chrétien, Ralph Klein, Lucien Bouchard, Mike Harris, Preston Manning, Paul Martin, and Sheila Copps, let alone a host of other provincial premiers, cabinet ministers, and even back-bench Members of Parliament. They are neither publicly elected nor publicly accountable. Compared to the politicians we elect to office, we know little or nothing about them. For the most part, they choose to live a life of relative obscurity in the boardrooms of their corporate headquarters in Toronto or Montreal.

Yet there are some, like Conrad Black, who are no strangers when it comes to political power. After all, it was Black who bankrolled Brian Mulroney's initial bid for the leadership of the Conservative party back in 1976. For Canada's media baron, exercising political power is as important as producing profitable newspapers. Says Laurier LaPierre, who once taught Black at Upper Canada College: "I don't think Conrad wants to be prime minister, but he really does want to be the power behind the throne and feels his money will buy him that."

In addition to the BCNI's policy task forces and corporate think tanks like the C.D. Howe, a sophisticated network of political lobbying machinery has been built up in Ottawa to provide direct assistance to corporations in terms of communication and advocacy work with the highest levels of government. Investigative journalists John Sawatsky and Stevie Cameron have documented stories about some of the intriguing personalities and events that have taken place behind the scenes on Parliament Hill, particularly during the Mulroney years. Indeed, Tom d'Aquino himself worked this circuit before being appointed head of the BCNI.

While the CEOs of the country's major corporations certainly have their own ways of securing direct access to key cabinet ministers, they depend on a battery of specialized consulting, strategic planning and public affairs firms in Ottawa to keep their operations plugged into deputy ministers and senior decision-makers on a regular basis. Political access is a vital dimension of the exercise of corporate power in Ottawa, and every major corporation has a lobbying firm on retainer. Two companies, Executive Consultants Limited (ECL) and Public Affairs International (PAI), dominated the Ottawa lobbying scene throughout the 1970s and '80s. During this period, their operations transformed the decision-making apparatus in Ottawa, from the prime minister's office to the departments of key cabinet ministers to the legislative committees themselves.

Although the BCNI and its member corporations are, by and large, the crème de la crème of the Canadian economic élite, they have not operated in a complete political vacuum since the early 1980s. In a number of ways, they were indirectly aided by right-wing citizen front groups. Prominent among these has been the National Citizens' Coalition, which was originally founded and financed in 1975 by London, Ontario insurance magnate Colin Brown. In essence, however, the NCC was neither meant to be a citizens' movement nor a coalition. Instead, it was run by a small advisory body and supported financially by individual donors with little or no direct voice in organizational policy decisions and actions.

As Murray Dobbin describes it, the NCC serves as "the pit bull terrier" of the corporate agenda. Rather than directly lobbying government or the Ottawa bureaucracy, the NCC concentrates its energies on media campaigns, spending millions of dollars on inflammatory advertising. Throughout the 1980s, they mounted

major advertising blitzes aimed at progressive tax reform, the
National Energy Program, Medicare, immigration policies, and
trade union rights. In 1984, the NCC was also successful in using court action to overturn federal legislation prohibiting corporations and wealthy individuals from spending large sums on
political advertising during election campaigns. In effect, this
action opened the flood gates for the massive corporate advertising blitz during the 1988 free trade election. Before the tide-turn-
ing party leaders' debate in the 1988 election campaign, the NCC
alone had spent over $400,000 on pro-free-trade advertising.

The BCNI, of course, has been careful to maintain an arm's-
length relationship with the NCC and other right-wing citizen
front groups. As the touchstone of the nation's economic and
political élite, it would not want to have its public image tar-
nished by association with some of the more extreme elements
of the political right. Still, it knows full well that these groups
play a vitally important role in changing people's' attitudes and
values.

A case in point is the Canadian Taxpayers' Association (CTF).
When big business was mounting its campaigns to make the deficit and social spending cuts the main priority of the Mulroney
government following their victory on free trade, it was groups
like the CTF which paved the way for dramatic shifts in public
opinion through their vociferous campaigns against "high" taxes.
During this period, the CTF developed a capacity to produce
ready-to-print articles for weekly newspapers in communities
across the country, spreading its message through the electronic
media regionally and nationally, and organizing anti-tax rallies
in both urban and rural communities.

While some of these CTF campaigns were to reach their peak
later during the Chrétien government's tenure, they began to stir
up anti-government hysteria in the latter years of the Mulroney
regime.

At the same time, Tom d'Aquino and his policy board of
CEOs had to steer their own ship of state through the whirlpool
of party politics. The popular opposition that had been mobilized
against the Mulroney government (much of it rooted in the build-
up of the anti-free-trade movement) had gained so much momentum that it forced big business to change its strategy. The
Mulroney Tories had become a political liability. To ensure that
the corporate agenda remained intact, it was necessary to con-

solidate support for big business interests within the Liberal party. Given the ability of the BCNI member corporations to bankroll parties and elections, most of them quietly shifted their political financing to fill the coffers of the Liberal party.

In ideological terms, they knew that the Reform party also had the interests of big business at heart and had become the country's loudest cheerleader for free market politics. But the BCNI and its members were well aware that it was unlikely the majority of Canadians would rally behind Preston Manning in the foreseeable future, and that it would therefore continue to be more fruitful to control the direction of the country through the two mainstream parties.

Ultimately, what counts for the big business barons is not which party forms the government but whether they can maintain their stranglehold over the levers of power and policy-making in the nation's capital and the provinces. As long as the BCNI, through its member corporations, had the ability to buy parties and elections, it would retain the power to steer the ship of state.

In some ways, it could be argued, there is nothing especially new in all of this. From the early land-holding seigneuries in Quebec and the Family Compact in Ontario to the building of the CPR across the West, big business played a decisive role in the origins and development of Canada. It has also been common practice in this century for business and political leaders to swap positions and for former cabinet ministers to sit on the boards of corporations. What is new today is that the power and influence wielded by corporate leaders over public affairs in Ottawa (and provincial capitals as well) is much more pervasive, systemic, and overpowering. Never before in this century has big business come so close to actually replacing the operations of government with its own apparatus.

After all, the BCNI was not organized so that big business could simply be consulted more regularly by government. Its intention has been to write and direct public policy in key areas affecting Canada's economy and society. Nor does it simply want to influence and change specific policies or pieces of legislation. Its ultimate aim has been to redesign the state itself. Here, the BCNI has certainly not been alone. Its counterparts elsewhere in the global economy have also been moving rapidly in the same direction. ❧

2. Global Managers

Sure looks like those big CEOs have an awful lot of clout, doesn't it?

...Yeah! No wonder this country's in such a mess.

...But we're not the only ones. Remember the news reports we heard a couple of years back about the powerful role that Shell Oil was playing in Nigeria?

... Do you mean the story about that writer Ken Saro-Wiwa and nine other environmental activists who were murdered by the Nigerian state police for organizing a protest against what Shell was doing to their land and resources?

...That's right. A whole lot of people from all over the world wrote letters to Shell Oil demanding that something be done to bring the murderers to justice, but they hardly lifted a finger. Not only that, but they tried to cover up the whole thing with all those full-page Shell ads in the newspapers.

... What bothers me is that this is only the tip of the iceberg. I read somewhere that Shell Oil is operating in over 150 countries around the world. So are a lot of other giant corporations like General Motors, Coca-Cola, Toyota, IBM, McDonald's, and hundreds more we don't even know much about. Just think about that for a minute.

... It's hard to believe that we're living in a world where a few giant corporations become so wealthy and powerful that they can take control of whole countries. Before you know it, they'll be managing and governing the world.

... We used to be told it was important for big business to grow and expand in order to make the world safe for democracy. Sure sounds to me like just the opposite is happening.

... Well, before we get too worked up, maybe we should try to find out what's really going on here.

Borderlesss World

THERE IS NOTHING NEW about transnational corporations exerting political influence over countries, particularly in the less industrialized regions of the South. By employing government officials, participating directly on key national economic policy-making committees, making financial contributions to political parties, as well as practising various forms of bribery, corporations have been able to exert a considerable amount of political leverage over governments in the South.

At times, transnationals have even called upon their own governments to provide military assistance, as, for example, when the U.S. launched an invasion of Guatemala in 1954 to prevent the Guatemalan government from taking over (with compensation and interest) unused land of the United Fruit Company for redistribution to peasants.

Perhaps the most notorious example of corporate meddling in the political affairs of a sovereign state occurred in the early 1970s when International Telephone and Telegraph (ITT) proposed to finance a campaign by the Central Intelligence Agency of the U.S. government to defeat the candidacy of Salvador Allende in Chile's national election. Although the offer was refused, ITT vigorously lobbied Washington and other corporations after the Chilean elections to mobilize economic pressures against the Allende government by terminating credit and aid and supporting Allende's political rivals.

Public disclosure of ITT's campaign to overthrow Allende prompted the United Nations to set up a Centre on Transnational Corporations and to draft a TNC Code of Conduct designed to establish some guidelines on corporate behaviour. At the same time, the growing economic and political power wielded by transnational corporations became one of the main themes in the UN's attempt to negotiate a New International Economic Order.

But these efforts were soon thwarted. The N.I.E.O negotiations never took off, and the UN Centre on TNCs became marginalized to the point where it was eventually decimated. In the meantime, the CEOs who ran the giant corporations promoted their own vision of a new economic order—that of a borderless world. As the global managers of the planet, they envisioned a world in which corporations could instantly move their operations from one country to another to take advantage of more profitable investment opportunities, unfettered by either the intervention or regulation of national governments.

In this new world order, transnational corporations would be granted immunity from the rule of law administered by democratically elected governments, and thus be in a position to replace nation states as the dominant and most powerful institutions shaping the lives of peoples around the globe. Through liberalized trade and regional economic integration over the past 20 years or so, this global managers' dream of a borderless world has taken concrete shape and form.

In many ways, this vision is personified by CEOs like Akio Morita, the dynamic founder and chairman of the Sony corporation. After tapping into the new world of transistors and semiconductors in the early 1950s, U.S. corporate watchers Richard Barnet and John Cavanagh recall, Morita consciously set about the task of building Sony as a global and not just a Japanese corporation. Half his time was spent in New York City where, surrounding himself with a coterie of American advisors, he worked on designing new products and markets.

Under Morita's leadership, Sony emerged as one of the world's major manufacturers of electronic entertainment equipment. By the 1970s, with manufacturing plants established in the U.S. and Europe, as well as Japan, Sony captured the imagination of people around the industrialized world by producing and marketing one new electronic gadget after another.

Indeed, the story of Akio Morita and Sony illustrates the rise of global corporations and the new world economic order. Just over two decades ago, the United Nations reported that there were approximately 7,000 transnational corporations operating throughout the world. Today, there are over 40,000 of them. According to a recent study by the Washington-based Institute for Policy Studies, the top 200 of these transnationls now control over a quarter of the world's economic activity.

With combined revenues totalling $7.1 trillion, these 200 corporate giants are bigger than the combined economies of 182 countries (out of a total of 191 countries). Indeed, the combined annual revenues of these 200 conglomerates amount to almost twice the combined income of the bottom four-fifths of humanity (which adds up to $3.9 trillion). Yet the world-wide employment of the top 200 totals only 18.8 million, which is less than one-third of 1 percent of the Earth's population.

Of the 100 largest economies in the entire world today, 51 are individual transnational enterprises (three years ago, it was

47). Only 49 of the world's biggest economies are nation states. Mitsubishi, the largest transnational conglomerate in the world, has more total revenue than the fourth most populous nation on the planet, Indonesia. Wal-Mart is larger than the economies of 161 countries, including Israel, Poland and Greece. Ford's economy is bigger than either Saudi Arabia's or South Africa's. Philip Morris's annual sales are greater than New Zealand's GDP, while General Motors' income is greater than Denmark's and Toyota's is larger than Norway's. And five transnationals alone control 50 per cent of the global market in seven industries (i.e., consumer durables, automotive, airline, aerospace, electronic components, electrical & electronic, and steel).

Regardless of their home base, the Japanese, American, and European giants have increasingly become stateless corporations juggling multiple national identities and loyalties to achieve their global competitive interests. No matter where they are operating in the world, these transnational conglomerates can use their overseas subsidiaries, joint ventures, licensing agreements, and strategic alliances to assume foreign identities whenever it suits their purposes. In so doing, they develop chameleon-like abilities to change their appearance to resemble insiders in whatever country they are operating. As one CEO put it: "When we go to Brussels, we're member states of the EEC, and when we go to Washington we're an American company, too." Whenever they need to, they will wrap themselves in the national flag of their home governments to obtain support for tax breaks, research subsidies, or governmental representation in negotiations affecting their marketing plans. Through this process, stateless corporations are effectively transforming nation states to suit their interests in global transnational investment and competitiveness.

In 1993, after having achieved the status of one of the most respected CEOs in the world, Sony's Akio Morita published an open letter to the heads of state who were about to attend the G-7 Summit meeting in Tokyo. Calling on the Summit leaders to lower *all* economic barriers to trade and investment between North America, Europe and Japan, Morita proposed "creating the nucleus of a new world economic order that would include a harmonized world business system with agreed rules and procedures that transcend national boundaries." He went on to say: "Over time we should seek to create an environment in which the movement of goods, services, capital, technology, and people throughout North America, Europe, and Japan is truly free and unfettered." Outlining a series of proposals for government action, Morita's message was quite clear: governments must, first and foremost, serve the "needs" of global corporations rather than the needs of their own people.

Morita's letter to the G-7 leaders simply reinforced a trend that was already well underway. Around the world, national governments were lowering economic barriers and deregulating their economies at a furious pace. According to the 1995 United Nations report on global investment, no fewer than 374 pieces of legislation were introduced by national governments throughout the world, between 1991 and 1994, which had to do with investment by corporations. Some 369 of these legislative initiatives were designed to eliminate regulations on corporate practices. In other words, 98.7 per cent of the legislation brought forward by national governments in this area was aimed at providing transnational corporations with a freer environment in which to "transcend national boundaries." By doing so, national governments, in effect, have been giving up the powers and tools they would need to regulate corporations and their investments so as to better serve the needs of their own citizens.

This is the vision of a "borderless world" that big business guru Kenichi Ohmae has been selling to his government clients. As managing director of McKinsey & Company Japan, Ohmae argues that the national economy is nonexistent and therefore governments no longer have a role as managers of the national economy. Instead, they have been eclipsed by economic globalization and the emergence of transnational corporations. Traditional policy tools for managing the economy, says Ohmae, such as raising interest rates to control inflation or slapping on import restrictions to restrict foreign competition, have become obsolete simply because globalized corporations can easily avoid or circumvent these measures.

The time has come, Omhae counsels, for politicians and bureaucrats alike to recognize that government itself has become largely "obsolete." It's time that government got out of the way and let capital flow freely in response to market forces.

The Trilateralists

The call to create a borderless world, however, was not generated overnight by the new global managers. On the contrary, it has taken more than 20 years to forge this corporate vision and the global strategy necessary to make it a reality. In the early 1970s, the CEOs of some of the world's foremost transnational corporations began meeting on a regular basis behind closed doors with political leaders from the major industrialized countries through what became known as the Trilateral Commission.

This was not the first international forum organized by and for big business. During World War II, the Council on Foreign Relations was formed which, in turn, had been instrumental in establishing the International Monetary Fund and the World Bank. Similarly, the Bilderberg Group was organized in the early 1950s to bring business and political leaders together around the goal of European unification. But the Trilateral Commission was the first body of its kind with the explicit goal of restructuring the global economy and redirecting the policies of nation states towards this end.

The Trilateralists were initially brought together in 1973 by David Rockefeller, then chairman of Chase Manhattan Bank, and Columbia University professor Zbigniew Brzeninski, who later became national security advisor under U.S. President Jimmy Carter. Their select membership comprised 325 top leaders, most of them CEOs of major corporations, along with a smaller number of heads of state, government bureaucrats, media, and a few union leaders from the industrialized countries of Western Europe and North America, plus Japan. Included were the CEOs of four of the five largest transnationals, five of the world's six international banks, plus the major media corporations in the industrialized countries. Prominent CEOs like Sony's Akio Morita served terms as president of the Trilateral Commission. Seed funding was provided by the Kettering Foundation and the Ford Foundation, with more sustained financing contributed later by such brand name corporations as General Motors, Exxon, Sears Roebuck, Coca-Cola, Honeywell, Weyerhauser, Bechtel, Texas Instruments, Caterpillar Tractor, Cargill, John Deere, Time, and CBS.

Throughout the 1970s, the Trilateralists developed a common agenda for restructuring the global economy and nation states. This agenda, says UBC sociologist Patricia Marchak, was based on two strategic objectives. First, in order to create conditions required for the restructuring of national economies in the global marketplace, the internal relationships between governments and peoples had to be completely reorganized. For the Trilateralists, this meant strengthening the hand of governments relative to citizens' movements and public interest groups. Second, in order to ensure greater freedom for the movement of transnational capital, changes were required in the international structures of nation states. In particular, the international monetary and trading system needed to be restructured to accommodate global capital. On both fronts, the common obstacle that had to be dismantled was the Keynesian model of the nation state and the international economy.

One of the first major studies commissioned by the Trilateralists had to do with the crisis of democratic governance which had become a major problem for global corporations. In a report titled "The Crisis of Democracy," the authors argued that in the history of democratic governance the pendulum has sometimes swung in the direction of either too much governance or too much democracy. In the 1970s, they warned, democratic governments had become bogged down by special interest groups, over-emphasis on social welfare programs, a top-heavy public bureaucracy, too much protection for workers in the economy, and too many critics in the media and universities. In short, the pendulum had swung too far in the direction of democracy. The central political problem was what the authors called "an excess of democracy" which, in turn, "means a deficit in governability." The main culprit was identified as the Keynesian welfare state.

Although the report did not call for an outright dismantling of the welfare state, the authors did propose some radical changes in the model of democratic governance. The solution to the crisis, they said, was a stronger government in a weaker democratic framework. In order to effectively coordinate and plan changes in national economies required to facilitate transnational investment, governments needed to have more centralized authority and be less susceptible to the diverse demands of citizens' movements. The media should be disciplined through stronger libel laws and restrictions put on public access to government information.

The report also recommended that mass education be curtailed (too many educated people for the jobs available) and measures taken to stifle critical voices from academic circles. Throughout, it was assumed that corporations should have the freedom to alter the rules of national economies.

At the same time, the Trilateralists commissioned a variety of studies and reports on the restructuring of the global economy.

In 1973 and 1974, for example, the Commission published reports calling for an overhaul of the international monetary system, the world trade system, and North-South economic relations. The common assumption behind all these reports was that the only solution lay in creating a global free market. Expanding economic growth, based on mass consumption, is essential. New markets need to be opened up for transnational corporations to invest and expand their operations. New technologies have triggered changes in consumption patterns in industrialized countries, while new consumer populations have emerged in developing countries. For these and related reasons, the Trilateralists insisted that major changes were needed in investment, trade, and monetary policies.

In proposing solutions, the Trilateral Commission focused its energies on the international institutions in which its members had the most effective control—the International Monetary Fund (IMF), the World Bank, and the General Agreement on Trade and Tariffs (GATT). In 1983, the Commission issued a report on North-South economic relations, co-authored by former World Bank president Robert McNamara, which deliberately sidestepped international forums like the United Nations Committee on Trade and Development that had been originally designed by nation states to deal with these issues. Instead, the McNamara report proposed that the economic problems of developing countries be resolved through the GATT, the IMF, and the World Bank.

Through GATT, the Trilateralists called for major reductions in tariff and non-tariff barriers to free markets, especially in textiles, clothing, footwear, radios, televisions, steel, ships, and chemicals. Similarly, the debt crisis that was crippling the economies of developing countries could only be resolved through the IMF and the World Bank rescheduling debt loans in exchange for "structural adjustments" in the economic and social policies of their countries.

In effect, this private body of non-elected CEOs and selected political leaders became the self-appointed architects of the new global economy. With the exception of Mexico, the developing nations of the South had no representation on the Trilateral Commission. Moreover, the Trilateralists both ignored and outflanked the United Nations. Unlike previous generations of business leaders, who maintained that business should not be directly involved in public policy-making, the Trilateralists saw themselves as self-proclaimed leaders with a mission to create an ideological con-

sensus around a new economic and political agenda. As powerful representatives of the world's élite, they felt they had not only
the privilege, but the obligation, to preside over the restructuring
of the global economy in the closing decades of the millennium.
At the same time, they knew they could not advance this agenda
without changing the direction of public policy-making and general public opinion within nation states.

Business Coalitions

One of the main offsprings of the Trilateral Commission was
the formation of big business coalitions, such as the BCNI, in
the major industrialized countries and regions. Composed of the
CEOs of the largest corporations, these business coalitions were
designed to develop new directions in economic and social policy-
making. Armed with a network of policy research institutes and
public relations firms, these mainline business coalitions are able
to mobilize facts, policy positions, expert analysis, and opinion
polls, as well as organize citizen front groups for their campaigns
to change national governments and their policies.

Once policy consensus is reached among its member corporations, massive lobbying and advertising campaigns are mounted
around key policy issues and aggressively promoted by networks
of trade associations.

In the United States, the Business Round Table, comprising
CEOs from 200 leading corporations, was set up in 1972. As U.S.
business analyst David Korten reveals, its membership includes
the heads of 42 of the 50 largest corporations in the world. Indeed, the Business Round Table involves seven of the eight largest U.S. commercial banks, seven of the ten largest insurance
companies, five of the seven largest retail chains, seven of the
eight largest transportation companies, and nine of the eleven
largest utility corporations. In this forum, the head of General
Motors works side by side with his counterparts in Ford and
Chrysler; the CEO at Exxon sits down with his rivals at Mobil,
Texaco, and Chevron; the head of Citicorp works with his counterparts at Chemical Banking, Chase Manhattan, and First Chicago; the president of DuPont collaborates with his competition
at Dow, Occidental Petroleum, and Monsanto.

Fortified by extensive resources for policy research, congressional lobbying and political advertising, the Business Round
Table has played a strategic role over the past two decades in

shaping the direction of U.S. policy, especially around free trade, corporate taxation, and the deregulation of the economy, along with reforms in welfare, health care, and education.

In Europe, a similar corporate-governmental regime has been operating on a continent-wide basis. The European Round Table of Industrialists (ERT) is composed of 40 men, all CEOs of major transnational corporations mainly based in the European Union. ERT membership includes 11 of the top 20 European companies—British Petroleum, Daimler-Benz, Fiat, Siemens, Unilever, Nestle, Phillips, Hoechst, Total, Thyssen and ICI—all of which are listed among the world's top 500 companies. Formed in 1983, the ERT has become the *eminence grise* behind the economic integration of the 12 countries that comprise the European Union.

In 1984, the ERT launched a campaign for the creation of a single European market through a five-year plan that called for the elimination of trade barriers, the harmonization of regulations, and the abolition of fiscal restrictions. With direct access to the top decision-makers in government at both the European Commission and its member countries, the ERT has been highly effective in influencing, if not directing, policy changes on a broad range of fronts, including competition, transportation, education, employment, environment, and social reforms.

In Japan, the leading coalition of big business is called the Keidanren. Its membership includes the big automakers (Toyota, Nissan, Honda), six of the world's top commercial banks (Industrial Bank of Japan, Sanwa Bank, Mitsubishi Bank, Fuji Bank, Dai-Chi Kangyo Bank, and the Long Term Credit Bank), six of the world's ten biggest electronic companies (Hitachi, Matsushita Electric, Toshiba, Sony, NEC, and Mitsubishi Electric), five of the world's ten leading electric and gas utilities (Tokyo, Kansai, Chubu, Tohoku and Kyushu Electric Power), and eight of the top ten life insurance companies in the world (Nippon Life, Dai-ichi Mutual Life, Sumutomo Life, along with Meiji, Asahi, Mitsui, Yasuda, and Taiyo Mutual Life Companies).

Indeed, 140 of the Fortune 500 corporations in the world are based in Japan. The Keidanren, however, differs from the U.S. Business Round Table and the European Round Table of Industrialists in the way it operates. In Japan, brand name corporations like Toyota are already intricately woven into the everyday life and culture. The country itself is largely governed like a corporation.

In both Europe and North America, the leading big business

coalitions have been fortified in their policy-making campaigns by the formation of corporate think-tanks. For example, the Kiel Economics Institute in West Germany, the Adam Smith and the Economic Affairs institutes in Britain, the Heritage Foundation, the American Enterprise Institute and the CATO Institute in the U.S., as well as the C.D. Howe and Fraser institutes in Canada are, for the most part, policy think-tanks heavily funded by big corporations in their respective countries. While the nature of their relationship with the big business coalitions vary, they have all played a pivotal role in arming corporate lobbying campaigns with background facts, policy options, expert analyses and related ammunition.

In Britain, for example, the Adam Smith Institute, which was formed in 1977 and specializes in policy advocacy, became one of the country's most influential think-tanks, particularly during Margaret Thatcher's government, when it was largely responsible for developing plans for the privatization of a wide range of nationalized industries and government services (including the National Health Service).

At the same time, says Korten, citizens' front groups were organized to advance the corporate agenda with a wider public. Studies in the U.S. document the operations of 36 business-sponsored citizens' front groups. They range from the National Wetlands Coalition, co-sponsored by petroleum and real estate corporations to fight for less government regulation over the conversion of wetlands into drilling sites and shopping malls, to groups like Consumer Alert which campaigns against government restrictions on product safety. In all these cases, the name of the game is to show that corporate interests are essentially public interests.

Moreover, big business coalitions and their member corporations have access to a battery of public relations firms whose job it is to marshall public opinion polls and create public image-building campaigns for corporate clients. For example, Burston Marsteller, the world's largest public relations firm, was hired by Exxon to turn public opinion around during the *Exxon Valdez* oil spill, and by Union Carbide for the same assignment in the wake of the Bhopal disaster.

In recent years, a larger annual international assemblage of business, government and media leaders has been initiated. Known as the World Economic Forum, it consists of a week-long conference in Davos, Switzerland. In attendance are some

1,000 CEOs, along with heads of state and senior government officials from over 70 countries, plus selected media and cultural representatives.

According to the Forum's own propaganda, Davos is the locale for "the pre-eminent gathering of leaders from the private and public sectors." Its structure involves two main groupings: 1) the "Industry Governors" composed of the CEOs from the most dynamic corporations in the world's industrial sectors; and 2) the "Executive Leaders" composed of heads of state, cabinet ministers, and officials from selected international organizations.

The Forum's other groupings include: the "Media Leaders' Club" (e.g., leading editors-in-chief)' "Cultural Leaders" (100 distinguished writers and artists); "Forum Fellows" (over 400 academics); and the "Global Leaders for Tomorrow" composed of 600 people under the age of 43 from various sectors.

Davos has become the meeting place for what social activist Maude Barlow calls "the new global royalty"—the world's economic, political and cultural élite who have far more in common with one another than they do with fellow citizens in their own countries.

According to the *Globe and Mail's* Madeleine Drohan, the main attraction of this prestigious annual event is the opportunity it gives to "the eager horde of political leaders seeking to persuade giant corporations to invest in their countries." In other words, government leaders and their officials from all over the globe descend on this quaint Swiss village every year to sell the advantages of their countries as havens for profitable transnational investment.

"This is the Davos culture," boasts Samuel P. Huntington, who co-authored the Trilateral Commission's report on "the crisis of democracy." Says Huntington: "Davos people control virtually all international institutions, many of the world's governments, and the bulk of the world's economic and military capabilities."

Corporate Libertarians

To mobilize public support for their agenda, however, the Trilateralists and their big business coalitions needed to change the dominant political culture in the industrialized countries. Here, says sociologist Patricia Marchak, the libertarian movement emerged to play a pivotal role in advocating a fundamental shift in political and cultural values.

The origins of the modern libertarian movement date back to the formation of the Mont Pélérin Society in Geneva in 1947 by people like Robert Nozick, Friedrich Hayek, Karl Popper, Milton Friedman, and Ludwig Erhard (then West German minister of economic affairs). Extolling libertarian ideals such as the cult of individualism, free choice, property rights, productivity, and competitiveness, the Society focused its main attack on government. As Marchak puts it, the overall message was clear: "Government was bad: the market was good." The economy should be freed of government intervention and regulation. The only valid role for government is the protection of property rights and the enforcement of law and order.

By the 1970s, the libertarian organizations had sprouted across Europe and North America, taking shape and form as a full-fledged social movement. In addition to the Mont Pélérin Society, European organizations included the Club de l'Horloge in France, the Kiel Economics Institute in West Germany, along with the Aims of Industry, the Adam Smith Institute, and the Institute of Directors in Britain. In North America, the libertarian movement included the American Conservative Union, Young Americans for Freedom, the Thomas Jefferson Center Foundation, the Reason Foundation, the Heritage Foundation, the CATO Institute, and the Society for Individual Liberty, along with the Fraser Institute in Canada.

While at first glance the emergence of these libertarian organizations appeared to be spontaneous, it later became clear that they were often backed by considerable planning, organization and funding.

The principal guru of the libertarian movement has been Friederich A.Hayek, the Austrian philosopher-economist whose work in the 1930s eventually became popular in the 1970s. For Hayek, progress depends on the freedom of individuals to act. Since all individuals are unequal when it comes to talents, inequality is both inevitable and necessary. In Hayek's view, this poses a fundamental political problem for democracy understood in terms of majority rule. It contradicts the primary value of individual liberty.

"There can clearly be no moral justification," argues Hayek, "for any majority granting its members privileges by laying down rules which discriminate in their favour." That is why libertarians must be "concerned mainly with limiting the coercive powers of all government..." In effect, Hayek saw democratic government as being a tyranny of the majority, which inevitably leads to economic decline and stagnation. "The Great Society," he argued, is one that is governed according to the rules and discipline of the market.

Throughout the 1970s and 1980s, Hayek's philosophy was spread far and wide by other, more popular writers. In Britain, Ralph Harris of the Institute for Economic Affairs, who defines himself as "one of Hayek's second-hand dealers in ideas," specializes in "proving" that governments are costly, inefficient and immoral (because they upset the natural balance of market forces). His colleague, Arthur Seldon, once a student of Hayek's at the London School of Economics, maintains that the common theme of the libertarian movement is "the rejection of the state as the source of the good life."

In the U.S., George Gilder developed a celebrated defence of Hayek's ideas, promoting (among others) the view that democratic governments should not respond to the demands of the masses, but rather to the interests of creative entrepreneurs who produce "real" wealth. While most libertarians had little to say about big corporations, Irving Kristol passionately defended them as the producers of great wealth in America and throughout the world. And Robert Nozick went so far as to argue that government taxation was a form of theft, stating that public demands on private wealth are morally wrong.

The libertarian message, which in many ways dovetailed with that of the Trilateralists, began to seep into mainstream political culture. Books written by Hayek and his disciples were published and distributed throughout the world. The movement's gurus were brought in to speak at scholarly forums in universities. Public speeches were organized and media events were staged. Perhaps, more significantly, popular magazines were produced to spread the message, including the *Libertarian Review, Plain Truth, Libertarian Forum, Reason, The Individualist, The Freeman, The Objectivist,* and *The Fraser Forum* (here in Canada). Whereas right-wing popular magazines in the past emphasized that communism was the main threat to individualism, the new libertarian publications saw their own governments as the enemy.

The libertarian message, however, was also plagued by contradictions. At the heart of the message is a paradoxical mix of both libertarian and authoritarian ideas. On the one hand, Hayek placed top priority on the value of individual liberty, but on the other hand the individual is bound by the dictates of the market.

For all intents and purposes, the market is a hierarchical mechanism with rules and disciplines that reward and punish individuals. Similarly, the strong attacks levelled by libertarians against government intervention and regulation of the economy are contradicted by a heavy emphasis on the role of government in protecting private property and law and order. Indeed, the extreme libertarians harboured a strong authoritarian streak portrayed by their blind obedience to impersonal market forces and their repeated demand for law and order government.

Although the libertarians largely endorsed and promoted the core values that underlie the Trilateral agenda advanced by big business, Marchak maintains that Hayek and his disciples were an independent movement. There were also, she says, some notable differences. Whereas the Trilateralists advocated a strong government with weaker democratic institutions, the libertarians insisted on a weakening of both government and democracy. Contrary to many libertarians, the Trilateralists did not see the role of government being limited to the protection of property and person, but rather promoted the idea that governments needed to be strong enough to restructure their national economies and create the conditions necessary for economic growth.

But, while there were divergent interests between the Trilateralists and the libertarians, what united them in a common cause was their rejection of the Keynesian welfare state.

As Marchak puts it: "The libertarian wing sought to free entrepreneurs from state restrictions; the corporate wing sought to free investment from national restrictions; both benefited from an ideological campaign against the welfare state." The glue that made the corporate alliance possible, in other words, was a common commitment to dismantle the Keynesian welfare state. It was this uneasy alliance that set the political stage for the 1976 election of the Thatcher government in Britain and the 1980 election of the Reagan government in the United States.

Transnational Regimes

In the meantime, the CEOs of the world's leading transnational corporations were busy consolidating their power bases within the new global economy. According to the UN's World Investment Report, total foreign direct investment surged 40 per cent by 1995 to $315 billion (US). The top 100 transnational corporations (led by Shell Oil, Ford, Exxon, General Motors and

IBM) accounted for one-third of all foreign investment flows. Through acquisitions and mergers, the giant corporations took steps to secure their control of the major sectors of the global economy, such as finance, resources, manufacturing, agriculture, retail, services, communications, and transportation. Through various forms of vertical and horizontal integration, these same corporate players were able to further consolidate their control. These moves, in turn, not only resulted in increasing the concentration of power in the hands of fewer and fewer corporations during the 1980s. It also set the stage for the establishment of a series of transnational regimes whereby a handful of corporations could virtually control all aspects of production, marketing and distribution within key sectors of the new global economy.

Take, for example, the resource sector where metal mining, forest production and petroleum development have become increasingly concentrated in the hands of fewer transnational resource companies. Petroleum production and refining became largely controlled by ten majors, five of which are U.S.-based (Exxon, Mobil, Texaco, Chevron, and Amoco), two British (Royal Dutch Shell, British Petroleum), two French (Elf Acquitaine, Total), and one Italian (Eni). While there were many companies world-wide involved in forest and paper production, the industry became concentrated in the hands of five majors, four of which are U.S.-based (International Paper, Georgia-Pacific, Kimberly-Clark, and Weyerhaeuser), and one Japanese (Nippon Paper Industries). Similarly, the big corporate players in metal mining included four major German companies (Thyssen, Fried-Krupp, Metallgesellschaft, and Degussa) and six Japanese companies (Nippon Steel, KKK, Kobe Steel, Sumitomo Metal, Kawasaki Steel, and Mitsubishi Materials).

In many cases, these resource industry giants also established joint ventures with national and local resource companies, thereby extending their control and multiplying environmental threats (e.g., oil spills, forest depletion, toxic waste, and global warming).

In the manufacturing sector, the production of autos, electronics, textiles and clothing became increasingly organized in a global factory system during the 1980s. World-wide auto production and parts manufacturing remained concentrated in the hands of the Big Three American corporations (General Motors, Ford Motor, and Chrysler), the Japanese majors (Toyota, Nissan, Honda, Mitsubishi, Mazda, and Isuzu), plus the major German

(Daimler-Benz, Volkswagon, and BMW) and French (Renault, Peugot) auto makers.

In electronics and electrical equipment, Japanese companies consolidated their control over the industry, securing seven of the top 15 spots (Hitachi, Matsushista Electric, Toshiba, Sony, NEC, Mitsubishi, Sanyo, and Sharp), along with two U.S. companies (General Electric, Motorola), two South Korean firms (Daewoo, Samsung), and German giants like Siemans. Throughout the 1980s, the major auto makers and electronic corporations shifted a substantial portion of their production lines from factories in the industrialized countries to plants in developing countries, to take advantage of low-wage, tax-free conditions. Within the auto industry, strategic alliances were also forged, with Ford and GM contracting with Mazda and Toyota to produce for each other's market.

In the retail sector, the ground was laid for the establishment of a global shopping mall. Leading the way were giant retailers like Wal-Mart, developing superstore chains designed to sell the largest range of retail consumer goods— food, clothing, hardware, furniture, pharmaceuticals, and other products. By the late 1980s, the top ten general merchandise chains in the world included six U.S. corporations (Wal-Mart, Sears-Roebuck, K-Mart, Dayton Hudson, J.C. Penney, and Federated Department Stores), two Japanese companies (Daei, Nichi), one German (Karstadt) and one French (Pinault-Printemps) firm. But it was clear that Wal-Mart had won the title as the world's most aggressive giant retailer.

At the same time, other global retailers like Coca Cola, Procter & Gamble, Philip Morris, RJR Nabisco, Kellogg, General Motors, Unilever, Pepsico, Nestlé, Kentucky Fried Chicken and McDonald's spent billions of advertising and promotion dollars each year with the intent of creating a steadily growing market based on mass consumption. The strategy was to create universally recognized brand names for their products around the world by "selling the same things the same way everywhere."

Transnational agri-business corporations and food proccessing companies were also busy preparing the way for the global supermarket. The world's leading food processing companies became further concentrated. The top food processser firms were Unilever (Britain, Netherlands) and Nestlé (Switzerland), followed by several U.S. companies including Congara, Sara Lee, RJR Nabisco, and Archer Daniels Midland. Two U.S. food service companies (Pepsico and McDonald's) were among the leaders in opening up global markets. Other brand name food corporations like General Foods, Kraft, Pillsbury, Philip Morris, Del Monte, and Procter & Gamble merged their operations and expanded their marketing strategies on a global basis.

Most of these food giants also demanded an end to the system of agricultural subsidies, regulation and protection that has maintained a relatively cheap food policy in the industrialized countries, while insisting that the developing countries turn over more of their agricultural lands and farming for cash crop exports. Meanwhile, the introduction of bio-technology in food production (e.g., laboratory vanilla, freeze-resistant tomatoes, bovine growth hormones) plus long-distance food transportation has opened the door to new corporate players as well as new threats to the quality and safety of food products.

Perhaps the most innovative developments took place in the service sector. As governments moved to privatize public services during the 1980s, transnational corporations began to innovate and expand their operations in fields like health care and education. The giant pharmaceutical corporations—Johnson & Johnson, Merck, Bristol Myers, American Home Products, Glaxxo Wellcome and Pfizer—had already secured control over a major portion of the health care industry. In the U.S., for example, the world's two largest private hospital companies, Columbia and Health Trust, merged to form a giant health care corporation with annual sales exceeding that of Eastman Kodak or American Express. Drug companies like Eli Lilly opened merger talks with insurance companies like PCS, aiming at the potential takeover of hospitals, pharmacies, free-standing clinics, nursing homes and doctors' practices.

In the field of education, the formation of the New American Schools Development Corporation in the U.S., designed to funnel corporate finances into profit-oriented elementary schools, was spearheaded by transnationals like AT&T, Ford, Eastman Kodak, Pfizer, General Electric and Heinz.

In addition to taking control of new sectors of the economy, the TNCs have also secured international protection for the patents and copyrights they hold on information and technology under the intellectual property codes of the WTO and NAFTA. This patent protection now includes genetic materials ranging from seed stocks to natural medicinals. The TNCs have even obtained monopoly rights over genetic research covering an entire species of animals or plants, plus any products derived from such research.

The W.R. Grace Corporation, for example, through its subsidiary Agracetus Inc., has secured a U.S. patent on all genetically engineered or "transgenic" cotton varieties (1992), a European patent on all transgenic soybeans (1994), and has applications pending in other countries to take control of 60 per cent of the world's cotton crop, including cotton grown in India, China and Brazil. Under these conditions, farmers who traditionally save seed from one harvest to replant for their next crop would find themselves charged with violating international patent law. In effect, farmers around the world are now prohibited from growing their own seed stocks unless they first pay a royalty to the TNC that owns the patented seed. India's well-known physicist, Vandana Shiva, calls this "biopiracy."

During this period, other sectors of the global economy have also been subjected to increasing concentration of ownership and control. They include the aerospace industry (Lockheed, United Technologies, Boeing, Alliedsignal, and McDonnell Douglas), the airline industry (American Airlines, Japan Airlines, United Airlines, Lufthansa, Delta, and British Airways), the chemical industry (DuPont, Hoechst, BASF, Bayer, and Dow Chemical), and the entertainment industry (Disney, Time-Warner, Capital Cities, ABC, CBS, Turner Broadcasting, and MTV).

But undoubtedly the most revolutionary developments have been in the globalization of the financial markets.

Casino Economy

The fuel that fanned the flames of this global corporate expansion came from "hot" money generated by a highly combustible mixture of unregulated financial markets and electronic cash flows. Back in the 1920s, John Maynard Keynes had warned against the dangers of an unregulated financial system built on excessive speculation. Keynes's fears were confirmed by the subsequent international lending boom of 1924-28, the crash of 1929, and the Great Depression. At the height of the Depression, he urged nation states to take concerted action to regulate international financial markets. "Above all," he exhorted, "let finance be primarily national."

While many of Keynes's recommendations were ignored, steps were taken to stabilize financial markets through banking regulations that included reserve requirements, deposit insurance, limits on interest rates, restrictions on the role of foreign banks, and the separation of commercial and investment banking. But the days of a regulated financial system quickly unravelled in the 1980s.

Following the Second World War, a network of powerful commercial banking institutions began to emerge. By the late 1980s, the world's leading 25 commercial giants included ten Japanese banks (Industrial, Sanwa, Mitsubishi, Fuji, Dai-ichi Kangyo, Sumitomo, Sakura, Norinchukin, Tokyo, and Long Term Credit); four British banks (Barclays, National Westminster, Lloyds TSB Group, and HSBC Holdings); three German banks (Deutsche, WestDeutsche Landesbe, and Dresdner); three French banks (Crédit Agricole, Crédit Lyonnais, and Paribas); two U.S. banks (Citicorp and Bank America); plus ABN Amro Holdings of the Netherlands, CS Holdings of Switzerland, and Banco Do of Brazil. The combined revenues from these top commercial banks during this period averaged close to US$600 billion a year. Having saturated their own national markets, most of these commercial giants began to demand an opening up of the international financial system.

Indeed, many of these national commercial banks started to deregulate themselves through various forms of corporate reorganization. In the U.S., commercial banks began to slip out of the legislative restraints set up for financial institutions under the New Deal by forming their own holding companies or through mergers. Citibank, for example, set up Citicorp as its own holding company, through which Citibank could operate as a credit card banker in all 50 U.S. states (rather than being limited to serving the communities of New York state as a chartered bank), and could outflank legal requirements for cash reserves by selling loans to Citicorp (which is not a bank under law and therefore not subject to the legal requirement of loaning only a percentage of its reserves).

By the 1980s, the major U.S. commercial banks were not only operating across state lines, but they also extended their operations to include insurance companies and brokerage firms. Long before Congress legally relaxed its regulatory measures, the fence that separated commercial from investment banking had been torn down.

At the same time, the commercial banks campaigned for legislated deregulation of the finance sector. The breakthrough occurred, says long-time corporate analyst Richard Barnet, in what became known as the "Big Bang" on October 27, 1986, when the London Stock Exchange was suddenly deregulated overnight, opening its doors to foreign banks and securities firms. An electronic marketing system was installed and banking institutions were given the green light to act as wholesale dealers and brokers. The Big Bang in London triggered an explosion in financial deregulation around the world, as laws which had previously barred banks from international investment came tumbling down. Global corporations in search of capital could shop in international financial markets, borrowing in diverse forms on a variety of terms. Foreign corporations could trade their stocks as global products in London, Amsterdam, Zurich, Paris or Frankfurt, while investors could hedge their bets in one national economy or industry by buying foreign stocks. As Big Bang spread, financial markets in New York and Tokyo were also opened up.

Simultaneously, the creation of electronic cash flows or cybermoney through revolutionary changes in communications technology served to accelerate the deregulation of financial markets and usher in a period of speculative investment. With one keystroke, currency speculators can move vast sums of money instantaneously around the world. The software used for electronic financial marketing today permits 24-hour trading in all kinds of money products. Here, vast fortunes are traded in the form of cybermoney made visible on computer screens through digital electronic information. Any multi-million-dollar transfer across the world can be completed for a mere 18 cents. Through these instantaneous electronic transfers, money not only becomes a global product. It also loses its linkages to former sources of value, such as commodities produced or services delivered in communities.

It is now estimated that as much as US$2 trillion dollars is circulated around the globe on a daily basis. When Keynes first warned against the dangers of finance markets dominating the real economy, financial transactions were about two times larger than international trade in goods and services. Now they are 60 times greater. Electronic transfer systems like CHIPS, a New York based bank clearing house, makes more than 150,000 international money transactions in a single day. The speed and frequency of these transactions—from Indonesia to Tokyo to Toronto to New York to Miami to the Cayman Islands to the Bahamas to Geneva—makes it virtually impossible to trace, let alone regulate.

According to the Bank for International Settlements, an estimated US$13 trillion can flow instantaneously around the world through present telecommunications systems. Moreover, global banking has become increasingly dependent on a few highly centralized data systems. Yet the big commercial banks are no longer the main players. Corporations themselves are fast becoming major financial institutions in their own right. General Electric, for example, is now recognized as one of the largest single financial institutions in the world.

In effect, this is the new global casino economy in which most investors have become speculators and gamblers. Instead of buying shares in a company engaged in production, investors tend to put their money into mutual funds where they can speculate or gamble on short-term fluctuations in prices. Speculative investment, in other words, has supplanted productive investment. All of this, in turn, has profound political consequences. As Toronto economic analyst John Dillon shows, basic market power in the hands of currency traders—which is estimated to be around US$1.3 trillion a day—far exceeds the combined resources available to central banks of national governments around the world, which is estimated to be about $US640 billion.

The potential power that can be exercised by individual speculators over nation states was dramatically illustrated in 1992 when financier George Soros, in order to win a bet with Prime Minister John Major, sold $10 billion worth of British pounds on world finance markets for a $1 billion profit, thereby single-handedly forcing a devaluation of the British pound and the break-up of a new exchange rates system which had been proposed by the European Economic Union.

Indeed, extravagant claims are being made today about the power wielded by the world's financial élite over nation states. The managers of hot money, say some observers, have emerged as a "disciplinary" force in global markets, compelling national governments to embrace stiff austerity measures. After all, currency speculators already play a major role in determining a broad spectrum of national government policies ranging from credit systems, money supply and interest rates to debt management, investment policies and taxation. As one New York banker put it: "Countries don't control their own destiny. If they don't discipline themselves, the world market will do it for them."

Walter Wriston, the former chair of Citicorp, America's leading financial institution and the world's sixth largest bank, was even more blunt when he boasted about the power exercised by "200,000 monitors in trading rooms all over the world (who conduct) a kind of global plebiscite on the monetary and fiscal policies of governments issuing currencies." Just look at what happened to François Mitterand, recalls Wriston, after he became President of France: "The market took one look at his policies and within six months the capital flight forced him to reverse course."

Structural Adjustment

The poor majority of the world who live in Africa, Asia and Latin America know all too well about the power wielded by the world's financial élites over their daily lives. Since the early 1980s, both the World Bank and the International Monetary Fund have used the renegotiation of debt loans as a club to compel developing countries in the South to make widespread structural adjustments in their economies. The new global managers needed such a lever to ensure that countries made the kinds of economic and social adjustments required for the new world order.

In renegotiating debt loans to developing countries, the Bank and the Fund would design a structural adjustment program for each country, calling for sweeping changes in their economic and social policies. The prime objective here was to restructure Third World countries into free market economies. As one observer described it, the main strategy of the Bank and the Fund was "to insist that debtor nations remove their government from the economy as the price for getting credit."

The structural adjustment medicine imposed by the Bank and the Fund, notes Third World analyst Waldon Bello, included the following prescriptions: (a) removal of all restrictions on foreign investment in local industry, banks and financial services; (b) reorientation of national economies to produce for export, rather than to meet the basic needs of their own populations, in order to generate foreign exchange to pay down their debt loads; (c) reduction of wage levels in order to provide a pool of cheap labour and make exports more competitive; (d) substantial reductions in government spending, especially social spending for health, education and social assistance; (e) elimination of tariffs, quotas and other restrictions on imports; (f) devaluation of local currencies against hard global currencies (such as the U.S. dollar) in order to make exports still more competitive; (g) sell-off of state enterprises to the private sector, thereby attracting more foreign capital; (h) deregulation of national economies, thereby freeing corporations from government measures to protect labour, the environment and natural resources.

In applying this "medicine," the World Bank and the IMF have been directly aided by the world's leading commercial banks, which play pivotal roles in both the borrowing and the lending operations of debt loans and structural adjustment programs for developing countries. Through a revolving door mechanism, loan agreements are routinely negotiated in secret between banking and government officials who, for the most part, remain unaccountable to the people on whose behalf they were obligating the national treasury to foreign lenders.

Jonathan Cahn, writing in the *Harvard Human Rights Journal*, argues that the World Bank and the IMF have become "governance institutions, exercising power through (their) financial leverage to legislate entire legal regimens and even to alter the constitutional structure of borrowing nations." Their own consultants often have the power, says Cahn, to "rewrite a country's trade policy, fiscal policies, civil service requirements, labour laws, health care arrangements, environmental regulations, energy policy, resettlement requirements, procurement rules, and budgetary policy."

By 1986, 12 of the 15 debtor nations targeted by the Bank and the Fund in the South had adopted structural adjustment programs (including Brazil, Mexico, Argentina and the Philippines). In all these cases, the net effect has been to emasculate the powers of Third World governments to meet the basic needs of their peoples, with the poor majority paying the heaviest price. Between 1980 and 1990, the numbers of Latin American peoples living in poverty rose from 130 to 180 million, while in sub-Saharan Africa some 200 million people are now classified as poor, with numbers expected to rise to 300 million by the year 2000.

To be sure, a select group of ten countries in the South (the so-called "emerging markets" of Mexico, China, Malaysia, Argentina, Brazil, Thailand, Indonesia, South Korea, and Turkey) were targeted for major increases in foreign investment during this period. While more than 70 per cent of North-to-South investment flows were earmarked for these countries alone between 1991 and 1992, this meant that the remaining 140 poorest countries of the South had a decreasing share of global investment. In 1995, for example, the UN's World Investment Report revealed that only 1 per cent of North-to-South investment flows went to the smallest 100 countries, while close to 70 per cent was concentrated in these ten "tiger economies," (including $38 billion to China alone). To make matters worse, developing countries in the South paid some $280 billion more in debt service to their Northern creditors than they received through new private loans and government aid between 1985 and 1992.

When it comes to structural adjustment, however, the developing countries of the South have not been alone. Northern industrialized countries like Canada were also targeted for structural changes in their economies to adjust to the demands of the new global free market. Whereas the debt crisis was used as a club to force countries like Mexico to restructure their economies as a necessary precondition to being accepted as a partner in free trade regimes like NAFTA, the reverse was true for several industrialized countries in the North. Here the main mechanism for structural adjustment was initially free trade followed by debt slashing.

What the free trade deals like the FTA, NAFTA and GATT did was to consolidate and entrench the rights and freedoms of transnational corporations. As Carla Hills, chief U.S. negotiator for both NAFTA and GATT, put it: "We want corporations to be able to make investment overseas without being required to take a local partner, to export a given percentage of their output, to use local parts, or to meet a dozen other restrictions."

In effect, the new free trade regimes were designed to impose the same basic medicine for structural adjustment on partner countries. In the FTA and NAFTA, for example, the investment code ensures that various regulations of the partner countries will be removed, including foreign investment requirements, export quotas, local procurement, job content, and technology specifications. Under the national treatment clauses, foreign investors are guaranteed the same rights and freedoms as domestic firms.

Under the new free trade rules, there are built-in mechanisms designed to harmonize social programs and public services of the member countries, generally moving from higher to lower common denominators. If, for example, a country like Canada has a higher standard of unemployment insurance or agricultural marketing boards or a publicly funded system of universal health care, these programs can be challenged as "unfair trade subsidies" by other member states or their corporations under the free trade agreements. At the same time, the logic of the free market itself generates harmonization through the mobility of capital and the immobility of labour and national governments. Furthermore, the legislative authority of GATT and NAFTA supersedes the economic and social legislation of participating nation states when they come in conflict.

This free trade medicine, in turn, has been reinforced by the fiscal crisis of national governments and prescriptions for deficit-slashing. With the new free trade regimes of NAFTA and GATT in place, the CEOs of the major corporations focused their energies on making the fight against government deficits the overriding public priority in most of the industrialized countries in Europe and North America. By successfully lobbying for sharp reductions in corporate taxes, big business had effectively engineered a critical shortfall in public revenues for most national governments in the industrialized North in the late 1980s. Instead of treating rising government deficits as primarily a revenue problem, the corporate élite defined it exclusively as a spending problem. The only solution, insisted big business, was to slash government spending, especially social spending.

As a result, national governments prompted by their corporate allies initiated sweeping structural adjustment programs like the Contract with America in the U.S. and the Canada Health and Social Transfer Act which inflicted deep cuts in public funding for health care, education, social assistance and environmental protection.

Whether we are talking about the Southern or Northern brand of structural adjustment, the net effect has been essentially the same. For the industrial North, structural adjustment amounts to the dismantling of the Keynesian welfare state. For both the North and the South, the name of the game has been to turn nation states into export-oriented, free market economies to serve the interests of transnational corporations, unfettered by government intervention or regulation. Driven by the twin goals of increasing profitable investment and international competitiveness, the end result of this economic model for the majority of people in both the North and the South is nothing less than "competitive poverty," or in other words, a "race to the bottom." With the winds of change blowing in this direction, the question became how to manage this corporate agenda effectively on a global scale.

Global Governance

Of all things, it took the prolonged Uruguay Round of negotiations on a new GATT treaty to come up with a way of handling the problem of global management. In the fall of 1994, legislators in countries throughout the world, with little or no public debate, voted in favour of establishing a new global entity called the World Trade Organization (WTO). Most legislators, let alone the citizens they represent, were unaware that they were approving the creation of what amounts to a global parliament that would be dominated by transnational corporate interests. Nor did they know that under the WTO, as Lori Wallach of Public Citizen in the U.S. warns, national governments and democratic legislatures would virtually find themselves in a permanent hostage situation.

At first glance, the idea of establishing a WTO was perceived as being a quite reasonable and necessary undertaking. Its central mandate was to promote global free trade by working for the elimination of all remaining tariff and non-tariff barriers to international investment and trade. To carry out this mandate, however, the WTO would have legislative as well as judicial powers. Under the WTO, a group of unelected trade representatives would, in effect, have the power to override economic, social and environmental policy decisions of nation states and democratic legislatures around the world. What this means is that national laws designed to foster economic justice, democratic participation, worker heath and safety, minimum wages, social security, and sustainable use of natural resources could be targeted as barriers to trade and investment and therefore struck down by the WTO.

In short, laws passed by national and sub-national governments (like provinces or states) can be directly challenged under the WTO by other member countries or their corporations on grounds that they are "trade restrictive." For example, a country wishing to ban the export of raw logs as a means of conserving its forests, or ban the use of carcinogenic pesticides in processing food products or dangerous bio-tech hormones in the production of milk and beef, can be charged under the WTO for obstructing the free flow of trade and investment. A secret tribunal of unelected bureaucrats would then decide whether these laws were "trade restrictive" under the WTO and should be struck down. Once the secret WTO tribunal issues its edict, no appeal is possible. World-wide conformity is required. A country is obligated to make its laws conform to the WTO or face the prospect of perpetual trade sanctions.

The WTO itself was crafted behind closed doors by trade bureaucrats and corporate lobbyists. A U.S. business coalition calling itself the Intellectual Property Committee, for example, composed of such corporations as DuPont, General Electric, Pfizer, and IBM, bragged in its public literature that it shaped the U.S. negotiating position on the WTO. At the same time, the highly influential U.S. Advisory Committee for Trade Policy and Negotiations was also mainly composed of transnationals, including such corporate giants as AT&T, Bethlehem Steel, Time Warner, Corning, Bank of America, American Express, Scott Paper, Dow Chemical, Boeing, Eastman Kodak, Mobil Oil, Hewlett Packard, Weyerhauser and General Motors—all of which are members of the U.S. Business Round Table. Along with their counterparts in Europe and Japan, these corporate-dominated advisory bodies played a decisive role in designing the WTO as an instrument for global governance and the promotion of transnational competition and investment.

In most countries, including Canada, the WTO was railroaded through the legislative process in the closing months of 1994 with little or no public discussion, let alone debate. But public opposition was mobilized in some countries. While the WTO was rammed through the U.S. Congress, it ran into considerable opposition, passing by a relatively close margin of 235 to 200 in the House of Representatives and 68 to 32 in the Senate.

Elsewhere, the opposition was more intense. In the Philippines, anti-GATT riots broke out in the streets, stalling the final vote before the deal was eventually pushed through the Senate. In Spain, public opposition managed to keep the vote on the WTO off the legislative agenda, but a rump session of Parliament organized on Christmas Eve slipped the deal through unnoticed. In Belgium, citizen protesters had to be dragged out of their Parliament so that the WTO could be rubber-stamped. And in India, public resistance compelled Parliament to eliminate key portions of its implementing legislation, to the point where no vote was taken on whether India should become a member of the WTO or abide by its rules. When the Indian Prime Minister tried to rectify this later by executive decree, his actions were vetoed by Parliament.

Immediately following the adoption of the WTO, the global corporate managers began to mobilize support for the establishment of a world-wide investment treaty. Just as the investment code serves as the organizing centre for free trade regimes like NAFTA, so it was imperative that an investment treaty be incorporated as the centrepiece of the WTO. Two major proposals were launched along two different tracks. Initially, the European Community (strongly supported by Canada and Japan) began promoting the adoption of a Multilateral Investment Agreement in the WTO. A process of negotiations was to have been established at the first ministerial meetings of the WTO held in Singapore in December, 1996, but growing opposition to the proposal surfaced from several developing countries.

According to Martin Khor of the Third World Network, countries as politically diverse as Tanzania, Malaysia, India, Egypt, Pakistan, Ghana, Haiti and Cuba, plus 11 other countries who make up the Southern African Development Community, realized that the incorporation of the proposed MIA at the centre of the WTO would strip developing nations of whatever powers and tools they still have left to control and regulate foreign investment by transnational corporations. Not only did they see an investment treaty posing a direct threat to their sovereignty, but also potentially being a new form of colonialism. What the WTO decided to do then was to set up a working group on trade and investment, with a mandate to report back in two years.

Meanwhile, the U.S. was busy promoting a different strategy. Its stated objective was to "obtain a high-standard multilateral investment agreement that will protect U.S. investors abroad." Instead of running the risk of achieving a watered-down investment treaty through the WTO, the U.S. chose to spearhead its Multilateral Agreement on Investment (MAI) through the Organization for Economic Cooperation and Development (OECD), which is the club of the rich industrialized nations. After all, 477 of the Global Fortune 500 corporations are based in the 29 countries that make up the OECD. For the past two years, secret negotiations have been taking place at the OECD headquarters in Paris to establish the MAI as a "high standard" global investment treaty.

The U.S. proposal would guarantee: freedom to all foreign corporations wishing to enter a country and undertake investments; "full national treatment" for all foreign investors (i.e., treated no less favourably than local firms); most favoured nation status for all foreign investors; free movement for key corporate personnel; removal of performance requirements on corporations; tighter rules on the behaviour of state enterprises; allowances for foreign corporations to participate in plans for the privatization of state or public enterprises; protection of foreign investor rights (notably, intellectual property rights, safeguards against expropriation, protection from strife, transfers of funds and taxation); and the establishment of a disputes settlement mechanism (not only between states but also between investors and a state) which is both legally binding and enforceable through penalties. In addition, corporations would have the right to sue governments through local courts.

In effect, the MAI amounts to a corporate rule treaty (see Appendix V). It is designed to constitutionalize a whole new set of global rules for investment that will grant transnational corporations the unrestricted "right" and "freedom" to buy, sell, and move their operations whenever and wherever they want around the world, unhampered by government intervention or regulation. Under the MAI, tight restrictions will be laid down on what national governments can or cannot do in directing their economies. The ability of governments, for example, to use investment policy as a tool to promote social, economic or environmental objectives will be strictly forbidden. What's more, once a country has signed on, it will be virtually locked into the treaty's market disciplines for 20 years.

Under the U.S. plan, the OECD investment treaty was to have been ready for adoption by May or June of 1997, but due to a series of complications its implementation will likely be delayed until some time in 1998. However, once the OECD members have signed and ratified this treaty, it will be open to non-OECD countries who want (or can be persuaded) to join. Like NAFTA, there will be an accession clause in the OECD investment treaty allowing other countries to come on board. Regardless of what happens in the WTO, the plan is to make sure that the OECD version becomes the basis of a world-wide investment treaty. In other words, through the OECD process, the stricter investment regime proposed by the U.S. may very well be adopted eventually as the cornerstone of the WTO. The global managers, after all, insist that a world-wide investment regime of this kind is critical for their strategic plans in the future.

In his "Farewell Lecture to the World Bank" in January, 1994, economist Herman Daly warned that the elimination of the nation state's ability to regulate commerce "is to wound fatally the major unit of community capable of carrying out any policies for the common good." This is precisely what the WTO and the MAI are designed to do. Already, in regions of the world like Africa which have been virtually written off the map by most global investors, there are ominous signs of government collapse and corporate takeover. In the sub-Saharan region, for example, countries like Sierra Leone are actually hiring military-based corporations to provide security and pave the way for foreign investment. Companies such as Executive Outcomes, equipped with ground troops and military hardware, offer to restore law and order to Sierra Leone in exchange for cash and shares in the country's rich diamond fields. ◖◗

3. National Surrender

Do you really think Canada's been taken over by these global giants?

...Sure looks like that to me. Remember that speech Chrétien gave in Vancouver last year at a meeting with other world leaders where he said: "We cannot stop globalization, we need to adjust to it."?

...Was that the time when he said something about "a sense of not being able to control our own destiny"?

...That's it. He also talked about the power of "international finance" and how, "when a crisis erupts, a nation state can seem powerless."

...Maybe that explains why they poured all of their resources into reducing the deficit instead of living up to their Red Book promises to create jobs, protect social programs, and preserve the environment.

...But do you really believe the global economy made them renege on their election promises? What about all those big Bay Street corporations? Didn't they have a role to play in changing government priorities?

...Yeah, just look at the more than $6 billion in profits the big banks raked in last year. Seems to me they had a vested interest in making sure the Chrétien government made the deficit their No. 1 priority instead of jobs. They sure found a way to cash in on the deficit.

...It's not only the banks, but most of the other large corporations that are piling up huge profits. If they all paid their fair share of taxes, there'd be no excuse for the government to keep cutting back on health care, education, and other social programs.

...Well, I'd sure like to find out more about what happened when the Liberals won the 1993 election. Seems to me that's when a lot of Canadians got fooled.

...Right! If they're going to keep running the government for another four years, we'd better find out what really happened.

Business Liberals

THERE IS, OF COURSE, NOTHING especially new about Canada's surrender to the economic forces of globalization. As we have seen, the corporate captivity of the Canadian state has been an ongoing process for the past 20 years or more. What was new is that the Chrétien Liberals rapidly accelerated the process begun by the Mulroney Conservatives, while consolidating a more systemic relationship between Ottawa and big business. Well before they took over the reins of office, the Chrétien Liberals knew that Corporate Canada had become entrenched in Ottawa. Within weeks of the 1993 election, it had become clear that many of the economic and social promises outlined in the Red Book would either be substantially watered down or jettisoned altogether. Soon the Red Book would be replaced by Paul Martin's Purple Book. The key to this dramatic turnaround, as Maude Barlow and Bruce Campbell document, lay in the fact that the business Liberals had regained full control over the party under the leadership of Jean Chrétien.

The Liberal Party has long been a hybrid of business and social factions, each with its own conflicting vision of Canada and the role of government. While all Liberals believe in promoting individual rights, free enterprise, and market competition, and subscribe to the tenet that economic growth is crucial to national development, business and social Liberals differ on points of emphasis in this vision and the role of government in implementing it. For business Liberals, creating a free market economy is essential for the health of the nation. To them, the best form of government is the least government. In a free market economy, they hold that the proper role of government is to create favourable conditions in which corporations can prosper, including lower taxes, social standards, and more lax competition rules.

For social Liberals, on the other hand, government has a moral responsibility to mitigate the harsh and inequitable effects of the free market system by providing a safety net to assist the poor, the unemployed, the young, the old, and the disabled. Although most reject a class analysis of society, social Liberals believe that individual rights need to be tempered by collective rights.

Although these two factions represent warring souls within the bosom of the party, the Liberals have usually gone to extraordinary lengths to minimize internal conflicts and seek compromise for the sake of unity. Yet, as political economist Duncan Cameron notes, while the Liberal party has held power in Ottawa for more than two-thirds of this century, it has been dominated by either its business or its social wings. During the Pearson and Trudeau era of the 1960s and 1970s, for example, the social Liberals predominated for the most part in setting the government's agenda. Surprisingly, a relative though uneasy balance between the two camps was maintained under the leadership of Bay Street's own John Turner, largely because of his strong and uncompromising opposition to free trade. But by the time the Liberals returned to power in the 1990s after the reign of the Mulroney Conservatives, the business wing had seized control over the party and its agenda.

As far as Corporate Canada was concerned, Jean Chrétien was the perfect candidate for prime minister after Brian Mulroney. While he had a populist image of being a politician from Main Street, his basic interests and vision for the country were firmly planted in Bay Street. Indeed, Chrétien had sterling business credentials. During his early years in Parliament, his mentor was Mitchell Sharp, a Trilateralist himself, who for decades was one of the strongest advocates of business Liberalism in Ottawa. In his previous cabinet posts, Chrétien had established close ties with big business leaders as president of the Treasury Board, Minister of Finance, and Minister of Energy, Mines and Resources. When he temporarily left politics in the mid-1980s (after losing his party leadership bid to John Turner), he went to work on Bay Street for the high-powered corporate law firm of Lang Michener, and served as special advisor to the investment house of Gordon Capital. At the same time, he sat on the boards of Toronto Dominion, Stone Consolidated, and Viceroy Resources.

When he made his second run at the party leadership in 1989, he turned to his close friend, Paul Desmarais, the wealthy and highly influential CEO of Power Corporation, to be his chief fund raiser. After becoming leader, he surrounded himself with political advisors from the business wing of the party like Eddie Goldenberg, Peter Donolo and Jean Pelletier.

The direction of Chrétien's leadership, according to Barlow and Campbell, was nailed down at the Aylmer policy conference of the party in the fall of 1991. Like the Kingston conference convened three decades before by Pearson, wherein the social

Liberals hammered out an agenda for advancing the welfare state, the Aylmer conference was mainly designed by the Chrétien team as an occasion for the business Liberals to develop policy and program directions for the building of a free market economy in an age of economic globalization. The vast majority of the participants were from the business wing of the party, while the social Liberals were largely conspicuous by their absence.

In one of the keynote speeches titled, "Nowhere to Hide: The Economic Implications of Globalization for Canada," Liberal policy guru Peter Nicholson outlined six "guideposts" for a Chrétien government: a fiscal program based on draconian cuts in government spending; an overhaul of social programs (utilizing largely forgotten recommendations from the Macdonald Commission Report); an adjustment program that balanced safety net and work retraining requirements; economic union between the provinces; and the expansion of free trade into the rest of Latin America and Asia. As it turned out, Nicholson's six guideposts provided criteria for choosing a cabinet, as well as setting a policy agenda.

Not surprisingly, Chrétien's choice of Paul Martin as finance minister was praised on Bay Street. As the son of a former Liberal cabinet minister who served under no less than four prime ministers, Paul Martin began his career in the business world at Power Corporation in Montreal under the tutelage of Paul Desmarais. In 1973, Desmarais handed over to Martin the responsibility for Canada Steamship Lines (CSL), Power Corp.'s giant transportation subsidiary. In 1981, Martin and a partner bought CSL and transformed it into the largest Canadian-based multinational shipping line, complete with shipbuilding yards, a corporate realty arm, and Voyageur, the No. 3 bus company on the continent. In 1989, to avoid paying Canadian taxes on some of its holdings, as well as lowering its operating costs, CSL registered several of its ships under foreign flags (now up to one-third of its fleet) and announced that new vessels for its deep sea routes would be built in foreign shipyards.

While Martin's corporate assets were all placed in a blind trust when he became minister of finance, officials presiding over the government's conflict code consider Martin's case to be the "most complex...ever faced in terms of the diversity of the companies involved, their size and their interrelationships." From time to time, as opposition critic, Martin certainly espoused social Liberal ideals by championing the cause of social programs, the environment and economic nationalism, but there was little doubt that his feet were always firmly planted in the business Liberal camp.

The choice of Roy MacLaren as minister of international trade also sent a clear signal to Corporate Canada that the Chrétien government would be putting top priority on free trade and the demands of economic globalization. After studying business-government relations at Harvard, serving as a Canadian diplomat for 12 years, working as a director for Massey Ferguson and Leigh Instruments, and later as president of the Toronto advertising agency Olgilvy & Mather, MacLaren had cultivated an impressive set of credentials as a business Liberal. In 1977, he became co-owner of the pro-free-enterprise magazine, *Canadian Business,* developed extensive contacts on Bay Street, and headed up the task force for the Trudeau government that led to a relationship with the newly formed BCNI.

As president of his own advertising firm, MacLaren sat on numerous corporate boards, including Deutsche Bank, London Insurance and Royal LaPage. To the delight of the Canadian Bankers' Association, MacLaren played a pivotal role as parliamentary secretary to Finance Minister Marc Lalonde in facilitating government approval of the banks' entry into the discount brokerage and investment business, during the early 1980s. Later, as opposition trade critic under Chrétien, MacLaren worked closely with his good friend Tom d'Aquino at the BCNI in developing a position on NAFTA, designed to appease the social Liberals who had strongly critiqued the new trade deal with Mexico, while assuring big business that nothing would be done to upset the basic components of the proposed agreement.

At the same time, other key cabinet posts were given to staunch business Liberals such as John Manley (Martin's protégé) at Industry, Doug Young at Transport, Art Eggleton at the Treasury Board, and Anne McLellan at Natural Resources. The only social Liberal to get the nod for a key cabinet post in the new Chrétien administration was Lloyd Axworthy who, as Minister of Human Resources, was assigned to overhaul Canada's social programs under the heavy influence of the Finance Department. Other social Liberals were given cabinet positions that were considered to be marginal to the Chrétien economic agenda, such as Sheila Copps at Environment, Brian Tobin at Fisheries, Sergio Marchi at Immigration, Alan Rock at Justice, and Herb Gray who as House leader served as peacemaker between the two camps.

In any case, it was clear from the outset that the business Liberals were in charge. For all intents and purposes, the Chrétien government was committed to the task of dismantling the remaining pieces of the Keynesian welfare state in Canada. Nor would there be any real opposition in Parliament. After all, the Reform party was essentially the ideological backbone of the same right-wing agenda. The voice of the New Democrats was effectively muzzled, the NDP having been reduced to a rump group with no party status following the 1993 election. The Bloc Québécois, as the official parliamentary opposition party, would occasionally challenge the big business agenda of the Chrétien Liberals, but only if it suited its own nationalist agenda. Meanwhile, the only other objections in Parliament would come from a few social Liberal dissidents like Warren Allmand, who were promptly and severely disciplined for their outbursts.

Corporate Gridlock

During a brief stint as finance minister in the early 1980s, Jean Chrétien himself declared that he "never prepared a budget without seeking the opinion of the Business Council on National Issues." A decade later, the BCNI was in the driver's seat when it came to directing Ottawa's overall economic and social policy agenda. In 1994, the BCNI outlined a ten-point blueprint for the Chrétien government that included: the elimination of the federal deficit by 1998-99 through massive cuts in government spending rather than tax increases which would "deter investment and kill jobs;" continued support of the Bank of Canada's battle against inflation and the maintenance of "non-inflationary growth...as a central tenet of national economic policy; the promotion of an "aggressive...international trade development and diversification strategy," with NAFTA as the centrepiece, as "the best hope for job creation;" an overhaul of Canada's social programs designed to "do more with less," target assistance to "those most in need," and provide incentives to encourage more individual self-reliance; changes in unemployment insurance (a "badly flawed" system) by reducing employers' premiums (considered a "tax on jobs") while ensuring that UI payments do "not act as a disincentive to work;" the creation of a more decentralized federation and economic union with the elimination of internal trade barriers between the provinces; and "reducing the overall burden of government in our lives" by ensuring that services are provided by levels of government closest to the people, while at the same time strengthening the "role of the central government in key areas of national and international competence."

The BCNI program, already reflected in the guideposts outlined by Nicholson at the Aylmer conference, established the broad policy direction for the new Chrétien government. In turn, the BCNI platform was further substantiated by a series of publications by the C.D. Howe Institute which, as author Linda McQuaig notes, served to put a more independent academic spin on the otherwise vested interests of big business. The 1994 Howe series included *The Courage to Act,* which called on the government to accelerate its deficit reduction timetable over the next three years, and *Social Canada in the Millennium,* which warned that our social security system was no longer affordable and that, if we did not make radical changes now, international finance markets would step in and do it for us.

While the Howe publications were aimed at public opinion and policy makers, the Fraser Institute continued to popularize the big business agenda by delivering broadsides against the deficit, UI, social programs, universal health care, taxes, and other sectors of the Keynesian welfare state. They pursued this agenda through conferences, the *Fraser Forum*, and by staging events like Tax Freedom Day, the Debt Clock, the Economic Freedom Index, and hospital waiting lists. Indeed, while a decade ago the views promoted by the Fraser were dubbed as "extremist," by 1994 they had become part of the mainstream in the national media.

This corporate hammerlock on Liberal policy-making in Ottawa was further fortified by campaign and party financing. The 13 largest contributors to the 1993 Liberal election campaign were the big five commercial banks (Bank of Montreal, Royal Bank, Toronto Dominion, C.I.B.C., Bank of Nova Scotia), plus eight investment and brokerage houses (Scotia McLeod, Cooper and Lybrand, Wood Gundy, Richardson Greenshields, Nesbitt Thomson, Midland Walwyn, RBC Dominion Securities, and Toronto Dominion Securities). When these major financial corporations make substantial campaign donations, they expect to see a return on their investment. In this case, the financial establishment was unanimous in its demand that top priority be put on deficit slashing through massive cuts in government spending.

What's more, all of the mainline banks and their investment houses sustained their funding of the party the following year.

The Bank of Nova Scotia, for example, gave the Chrétien Liberals $44,512 in 1994, while their own brokerage house, Scotia McLeod, contributed another $66,310. C.I.B.C. gave $49,340 along with an additional $65,897 from its brokerage firm, Wood Gundy. Toronto Dominion and TD Securities contributed $42,180 and $40,000, respectively, while the Royal Bank and RBC Dominion Securities each gave well over $44,000.

In short, the full court press from banks, trust, brokerage and insurance companies amounted to more than $700,000 out of a total of nearly $6 million in corporate grants to the Liberals in 1994. The remaining big corporate donors to the party that year came from a variety of key sectors of the economy including: the mining industry (Inco, Barrick, Brascan), the petroleum industry (Imperial Oil, Husky Oil), pipeline companies (Trans-Canada Pipelines, Interprovincial Pipelines), the telecommunications industry (B.C.E. Inc., Rogers, Northern Telecom), transportation companies (Canadian Pacific, Bombardier, Canadian Steamship Lines), tobacco companies (Imasco, Rothmans), the airline industry (Air Canada, Canadian Airlines), and management consultant firms (Price Waterhouse, Poissant Thibault/Peat Marwick Thorne, WGM Management). In addition, contributions came from family-based empires like the Desmarais group through Power Corporation and Great West Life and the Bronfman group through Seagrams and London Life. Like their financial cousins, these and other major corporate donors also would expect a return on their investment.

One of the most powerful weapons in the arsenal of Corporate Canada has been its manipulation of the tax system. Since the Mulroney government's tax reforms of the 1980s, corporate tax contributions had dropped from approximately 15 per cent to as low as 5 per cent of overall federal revenues, the lowest rate among the G-7 countries. More than 80,000 profitable corporations in Canada end up paying no income taxes at all due to numerous tax loopholes and write-offs.

It was the Trudeau government, however, that originally introduced the device known as "deferred taxes" which, as Osgoode Hall tax lawyer Neil Brooks explains, was intended to ease the tax burden on corporations in return for their support. This device allows corporations to depreciate their assets more quickly than with the general accounting rule used to prepare annual corporate reports. In 1994, deferred taxes owing to the federal government amounted to over $40 billion. That year, the big three corporations using this device—B.C.E. Inc., Canadian Pacific and Imperial Oil—together owed Ottawa over $5 billion. In other words, the federal government freely gives to corporations what it would never give to other taxpayers—enormous interest-free loans.

In effect, Corporate Canada had been able to use the tax system to exert a form of fiscal strangulation on Ottawa. Even if the Chrétien Liberals had the political will to strengthen government spending on job creation and social programs in 1994, they lacked the fiscal capacity to do so. The reforms in corporate taxation had drained Ottawa of a much-needed source of public revenues. They also had been a principal cause of the federal government's galloping debt and deficit. To date, fiscal strangulation through the tax system has proved to be an effective strategic device for big business in compelling the Canadian state to undergo the kinds of structural changes business demanded.

By significantly reducing public revenues, Corporate Canada was in a position to reshape and redirect the role of government in the future. To make matters worse, the percentage of Ottawa's bonds and Treasury bills held by foreign investors had soared from 8 per cent to 28 per cent, giving offshore banks and bond agencies new powers to set government policy in this country. But even more consolidation and momentum would be necessary for this corporate stranglehold to take full effect. On this, Ottawa's finance department and the international finance markets were only too willing to lend a hand.

Finance Dictates

Paul Martin wasted no time in consolidating his own power base at the department of finance and seeing to it that this base was firmly entrenched at the centre of the new government's agenda. In so doing, he was aided and abetted by key department bureaucrats like David Dodge, who was deputy minister of finance under Michael Wilson. In the later years of the Mulroney government, Dodge had begun to spearhead an internal restructuring process in Ottawa designed to make government more responsive to the demands of "corporations that operate internationally" and to give finance a more central role. At Martin's request, Dodge agreed to stay and complete the process.

Months before the Chrétien team took office, Dodge had identified the prime targets for major cuts in government spending that would have to be tackled by whichever party won the 1993 election. Included in the Dodge target list were: pensions, unemployment insurance, transfers to the provinces, welfare payments, farm and some business subsidies. Operating on the assumption that social policy reform in the future would be driven by the finance department, Dodge later pronounced that Old Age Security, the Canada Pension Plan and Medicare would all have to be overhauled.

To develop an overall policy framework at Finance, Martin brought in Peter Nicholson, the Aylmer conference keynoter who had been on leave from his position as senior vice-president of the Bank of Nova Scotia designing a government relations strategy for B.C.E. Specifically, Nicholson was given the task of drafting a major policy and strategy document for Finance called *A New Framework for Economic Policy,* which the department released in October, 1994. Known as the Purple Book, its objective was to make deficit fighting the No. 1 priority of the Chrétien government. "Restoring fiscal health" was billed as the prerequisite for moving ahead with all other priorities on the government's economic and social policy agenda.

For Finance, there was only one road open to restoring fiscal health, and that was the elimination of the deficit through massive cuts in government spending, especially social spending. By taking this position, Nicholson and his colleagues at Finance had managed to overturn the logic of the Red Book which had called for increased economic growth and job creation as the best way to go about deficit reduction.

Preparing the ground-work for this policy shift, Martin and his bureaucrats first organized a nationally televised "think- tank" at the Ottawa Conference Centre in December 1993 to share advice on budget-making. Of the 40 invited participants, only a handful were considered to support the mainline economic policy direction outlined in the Red Book. The rest, many of whom were either neo-liberal academics or economists from banks, investment houses, and business-funded think tanks or lobby firms, strongly advocated that top priority be put on deficit reduction through program spending cuts, along with a "rethinking" of the role of government in an age of economic globalization. Later, Earnscliffe Research and Communications, a consulting firm with close ties to Martin (through his campaign manager, Mike Robinson), was hired to conduct what turned out to be the most elaborate pre-budget polling in the department's history. Through extensive use of polling and focus groups, a precise communications plan of action was developed for Martin and Dodge to pursue.

What the focus groups revealed was that, while most Canadians had come to the conclusion that the debt and the deficit were serious national problems, and would therefore be prepared (even if reluctantly) to accept program spending cuts, they were in no mood to swallow a dose of tax increases. This became the central message of Martin's communication strategy. In mid-October of 1994, he went before the Commons Finance Committee to sound the alarm bell about the financial crisis on the horizon. Armed with overhead charts and statistics, Martin declared: "We are in hock up to our eyeballs." If we don't take decisive action now, he warned, the country will soon be in financial ruins.

In the months that followed, Martin took this message on a speaking tour across the country, raising expectations that the budget might have to include tax hikes in order to deal with the mounting fiscal crisis. Allowing tax hysteria to fester and grow was, as Barlow and Campbell show, key to Finance's communication strategy. For, when the budget finally came down with no tax hikes but instead the deepest program cuts in history, people would be much more inclined to swallow the bitter medicine.

It was clear to Ottawa insiders that Finance had consolidated its power base at the centre of the Chrétien government. To enhance Finance's authority, the PMO abolished most of its committee structure, thereby eliminating any countervailing power bases. The prime minister had made it quite clear in the June cabinet meeting that he was backing his finance minister all the way. As Ottawa political scribes Edward Greenspon and Anthony Wilson-Smith tell it, Martin teamed up with Marcel Massé (a former bureaucrat who had been given the post as minister in charge of public service renewal) on "a joint project of slashing spending and reinventing the government of Canada."

With Martin and Massé taking the lead, a powerful program review committee of cabinet was set up which included Eggleton, Copps, Tobin, Ouellet, Marchi, Gray, and newcomer Anne McLellan. The prime objective, for Martin and Massé, was to get these ministers firmly onside with their plans for a massive overhaul of government. Three days a week, they locked themselves in a room for four hours a day, where they were briefed on "the big picture" by Martin and Dodge. After a heavy dose of

insider briefings (rarely heard outside of Finance) on the state of
the country's finances, Massé outlined his plans for a massive 20
per cent cut in program spending over a three-year period, including the elimination of 45,000 public service jobs. The size
of the federal government, in other words, was to be reduced to
what it had been during the immediate post-war years.

In short, Martin saw Massé's plan as the major vehicle for
his deficit battle. Getting the program review committee onside
was the key to winning widespread support from cabinet. Martin, along with Massé and Dodge, then met one-on-one with each
cabinet minister, presenting them with their target figures for cuts
in program spending over the three-year period. Once this was
accomplished (admittedly not without some internal struggles),
the stage was all but set for Martin to bring down his 1995 deficit-slashing budget and unveil his strategy for the restructuring
of government. Young would oversee the sale of some three-quarters of the government's railway and transportation services.
Goodale would take on the task of explaining to rural communities the loss of their grain transportation subsidy and other farm
support programs. Eggleton would have to pull back from implementing the rest of the government's much touted public infrastructure program. Copps would have to cut the Environment
ministry budget by a third, while McLellan would oversee major
reductions in personnel at Natural Resources. The only department that did not fall lock-step in line behind Finance's agenda
before the 1995 budget was Lloyd Axworthy and Human Resources and Development.

Axworthy was in charge of carrying out the government's
review and overhaul of the country's social security system. In
doing so, Human Resources was to work in collaboration with
Finance. It was agreed that Human Resources would go first, dis-
playing the government's concerns about social programs and
putting a human face on the issues, with Finance following up in
the second phase with cuts in transfer payments which, in turn,
would force the restructuring required in the country's social security system. The strategy broke down in October 1994 when
Axworthy's newly released Green Paper went too far in outlining detailed proposals for overhauling specific programs, identifying programs to be targeted for cuts, and designating the funds
saved for new programs such as reducing child poverty.

For Martin, the only politically feasible way of changing the
social security system was through cuts in transfer payments to

the provinces, not by openly targeting specific programs for cuts. Nor had Finance agreed that revenues saved from program cuts would be allocated for new social initiatives.

As it turned out, Axworthy's plans were doomed from the outset. He and his officials hadn't quite got the message as to who was really in charge of social security reform. Just as the Green Paper was being released, leaks to the press indicated that forthcoming budget cuts to social programs would amount to as much as $7.5 billion. Social advocacy groups, whom Axworthy desperately needed onside to win public support for his reforms, felt betrayed. The Commons Social Policy Committee became the lightning rod for growing anger and hostility as it travelled across the country in late 1994, hearing the views of Canadians on Axworthy's proposals. But even before his Committee had a chance to table its report, Axworthy threw in the towel, announcing to reporters that the review had been shelved and that, from now on, social security reform would be driven by Martin's fiscal agenda. The rift between Martin and Axworthy, which had been brewing for months behind the scenes in Ottawa, had erupted in public. Not only had Axworthy's foredoomed initiatives cost him support from Chrétien and the PMO, but they had also served to solidify Martin's political upper hand in cabinet.

By early 1995, it had become abundantly clear that Martin and Finance had seized complete control of the nation's economic and social agenda. The Purple Book, for all intents and purposes, had replaced the Red Book in providing the organizing principles for the Chrétien government's basic program of action. As Martin reportedly quipped at one point: "Nothing so wonderfully concentrates your mind as the feeling that the Department of Finance is breathing down your neck." But, just to make sure that Martin stuck to his strategy of bringing down the toughest budget in Canadian history, moves to stir the pot of debt hysteria were intensified.

Debt Terrorism

Throughout the fall of 1994, a more or less orchestrated campaign of deficit fear was mounted as a lead-up to the 1995 budget. In speech after speech, Martin warned Canadians that, if this country did not take a heavy dose of strong fiscal medicine soon, then the international financial market along with the IMF would intervene directly in Canada's economic affairs. At the same time,

Reform leader Preston Manning was going around the country preaching that the world's financial markets would punish Canada if we did not wipe out the deficit in three years.

Not to be outdone, the Fraser Institute publicly highlighted the theme, "Hitting the Debt Wall: Is Canada Bankrupt?," at a conference in Toronto co-sponsored by the Toronto Dominion Bank, MacMillan Bloedel and Sun Life. For its part, the C.D. Howe Institute released its report, *The Courage to Act*, calling for a $17 billion cut in transfer payments to the provinces for health, education and social assistance. Taken together, these activities created a climate of debt hysteria which, in turn, was compounded by a series of dramatic events in international financial markets.

The sudden collapse of the Mexican peso on December 20, 1994, poured oil on the rising flames of debt fire that had been ignited across the country. The rush of speculators to evacuate Mexico destabilized finance markets all over the world. On January 12, 1995, the *Wall Street Journal* warned in an editorial that Canada "has become an honourary member of the Third World" because of its failure to manage its growing debt problem. If decisive action were not taken, the editorial declared, "Canada could hit the debt wall...and have to call in the International Monetary Fund." This editorial was reprinted the next day by the *Globe and Mail* under the title "Bankrupt Canada."

In a widely reported speech to his shareholders, the CEO of the Toronto Dominion Bank declared that Canada was on the brink of a Mexico-like crash if urgent action was not taken on the country's debt problem. The pot was stirred up again when Toronto currency speculator Albert Friedberg pronounced that Canada was on the verge of a major currency collapse like Mexico, provoking another run on the Canadian dollar in international markets. To calm down the money markets, warned the banks and investment houses, Ottawa had better come across with big cuts in government spending in Martin's upcoming budget.

Less than two weeks before Martin was to bring down his 1995 budget, the New York bond rating agency, Moody's, publicly announced that it was putting Canada on a credit watch. Moody's sudden announcement sent shock waves throughout the market. At first, Martin seemed to respond to the news with dismay, exclaiming that "Moody's certainly could have waited until this government brought down its budget." But, as Linda McQuaig later revealed, Moody's was not simply giving an independent assessment. As it turns out, Canadian investors from Bay Street had been "hounding" Moody's senior Canada analyst to downgrade Ottawa's credit rating as a means of applying pressure for more aggressive action on the deficit.

"It's the only country I handle," said the Moody's analyst, "where...nationals from that country want the country downgraded even more—on a regular basis." Still, the Moody's announcement should not have come as a surprise, since Finance officials communicate directly with the bond rating agency on a weekly basis. It is safe to assume that there was an understanding by both parties that Martin's task in selling such a harsh budget to the Canadian public would be aided if the Moody's announcement was made before, rather than after, budget day.

"Authoritative voices" ranging from the prime minister to Bay Street CEOs are quick to emphasize that Canada has "no choice" but to respond to the demands of international finance markets. As C.D. Howe Institute president Tom Kierans contends: "We're losing our sovereignty. We are living on the edge...[We are] prisoners to the international markets."

What Kierans forgets to add is that Ottawa, aided and abetted by big business in this country, has surrendered many of the powers and tools it once had to deal effectively with international markets. Take, for example, the Bank of Canada. As the country's central financial institution, the Bank of Canada used to have the ability to chart the country's own course on monetary policy. By 1994, however, the central bank had all but abandoned its capacity to influence the bond market. It no longer intervened in the market by buying and selling long- term bonds on a regular basis. It had also drastically reduced its purchase and sale of three-month Treasury bills. Instead, the bond market was left wide open to the big five commercial banks which, since amendments made to the Bank Act in 1991, were no longer required by Ottawa to keep a minimum amount of their reserves with the Bank of Canada.

As Ottawa University's Duncan Cameron, testifying before a parliamentary committee in 1995, warned: "The Bank of Canada, rather than being a servant of Parliament, has become its master."

At the same time, these "authoritative voices" turned their backs on alternative fiscal strategies or solutions for reducing the country's debt. When it was suggested that, based on a 1990 landmark study by Statistics Canada's Hideo Mimoto, it would be much more effective if Ottawa's deficit-fighting strategies were focused on the two main causes of Canada's rising debt between 1973 and 1989—the 50 per cent rise caused by tax breaks to wealthy individuals and profitable corporations, and the 44 per cent increase caused by excessively high interest rates—the advice was not only ignored but often ridiculed. Both the Mulroney and Chrétien governments were fixated on targeting government spending alone (which was responsible for only 6 per cent of debt growth).

In other words, Ottawa, at the behest of big business, has totally ignored the two predominant causes of Canadian debt (i.e., corporate tax breaks and high interest rates) which were, in turn, the two very policies that the BCNI had campaigned for in the first place on behalf of domestic and international investors.

Nor did it matter that the Mimoto report was later reinforced by other studies, including one by the Dominion Bond Rating Service. While only tracking the role of interest rates (not tax breaks), Dominion still concluded that 84 per cent of the increase in Canadian government debt between 1984 and 1994 was due to soaring interest rates. Yet the Finance Department and the Bank of Canada stubbornly stuck to their policy of maintaining high interest rates in their never-ending battle to keep inflation rates low. Why? Because that's what the bond holders and finance market told them to do. The last thing they wanted to see was the Bank of Canada leading the charge against high interest rates, which after all mean rising profits for bond holders and financial markets.

The same could be said for Ottawa's policy of maintaining relatively low corporate tax rates. To keep big business happy, Finance had absolutely no intention of targeting corporate taxation as a principal cause of debt growth. As far as big business is concerned, high interest rates and low corporate tax rates are sacred cows. They were not to be touched by Ottawa's deficit-fighting crusade.

All of this was part of the debt terrorism to which Canadians were subjected in the months leading up to February 1995, when Paul Martin brought down the harshest federal budget in the history of this country. Not only had Martin, along with Dodge and Nicholson at Finance, engineered a 180-degree U-turn in the Chrétien government's agenda by making the deficit the mother of all issues and priorities, but there was only one way to deal with the problem, they repeatedly told Canadians, and that was by slashing government spending, especially spending on social programs and public services.

The fact that corporate tax breaks and high interest rates were by far the main causes of debt growth had no bearing whatsoever. Nor would the Bank of Canada be called upon to buy back a substantial portion of the country's foreign debt or tackle high interest rates. Instead, Ottawa's prime objective was to whip Canadians up into a deficit frenzy, so they would accept massive government spending cuts as the only viable solution. In short, this is what Canadian corporations and the bondholders in Canada's financial markets demanded.

Yet, in the final analysis, neither the bondholders nor the finance markets could make real on their threats. Despite the propaganda, Canada was far from being "bankrupt." As McQuaig demonstrated from her interviews with senior analysts on Wall Street, reports about Canada's debt crisis had been "grossly exaggerated." Said Moody's senior analyst, "several recently published reports have grossly exaggerated Canada's fiscal debt position. Some of them have double-counted numbers, while others have made inappropriate international comparisons...These inaccurate measurements may have played a role in exaggerated evaluations of the severity of Canada's debt problems."

In other words, Canada was not facing the "debt wall" and Ottawa's fiscal position was not "out of control." Nor were the IMF and international markets about to foreclose on Canada. Nevertheless, this was the kind of debt hysteria being fomented by big business and Finance. In turn, these were the same corporate and financial interests that solidly backed the Chrétien Liberals in the 1993 election and since. In return, through its 1995 budget, the Chrétien government sacrificed the entire country to this debt terrorism.

Job Killers

The 180-degree U-turn engineered by Finance through its Purple Book platform also wiped out the Chrétien Liberals' foremost election promise of jobs! jobs! jobs! By making deficit reduction the top priority and operating principle for all government programming, Finance had effectively eliminated any direct role by Ottawa in job creation. Not only was the public infrastructure program put on hold by Martin's 1995 budget, but the Chrétien government had also become the nation's No. 1 job killer by announcing that 45,000 federal public service jobs would be terminated by 1998.

According to the business Liberal agenda outlined in the Purple Book, it was not Ottawa's responsibility to be directly involved in job creation but, instead, to create the conditions for corporations and the private sector to generate new jobs. It soon became clear, however, that there was little or no substance to this strategy. With few exceptions, the country's major corporations were not only not creating new jobs, but most of them were engaged in a downsizing frenzy of their own.

The year 1995 was the most profitable year on record for Corporate Canada. Yet, as Canada's corporations raked in a total of $66 billion in profits, they were also laying off thousands of workers. Bell Canada, for example, took in $502 million in profits and cut 3,100 people from its work force. INCO boosted its profits by 3,281 per cent while chopping 1,963 jobs. C.I.B.C. increased its profit margins by over a billion dollars, yet laid off 1,290 workers. Canadian Pacific's profits climbed 75 per cent, but 1,500 of their workers were dismissed. Petro-Canada terminated 564 jobs while recording profits of $194 million. The Bank of Montreal axed 1,428 employees while increasing its profit margins by 20 per cent. And General Motors Canada broke its own record in profit-making with $1.39 billion, yet eliminated 2,500 jobs.

The problem was further complicated by the way the stock markets began to treat this massive corporate downsizing as "good news." When AT&T, for example, announced on the first working day of 1996 that it was going to eliminate 40,000 jobs over the next three years, its stock prices shot up on the Dow Jones Industrial. Subsequent announcements of new job growth figures in the U.S. were also labelled as "bad news" by investors on Wall Street, sending the market into a nosedive. Similarly, here in Canada, announcements of major corporate layoffs have frequently been greeted on the stock market as "good news" and reflected as such by rising share prices.

Large-scale downsizing used to be a public relations nightmare for companies, but now corporations were being promptly rewarded by the stock market for laying off workers. The goal of maximizing shareholder returns *along with* maintaining the well-being of their workers and the communities in which they operate is now no longer seen as the prime responsibility of most CEOs. As one Canadian CEO put it, "Companies aren't put together to create jobs. The No. 1 priority is creating shareholder wealth."

Meanwhile, the jobless rate continued to soar. Despite claiming that over 600,000 jobs had been created three years after it assumed office, the Chrétien government conveniently overlooks the fact that nearly all these new jobs were part-time, low-paying, insecure forms of employment, with little or no benefits. The official unemployment rate remained locked in at 10 per cent, comprising well over 1.5 million jobless (which, in turn, does not include the more than half million discouraged workers who have given up looking for work, and the estimated one-third of part-time workers who want, but cannot find, full-time employment).

Moreover, the polls show that Canadians were upset by recent announcements of large-scale corporate downsizing. According to an Angus Reid poll early in 1996, more than three-quarters of Canadians (77 per cent) disapproved of large, profitable corporations laying off workers, while 54 per cent said that profitable corporations who lay off workers should be punished through higher taxes or other measures.

In response, the Chrétien regime tried to piece together some sort of damage control strategy. By March 1996, the speech from the throne was pleading with big business to work with the government in making "the collective investments required to produce hope, growth and jobs." The prime minister followed with a major speech in the Commons urging business to help deal with "the human deficit of unemployment." Referring obliquely to the Liberal government's compliance with big business in carrying out its corporate agenda (i.e., deficit slashing, social spending cuts, free trade, privatization and deregulation), Chrétien declared the time had come for the private sector to do its part. Two days later, Industry Minister John Manley appeared before a gathering of business leaders at the Empire Club in Toronto and sheepishly repeated the question that had come to plague the Chretien government: "What are we going to do about the fact that corporations are making record profits and laying off people in droves?"

Using a soft stick approach, the Chrétien Liberals began to inveigle big business into becoming key players in their "First Jobs Initiative," a modest program targeted at unemployed youth. Conceived by a Boston consulting firm, the program was initially designed to create 50,000 one-year internships in Canadian businesses for new high school graduates who would be paid close to the minimum wage. Following a meeting with a small group of business leaders, Martin, Manley and Doug Young (then in his brief stint as Human Resources Minister) began to promote the project as the means for stimulating corporate responsibility for job creation. Big business, Martin claimed, "recognize(s) the problem and (is) prepared to come to the party." But Corporate Canada's reaction was less than enthusiastic. When little more than 30 companies signed on to First Jobs, the target number of internships had to be scaled back to a mere 10,000, barely making a dent in the problem of unemployed or underemployed youth, now numbering some 600,000.

As BCNI chief Tom d'Aquino explained: "A lot of people in the private sector are cynical about the prospect of government having made promises of jobs, jobs, jobs, saying now, 'It's not our fault. It's business who haven't created jobs.' What's more," says d'Aquino, "big business is not interested in responding to something because it's the political flavour of the month."

A review of the *Financial Post's* Top 500 listings shows why. In recent years, many of Canada's biggest corporations have been the country's leading job killers. Between 1988 and 1994, the top 15 "downsizers" comprise a cross-section of big corporations from several major sectors of the economy, including transportation companies like Canadian Pacific with 49, 000 job cuts; auto makers like Ford (13,200) and General Motors (7,230); retail chains like K-Mart (20,553) and Sears (10,690); mining corporations like Noranda (13,000) and Alcan (6,500); forest products companies like Abitibi-Price (9,919) and Stone Container (formerly Consolidated Bathurst) (9,061).

Most of these corporate job killers were ranked by the *Financial Post* listing to be among the most prosperous in 1995. Five of the top 15 "downsizers" between 1988 and 1994—General Motors, Ford Motor Co., Alcan Aluminum, Ontario Hydro, and Imasco—were ranked among the first ten corporations in Canada in terms of revenue sales in 1994. Of the 15 major downsizers, eight were in the top 20 in sales revenue in 1994. Despite making substantial cutbacks in their work forces, at least six of these corporations experienced significant growth in sales and revenues during this period (i.e., General Motors, Ford, Imasco, Alcan, Domtar and Dofasco).

Ottawa's tax system often rewards corporate downsizing. In

1993, for example, Canada's leading corporate job killer, Canadian Pacific, not only paid no tax on pre-tax income of $442,100,000, but actually received a tax *credit* of $5,700,000. One year later, Canadian Pacific was taxed at the low rate of 4.2 per cent on $720,200,000 in profits. Many of Canada's top corporate downsizers also take advantage of the deferred tax device, including the top three tax-deferring corporations in 1994— B.C.E. Inc., Canadian Pacific, and Imperial Oil.

On top of all this, Canadian corporations are reportedly making increased use of tax havens outside the country. A 1996 study by Revenue Canada concluded, for example, that corporations hid an estimated 20 per cent of their 1991 international transactions from tax officials, transferring $17 billion to offshore tax havens and hiding another $60 billion with their foreign affiliates through a device known as "transfer pricing." As well, compared with the previous year, there was a 46 per cent increase in transactions with tax havens ranging from Switzerland to the Cayman Islands.

Indeed, Corporate Canada has been gradually stripping Ottawa of not only the fiscal resources but also the policy tools it requires to launch a comprehensive job creation strategy. Under NAFTA, as we have seen, the federal government can no longer apply foreign investment criteria such as job content specifications or technology transfer requirements when it comes to transnational corporations seeking access to our resources or our markets.

Nor has free trade, coupled with a more deregulated economy, resulted in more job-creating forms of U.S. investment in Canada. On the contrary, from the introduction of the new free trade regime in 1988 through 1994, Canadians invested $10.6 billion more in the U.S. than U.S. investors placed in Canada. Some 93 per cent of all foreign investment in Canada between 1989 and 1991 was used to acquire Canadian firms rather than establish new businesses. Not only do acquisitions mean no new jobs, but they often lead to more layoffs as new owners streamline their operations. Moreover, in keeping with the new casino economy, the pattern of U.S. investment has shifted dramatically from productive (job-creating) to speculative (non-job-creating) investment.

Social Assault

Even before Axworthy's ill-fated Green Paper made its way onto the political agenda, the C.D. Howe Institute had already set the terms of the debate for social policy reform with the release of its report on *Social Canada in the Millennium*. As the leading business think tank in official policy-making circles, the Howe had commissioned Tom Courchene of Queen's University to prepare this report in 1994 as an update on his 1989 report for the Institute on *Social Policy in the 1990s*. What Courchene did, in effect, was to outline a platform of what big business wanted to see in terms of changes in Canada's social security system.

This platform included: termination of the Canada Assistance Plan, coupled with the transfer of total responsibility for welfare to the provinces and the reintroduction of workfare; elimination of health care transfers to the provinces, along with the granting of new tax powers to raise revenue at the provincial level; withdrawal of transfer payments to the provinces for post-secondary education, to be replaced by student vouchers; restricting UI benefits by doubling or tripling both the qualifying period and the work period as preconditions; and replacing the minimum wage to be paid by all employers with a system of public subsidies to top up wages where necessary.

To a remarkable degree, Axworthy's Green Paper fell in line with the business agenda for social security reform outlined by the Howe. On social assistance, the Green Paper proposed a shift from the cost-sharing program targeted for welfare to a more open-ended bloc transfer allowing provinces to use the funds for other purposes, which in effect meant removing national standards and opening the door to workfare. On post-secondary education, most of the transfers would be eliminated and replaced by a student loan program set up with the commercial banks.

While the Green Paper did call for a new program to combat child poverty, based on a more targeted child tax credit and an expansion of child care spaces, this initiative was quickly dropped when it became clear that Finance planned to cut $7.5 billion from social programs. But much of Axworthy's proposals focused on changes in UI. Drawing upon a recent OECD study on jobs, the Green Paper concluded that Canada's UI program was "too generous" and was "destroying the incentive to work." The objective, as the OECD study urged, was to get the unemployed to "price themselves into jobs" by compelling them to accept lower wages. In turn, this meant getting rid of certain market "rigidities" such as "generous UI benefits" and "high minimum wage" laws.

The Green Paper was immediately praised by the BCNI's d'Aquino as "sweeping reforms that essentially embrace the principles I have outlined." But it was Paul Martin's Canada Health and Social Transfer (CHST) in his 1995 budget that engineered the real "sweeping reforms." Under the CHST, cash transfers to the provinces for health, education and social assistance would be combined into a single, smaller block grant. By 1997, federal cash transfers to the provinces for these programs would drop from $17.3 billion to $10.3 billion, representing a 40 per cent cut in just two years.

While the provinces, in exchange, would be given tax points to raise additional revenues, the CHST effectively takes away the capacity of the federal government to maintain national standards, particularly in relation to health care and social assistance in this country. By withdrawing as the principal funding partner in these social programs, Ottawa relinquishes the authority and tools it needs to ensure that national standards are met in all the provinces across Canada. By targeting its social reforms to the most vulnerable in society (as the Green Paper advocated), Ottawa is also relinquishing its commitment to maintain social programs that are *universally* available to *all* citizens.

From the standpoint of big business, the social reforms generated by the 1995 budget served to remove some of the "rigidities" and "disincentives" from the market, thereby laying the groundwork for a cheap labour policy in Canada. By shifting from a 50-50 cost-sharing to a block-funded program, the CHST effectively killed the Canada Assistance Plan as a national program that was originally designed to provide social assistance to poor people on the basis of need. At the same time, by eliminating national standards for social assistance, the CHST allows the provinces to introduce workfare programs that force poor people to take jobs for even less than the minimum wage.

In effect, workfare forces people on welfare to compete with other workers in the job market and thus put downward pressure on the entire wage structure. The combined result is the creation of conditions for cheaper labour. Here, big business has the support of most small and medium-sized businesses which, in turn, are not only actively lobbying their provincial governments to adopt workfare schemes, but are also calling for the abolition of the minimum wage.

Deep cuts in UI have reinforced these trends. In 1989, due to mounting pressure from a consortium of U.S. corporations which had targeted Canada's UI program as an "unfair trade subsidy" under the new free trade agreement, the Mulroney government withdrew as a major UI funding partner and proceeded to radically overhaul Canada's UI program. By the time the Chrétien Liberals took over, Canada's UI had been scaled back in line with the inferior American UI program. But the BCNI and its allies were still not satisfied. Using their rhetoric, Martin described UI premiums as a "payroll tax on employers" which amounts to "a cancer on job creation." By further lowering payments and reducing the time span for benefits, plus introducing means testing and disqualifying people who "voluntarily" quit their jobs, the so-called "disincentives to work" are taken out of UI.

While this satisfies the demand of big business, the social costs are staggering. The proportion of unemployed workers collecting UI payments has dropped dramatically from 87 per cent in 1990 to around 40 per cent in 1997. What's more, Ottawa has been reallocating the savings from these cutbacks in the UI fund (which is now directly financed only through payments by workers and their employers) to pay down the deficit rather than give the unemployed the help they need and have paid for through their premiums.

By the same token, the massive cuts in Ottawa's transfer payments for health care under the CHST provide new opportunities for private, profit-oriented health care corporations (largely U.S.-based) to move in and take over pieces of Canada's Medicare system. Viewed from the perspective of the private health care industry, Canada has a lucrative $72 billion dollar market, 72 per cent of which comes each year from governments. With the massive cuts in transfer payments, hospitals are being closed all across the country, while health services and drugs previously covered by Medicare are being de-listed and de-insured. As a result, major segments of our public health care system are now being privatized.

When medical services and drugs are de-listed from the public health care system, for example, it opens up a market for private insurance companies like Liberty Mutual, Blue Cross/Blue Shield, and Metropolitan Life. When hospitals are shut down, a market is potentially opened for corporations like Columbia/HCA, the largest for-profit hospital chain in the U.S., to come into Canada and set up private hospital facilities that would provide services, not on the basis of people's need but on their ability to pay.

Meanwhile, major pharmaceutical companies like Eli Lilly, Merck, Pfizer and Bristol-Myers have already been reaping profits from rising drug prices in Canada. Following a strong lobbying campaign in 1993, these and other giants in the pharmaceutical industry succeeded in winning monopoly protection over their drug patents in this country, a monopoly which was later cemented in the intellectual property rights sections of NAFTA. As a result, drug prices have been skyrocketing and Canada's generic drug industry, which used to reproduce patented pharmaceutical products at reasonable prices, has been damaged.

As the only major component of health care spending which has been steadily rising, prescription drug costs are now considered to be the main destabilizing factor in Canada's public health care system. Now these same pharmaceutical giants, along with newly acquired drug management companies, are offering packaged deals to cash-strapped hospitals and provincial drug plans.

To make matters worse, adds health care analyst Colleen Fuller, a Canadian-owned corporation, MDS, has suddenly emerged as a major player in the private health care industry, providing services to 17,000 physicians and institutions through 380 locations in seven provinces. In 1996, MDS announced joint ventures with HCA/Columbia (the giant international private hospital chain) and Bristol Myers Squibb (one of the world's largest pharmaceutical companies). Aided by the influential public relations firm Hill & Knowlton, MDS has also played a key role in lobbying the governments of New Brunswick and British Columbia to protect and enhance the interests of the private sector in health care.

In short, big business has been positioning itself to take over key components of Canada's social security system. What was once a viable, publicly-funded, largely universal system of social security has been subjected to a process of fiscal strangulation. Corporate Canada has managed to pull off this underfunding strategy by draining public revenues through a series of measures, including tax write-offs that allow over 80,000 profitable corporations to avoid paying taxes every year, deferred tax schemes that result in corporations owing over $40 billion to the federal government alone, plus the $11 billion that Ottawa pays out to businesses each year in the form of subsidies.

Once the suffocation strategy takes hold, the process of privatization kicks in, opening up new public sector markets for corporations. This corporatization of social security is already under way, not only in Medicare and other social programs, but even in the Canada Pension Plan, which would soon find the investment of its funds turned over to the private sector.

Green Machine

No, we are not talking here about the TD bank's instant teller service. For years, Ottawa has had its own "green machine" known as the Department of the Environment. The trouble is, Ottawa's green machine has been falling apart. Which brings us back to the connection with the TD bank. The Environment Ministry has been stripped of the powers and tools it needs to do its job by the same fiscal agenda that the TD bank and its allies have established as the cornerstones of public policy-making in Ottawa. In turn, the prime beneficiaries of the collapse of Ottawa's green machine are the major resource industries—mining, petroleum, forestry—which have manouvered themselves into a position where they now, to a large extent, set the terms and conditions of the country's ecological management.

Driven by Paul Martin's fiscal program, Environment Canada has been squeezed through the "Three-D" wringer of downsizing, decentralization and deregulation, all at once. Through deregulation, environmental standards have been reduced to a patchwork across the country, with weak enforcement measures. Through downsizing, Environment Canada has lost some 1,400 workers as a result of recent budget cuts, thereby further weakening the department's capacities to monitor performance and enforce standards, especially in the major resource industries. Through decentralization, the mandate and responsibilities for environmental protection have been increasingly shifting from the federal government to the provinces, and to business itself.

Even Ottawa's annual report on *The State of Canada's Environment*, which has provided the most comprehensive picture of what is happening to our wildlife, air, soil, forests and waterways, has been scrapped. Sheila Copps, Chrétien's first environment minister, along with her successor, Sergio Marchi, appear to have done little to resist, let alone reverse these trends. Indeed, the power in dealing with environmental matters in Ottawa has been shifted to the Ministry of Natural Resources and to the corporations it represents.

As Chrétien's natural resources minister, Anne McLellan has

become the darling of the resource industry, which includes mining, forestry and petroleum companies. When she took on her new assignment in 1993, the former University of Alberta law professor had little knowledge or experience with the resource sectors. But she proved to be a fast learner. Says David Manning, former Alberta deputy minister of energy and now president of the Canadian Association of Petroleum Producers, "She's come up the learning curve at a tremendous pace, in a neighbourhood where learning curves are severe by definition."

What this means, of course, is that she has become a strong advocate of the resource industry's major priorities, especially the elimination of government intervention and regulation. As McLellan herself put it: "I think I'm doing quite a good job of helping government get out of business." She engineered the sale of Petro Canada and the government's equity interest in Hibernia, the introduction of a voluntary system of environmental regulation within the resource industries, as well as an exemption for the oil and gas industry from national environmental standards.

From the perspective of the petroleum industry, one of McLellan's major "achievements" was to prevent Ottawa from imposing a carbon tax. As one of the first nations to be a signatory to the Convention on Climate Change at the Earth Summit in 1992, Canada had pledged to stabilize greenhouse emissions at 1990 levels by the year 2000. In the Red Book, the Chrétien Liberals promised to follow up this commitment. Ottawa began to give serious consideration to a proposal for a carbon tax on fossil fuels as a way of compelling the oil and gas industry to start reducing greenhouse emissions. Alberta's oil patch, the home of Imperial Oil, TransCanada Pipelines, and a host of other petroleum companies who supported the Liberals financially, were furious about such a proposal. Fearing that a carbon tax would pose an even greater threat to their industry than the National Energy Program a decade earlier, some company representatives, along with the Reform party, targeted Environment Minister Sheila Copps as the villain. In the end, however, McLellan handily won the battle in cabinet, and the proposal for a carbon tax was quietly dropped from Martin's budget plans.

At the same time, the downsizing and decentralization of Environment Canada further strengthened the hand of McLellan and the interests of the major forestry and mining corporations. Eliminating some 1,400 jobs, along with the closure of 16 forestry centres and 20 regional forestry offices, greatly reduced Environment Canada's regulatory capacity across the country. Withdrawal of federal funding from reforestation projects meant that Ottawa was leaving to the provinces and the industry the responsibility of ensuring that Canada's forests are treated as a renewable resource for future generations.

Federal ministers like McLellan were also given the authority to make deals with particular corporations that would exempt them from specific environmental regulations under certain circumstances. Similarly, the devolution of powers to the provinces for environmental protection in the mining industry allowed mining companies greater freedom to operate because of lax laws concerning toxic waste disposal in most provinces. In Ontario, for example, provincial restrictions on waste management were drastically reduced under the Conservative government of Mike Harris, allowing mining corporations to devise their own waste disposal methods for mine tailings rather than having them inspected and approved by provincial authorities.

In any case, Environment Canada had already racked up a dismal record when it came to monitoring and enforcing pollution standards. In 1994, Environment Canada caught a total of 169 companies and government agencies breaking the standards outlined in the Canada Environment Protection Act. But only 15 of these companies were prosecuted; the other 154 corporate polluters got off scot-free. Since Canada's pollution laws are considered to be a great deal weaker than those in the U.S., it is reasonable to assume that there are many more corporate polluters operating without restraint across the country. Little wonder that a Washington-based public policy agency, in a report documenting the environmental performances of countries throughout the industrialized world, rated Canada as having the second worst record. Even if Ottawa were to upgrade its pollution abatement standards, ministers like McLellan and Manley would still be able to exempt companies from having to meet those tougher limits.

The one case where the Chrétien government has notably taken action is in fisheries. As minister of fisheries and oceans, Brian Tobin launched an all-out campaign in 1995 against deep sea Spanish trawlers which were overfishing the already depleted turbot stock just outside the 200-mile limit off the Grand Banks of Newfoundland. Although Tobin's actions were praised by environmentalists around the world and a compromise was finally

reached with the European Community, the fact remains that foreign fishing corporations continue with impunity to use deep sea
trawlers to drag and scrape the ocean floor off the coasts of
Canada.

To be sure, the Chrétien government, preceded by the
Mulroney government, finally took action to shut down the cod
fishery on environmental grounds. But little has been done to
assess what role was played by the giant fish corporations, as
well as the federal government, to create or tolerate the conditions that led to the depletion of the fish stocks in the first place.
Nor are there any assurances that corporations like National Sea
will not regain control over the industry once the fish stocks return.

Trade Warriors

Nothing quite portrays the big business takeover of Canada
as much as the missionary zeal with which the Chrétien government has been promoting international trade. Enter Roy
MacLaren, the Liberal champion of free trade and the global
spearhead of Paul Martin's fiscal agenda. It was MacLaren who
worked out a deal with Tom d'Aquino of the BCNI on how the
Liberals should handle the NAFTA issue. Ever since the 1988
election, which the Liberals lost when campaigning against free
trade with John Turner at the helm, the business wing of the party
had been trying to find a way to weaken and eventually reverse
the official party line. Instead of calling for abrogation of the
FTA, as Axworthy and other social Liberals had been doing in
opposition, Martin and MacLaren proposed that the party outline conditions to be negotiated for improvements in NAFTA. A
list of five improvements were identified, which largely coincided with proposals made by the BCNI before the Parliamentary committee in the Spring of 1993. However, as Greenspon
and Wilson-Smith explain, while the Liberals favoured renegotiating NAFTA in their Red Book, they put low priority on the
issue during the election campaign.

With the Liberal victory, the Clinton administration in Washington suddenly became nervous, especially since the crucial vote
on NAFTA was looming in Congress. But the new government
in Ottawa did not have the political will to press forward with a
renegotiation of the NAFTA package. Instead, Chrétien and
MacLaren simply tried to work out some face-saving resolutions

with Washington on cultural protection, energy security, and rules on subsidies and dumping. In the end, nothing was changed in the 2,000-page text. All they got was three pages of toothless side agreements.

It was also MacLaren who worked with some of the top CEOs from Bay Street to organize "Team Canada" trade missions, led by the prime minister and provincial premiers, along with hundreds of business leaders, to open up new markets in Asia and Latin America. In November 1994, the first Team Canada trade mission focused on China. In Beijing, Chrétien presided over the signing of $5.1 billion worth of new business ventures involving more than 50 Canadian companies. Among the corporations signing commercial contracts and agreements were Power Corporation, Barrick Gold, Northern Telecom, Dominion Bridge, Mitel, SNC Lavelin, Pacific Entertainment and Spar Aerospace. In addition, a $3.5 billion agreement was signed by Atomic Energy of Canada Ltd. to provide two CANDU nuclear reactors to China's nuclear power corporation.

The sole purpose of the China mission was business. Canada's top political leaders were more than happy to wine and dine the same Chinese leaders who had ordered the student massacre in Tiannamen Square, enforced labour prison camps, and conducted the outrageous trade in human body parts from executed political prisoners. Yet none of these human rights issues was on the agenda. Says one Foreign Affairs official, "We used to go with lists of political prisoners we wanted released. Now we go with lists of companies that want contracts."

Less than three months later, Chrétien and MacLaren led another Team Canada trade mission of premiers and business leaders to Latin America, where a potential $2.7 billion worth of commercial agreements were signed. More than 250 business leaders were involved in the trip to Brazil, Chile and Argentina. In Brazil, contracts were signed with Brascan, Hydro Quebec, the Canadian Wheat Board, Newbridge Networks, and 29 other corporations. In Chile, Barrick Gold, Inco, Noranda, SNC Lavelin, Methanex, Bema Gold, and 27 other Canadian corporations signed contracts worth $1.7 billion. In addition, 33 Canadian companies also signed business contracts in Argentina.

Nothing was said by Chrétien or the premiers about the misery and deprivation inflicted on the majority of Chileans by the economic policies of Chile's General Augusto Pinochet, let alone the widespread repression of human rights perpetrated under his regime. Indeed, Peter Munk, the CEO of Barrick Gold, which has extensive investments in Chile, has been quick not only to defend but to praise Pinochet's economic model in Chile, saying, "Perhaps Canada and the U.S. should check exactly what it is the Chileans are doing right."

A year later, Team Canada was in Asia signing prospective business ventures with India, Pakistan, Malaysia and Indonesia. In India, business contracts and agreements worth some $3.44 billion were signed with over 70 Canadian companies, including Bell Canada, Dominion Textiles, Mitel, SNC Lavelin and Ontario Hydro. Another $2 billion worth of business contracts were signed by Alcan Aluminum, SNC Lavelin, Sunora Foods, Teleglobe Canada, World Tel and 15 other Canadian companies. Another 44 were signed in Malaysia worth close to half a billion dollars. In Indonesia, 54 business contracts and agreements totalling $2.76 billion were signed with Canadian firms, including Atomic Energy of Canada, Northern Telecom, SNC Lavelin, Sun Life Assurance, LanSer Technologies, Interprovincial Pipelines, and the Sydney Steel Corporation. While Chrétien did sign an agreement to provide technical and financial support for the Indonesian Human Rights Commission, the Canadian government is still prepared to promote business deals with the brutal Suharto regime which has been responsible for the genocide of 200,000 people in East Timor.

These trade contradictions in Canada's foreign policy were further heightened when the third Team Canada mission went to South Korea, the Philippines and Thailand in January, 1997. Heralded as the largest trade delegation in Canadian history, the prime minister and the premiers, plus 500 assorted CEOs, politicians and educators, landed at the military airport in Seoul just as riots were breaking out in the streets over South Korea's harsh new labour legislation. While the Canadians were herded into trucks decorated with red maple leaves and whisked along a city route lined with armed police equipped with helmets and shields, other squads of military police were throwing tear gas into a demonstration of 3,000 Korean workers. When asked to comment, the only words Chrétien reportedly could muster were, "It's a local concern." His only concerns were the 73 business contracts totalling $600 million that were going to be signed during the mission's first full day.

More than anything else, the Team Canada trade missions demonstrate the extent to which the Canadian government has

become a tool of big business used to promote profitable investments in the new global economy. Although several billions of
dollars in contracts were announced, many of these were decla-
rations of intent rather than actual deals. To be sure, increased
exports to Asian and Latin American markets would translate into
some jobs back in this country. But government institutions like
the Export Development Corporation were originally established
to assist Canadian businesses to develop markets for their exports abroad. Now the CEOs are able to summon Canada's highest political leaders to do their bidding for them in international
markets.

At the same time, the BCNI has positioned itself to play a
quasi-ambassadorial role by signing "strategic alliance agreements" with like-minded big business coalitions in many of these
regions, including the Confederación de la Producción y del
Comercio in Chile, which actively supported the Pinochet regime's repressive economic measures. What's more, Ottawa also
turned a blind eye when Peter Munk's Barrick Gold of Toronto,
aided by an intervention from Brian Mulroney (as well as former
U.S. President George Bush), tried to strike a deal with the repressive Suharto regime of Indonesia to develop what was then
being touted as the world's richest untapped gold deposit.

Meanwhile, MacLaren had also led the way in spearheading
a new round of free trade negotiations on behalf of Canadian
corporations, starting with the expansion of NAFTA to include
Chile. When the Clinton Administration in the U.S. was blocked
by the Republican-dominated Congress from proceeding with
agreements reached at the Summit of the Americas in December
1994 to expand NAFTA throughout Latin America, Canada agreed
to go ahead and negotiate a bilateral deal with Chile under the
NAFTA framework. But when Art Eggleton, who had succeeded
MacLaren as Canada's trade minister in the spring of 1996, was
pressed by the Canadian Labour Congress to use the Chile negotiations to reopen NAFTA for the purpose of inserting stronger
and more effective labour and environmental codes, he made it
clear that no attempts would be made to change or improve on
the existing NAFTA rules and standards. The reason, he said,
was that the U.S. was unlikely to support such changes to the
NAFTA model. Yet, by signing a bilateral deal with Chile in
November 1996, Canada accommodated itself to Chile's own
laws, which permit flagrant violations of workers' rights and the

use of pesticides and chemicals that are banned here in Canada.

Similarly, Canada has become an increasingly active player in promoting the Asia Pacific Economic Cooperation (APEC) forum, along the lines of the NAFTA model of free trade. Since Asia has been designated as the centre of growth for the world economy in the 21st century, Japanese and U.S. corporations are scrambling to gain control over the region. Canadian businesses, too, want to get a piece of the action. Yet, as U.S. Under-Secretary of State Joan Speers stated before a Congressional committee: "APEC is for business. Through APEC, we aim to get governments out of the way, opening the way for business to do business."

This also appeared to be the position adopted by Ottawa at a summit meeting of APEC leaders in the Philippines in November 1996, when Trade Minister Eggleton submitted Canada's plan of action, calling for accelerated privatization and deregulation in order to create more favourable conditions for the flow of foreign investment in the region. This was essentially the same message delivered by Chrétien when he gave a keynote address to a parallel summit meeting of corporate CEOs in Manila, calling for even more direct participation of business leaders in the future development of APEC.

Indeed, the Chretien government has become one of the world's most vocal cheerleaders for free trade in the interests of big business. More recently, it has placed Canada at the forefront of a European-led campaign to develop an investment treaty as the centrepiece of the World Trade Organization. Through 1996, Canada emerged as a key player, working closely with the European Community and the U.S., in promoting the proposed MAI with other nations, notably the developing countries of the South. It seems to matter little to the Chrétien government that the investment code in the FTA and NAFTA has done little to promote job-creating production in Canada. Nor does it seem to matter that it's not only Canadian exports that have risen sharply as a result of free trade, but so have foreign imports, a trend which has had a negative impact on Canadian manufacturers who produce primarily for our domestic market. According to the Alliance of Manufacturers and Exporters Canada, manufactured goods from Canadian producers sold in Canada plummeted from 73 per cent in 1980 to 40 per cent in 1996. Imports made up the remaining 60 per cent. Little wonder that free trade has turned out to be a nightmare for most Canadians.

Ottawa has clearly become a stalking horse for both Canadian and U.S. transnational corporate interests on the global trade investment front. As if surrendering our own national sovereignty was not enough, the Chrétien government is now in the business of helping other countries do the same. ✪

4. Corporate Rule

*Does this mean we've had
a coup d'état in this country?*

...Sure seems like it. But it's obviously not the kind of coup d'état we're used to hearing about in other countries. This isn't a coup by the military or armed revolutionaries.

...No. And it's not an invasion by a foreign country. It's a coup that was slowly and quietly pulled off by big business. They've done it with the help of their political minions in Ottawa and the provinces, as well as their allies in universities and the media, and in global corporations around the world.

...Talking about this reminds me of what Brian Mulroney promised a few years ago: "Give me 20 years and you won't recognize this country any more." Well, between Mulroney and Chrétien, it hasn't even taken that long.

...They obviously know something the rest of us don't—that it doesn't matter any more what political party forms the government. So much so that there's no longer any difference between what big business wants and what governments say and do. The real agenda is being set behind the scenes by the transnational corporations.

...It sure looks like our whole political system has been reshaped on the assumption that what's good for General Motors is automatically good for the rest of us.

...A questionable assumption, to say the least. It used to be that the politicians we elected were accountable to the voters, so we could get a real change of policies and priorities by changing the governing parties. But what do we do in a system where all governments are held hostage by corporations that have no public accountability?

Counter-Revolution

WHEN POLITICAL AUTHOR Peter C. Newman criss-crossed the country in 1996 promoting his latest saga on the Mulroney years, he left a slightly mistaken impression in the minds of Canadians as to what had been achieved under the Conservatives. This was not, as Newman had characterized it, "A Canadian Revolution." What Mulroney, and later Chrétien, were party to was more a "counter-revolution." The same could be said of Mike Harris's "Common Sense Revolution" in Ontario and the Klein Revolution in Alberta. No matter which way you look at it, these and other political leaders are engaged in nothing less than the systematic dismantling and restructuring of the socioeconomic system that was built up in Canada over the past 60 years. Corporate Canada has all but succeeded in its mission to eradicate the Keynesian social welfare state in this country.

The goal is to restore Canada to an unimpeded free market economy. At the heart of this counter-revolution is the destabilization of the public sector and the crowning of the private sector as the engine of economic and social development. When it comes to Canada's future, the free market is to reign supreme, unfettered by government intervention and regulation. To paraphrase Maude Barlow, the Canadian experiment of a "social nation state" is being dismantled in favour of a "corporate nation state."

Like most counter-revolutions, this too was carried out through an organized coup d'état. But this was no ordinary political coup. It was not engineered by an armed military assault on Parliament Hill in Ottawa. Instead, it was finessed by a band of CEOs from Bay Street in pin-striped suits. The takeover was hostile, but not violent. There was no overthrow of the prime minister or the minister of finance or the rest of the cabinet. On the contrary, these politicians were seen by the BCNI and its allies as useful servants for implementing the counter-revolution.

As we have seen, the strategy of big business was to seize control over the levers of public policy-making at both national and provincial levels. Coordinated by the BCNI, the country's leading corporate CEOs mobilizd a powerful shadow cabinet in Ottawa to oversee and direct the basic reorientation of fiscal, economic, social, and environmental policy-making in Canada. Nor was this political coup carried out through a sudden, dramatic action. It was gradually developed by the BCNI and its allies through a series of actions on multiple policy fronts over a period of no less than 20 years.

In effect, this is what John Ralston Saul, one of Canada's leading contemporary political philosophers, means when he says that "we are now living in the midst of a coup d'état in slow motion." In his 1995 Massey Lecture series, Saul lamented the growth of corporate power in our society which, he says, is disfiguring the ideal of the public good, turning citizens into consumers, and weakening the fabric of democracy. Instead of citizens making a conscious choice to move down this path, Saul deplores the fact that what we have called a counter-revolution has been planned and pulled off by economic and political élites. Even in the United States, he notes, a president can be elected on a mandate to bring in comprehensive health care, only to find that his plans to do so are thwarted, not so much by Congress itself, but by the mobilization of what he calls the "corporatist forces."

"What the corporatist system is telling us," says Saul, "is that the democratic system is no longer appropriate." This is the same message which the Trilateralists started promoting almost 20 years ago when they attacked the Keynesian state for creating "excess democracy."

All of which leads to the question of whether this counter-revolution has been the product of a conspiracy. After all, as we have seen, well-orchestrated attacks on the Keynesian social welfare state, based on the strategic vision outlined by the Trilateralists and the libertarians, have been taking place all over the Western world, starting with Margaret Thatcher's Britain and Ronald Reagan's United States. We also know how this same strategic vision was used to whip the poor countries of the South into line through structural adjustment programs imposed by the World Bank and the IMF.

So was the coup engineered by the BCNI and its allies a conspiracy? For sociologist Patricia Marchak, a lot depends on how the term "conspiracy" is being used. If, by conspiracy, we mean a gathering of big business interests to more effectively influence, if not direct, government policy-making, then the answer is "yes." But if conspiracy means a secret, clandestine operation plotted by big business to seize control of the reins of government in Ottawa, then the answer is "no." In general, the plans of the BCNI and its allies have been relatively transparent.

In any case, what's most important here is that Canadians come to grips with the realities of corporate power in the social and political life of this country. As we move into the 21st century, the transnational corporation has emerged as the single most powerful institution dominating our times. More than any other institution, the transnational corporation possesses the two main instruments of power in the new global economy: capital and technology.

Utilizing advanced communication and production technologies, along with direct access to global pools of finance capital, these institutions can shift production and services instantly around the world to take advantage of ever more profitable investment opportunities, outflanking not only the interests of workers and communities, but of nation states as well. This is true whether we are talking about domestic or foreign-based transnationals. These same institutions have gained control over much of our political life, not only in this country but elsewhere in the world. In effect, the transnational corporation has moved into the very centre of our history as a dynamic social force reshaping the destinies of nations and peoples.

Indeed, the turning of the millennium signals the dawn of a new political era, the age of corporate rule. The common theme running through all of Corporate Canada's strategies and campaigns—from privatization and deregulation to free trade, from corporate tax reforms to deficit-slashing and the dismantling of public services and social programs—is the re-invention of the role and powers of government.

The BCNI calls it the return to "minimal government." But what is really going on is that the Canadian state is being completely reorganized and restructured to serve the interests of transnational competition and investment in the new global economy. And with this, the fundamentals of our political life—the nation state, citizenship, and democracy itself—are being radically reshaped in the image of the corporation and free market economics. This is the trajectory along which the counter-revolution is now moving and taking us in its wake.

Yet somehow Canadians seem to be sleepwalking through this critical moment of our history. As Saul puts it, "We are engaged in an unconscious process which can be described as slow, masochistic suicide. And suicide", he adds, is usually "the product of an inability to see ourselves in the context of our reality."

Drawing on the insights we have gleaned so far about the political agenda of big business here in Canada and throughout the world, the task before us now is to try and come to grips with the emerging realities of corporate rule that are reshaping our destiny as a nation.

Corporate Citizenship

One of the cornerstones of this new political era is the fact that corporations themselves have achieved a legal status as "persons" and as "citizens," with political rights through both national and international law. Throughout the 20th century, a vast body of corporate law and legal doctrine has been put in place which now serves to both recognize and protect the political rights of corporations as citizens with respect to property, investment, markets, and related aspects of their operations.

While the law refers to corporations as "fictitious persons" or "fictitious citizens," this legal status gives them rights not only in the domain of market transactions such as the buying and selling of property, but also free speech through political advertising, as well as the right to sue for injuries, slander and libel. As a result, the rights and freedoms of corporations as "citizens" have been guaranteed protection under the law at a time when people increasingly find themselves losing their rights and freedoms as citizens in a democratic society.

Initially, it was governments themselves that gave corporations the legal permission to operate by granting charters. In Canada, corporations like the Hudson's Bay Co. and the Bank of Montreal were granted royal charters by the King of England through Parliament in Westminster, which provided a legal mandate to operate in what was then called British North America. While the practice of granting royal charters continued after Confederation, Ottawa and the provinces eventually assumed the responsibility of legally chartering corporations. In the U.S., state legislatures were given the power to grant charters or certificates of authority to corporations operating in their jurisdictions.

Without such a charter, no corporation has the legal right to own property, borrow money, sign contracts, hire or fire, accumulate assets or debts. As Richard Grossman and Frank Adams explain, corporations existed at the pleasure of the state legislature to serve the common good. State charters often specified social obligations to be performed by a corporation in exchange for the right to operate. And if a particular corporation failed to live up to its obligations, the state legislature would often revoke its charter. Through this chartering process, citizens effectively had sovereignty over corporations.

By using the courts, however, big business gradually turned the tables, gaining legal sovereignty superior to that of citizens in general. Hiring their own law firms, corporations tackled charter legislation in the courts at every turn. Once the U.S. Supreme Court ruled that corporations were to be recognized as "natural persons" under that country's constitution, they successfully used the Bill of Rights and the 14th Amendment to strike down hundreds of local, state and federal laws that elevated the rights of citizens over those of corporations. The courts gave corporations more protection over property rights, declaring that corporate contracts and the rate of return on investment were property that could not be meddled with by citizens or by their elected representatives.

Corporations were also granted powers of "eminent domain" under the law, with the result that jury trials were eliminated for determining whether corporate practices cause harm or injury and, if so, what damages should be assessed. The courts also ruled that workers were responsible for their own injuries on the job in the U.S., and regulatory agencies overseeing prices and rates of return were made answerable to the courts, not to Congress.

Although the process differed in Canada, the results were similar. Originally, Canadian citizens were not accorded as much constitutional protection from corporate power under British law as U.S. citizens. Nevertheless, big business was successful in establishing legal status and protection by building up a body of corporate law in the Canadian legal system. As in the U.S., close links were developed between business and law schools in universities which, in turn, served as engines for the production and expansion of corporate law.

Although the legal recognition of corporations as "persons" and "citizens" was fictitious, corporations were able to use this artificial creation to enhance their rights and privileges under the law. Through the system of corporate law that had been built up, decisions affecting ownership, production, work and money have been effectively kept beyond the reach of citizen action and democracy. At the same time, the "common good" has increasingly been redefined by the courts in favour of maximizing corporate production and profits.

More recently, corporations in Canada have successfully invoked the Charter of Rights and Freedoms to further consolidate their fictitious legal status as persons and citizens with political rights. As Toronto law professor Michael Mandel has shown, the Charter has become "a potent symbol" in "transforming business rights into moral rights." In the 1987 *Irwin Toy Ltd. v. Quebec* (A.G.) case, says Mandel, the Supreme Court ruled that "business advertising comes within the protection of the Charter as a fundamental freedom." A few years later, in the *Rothman's* case, the Charter right of "freedom of expression" (free speech) was used to strike down federal laws restricting tobacco advertising. The Charter has also been effectively used by retail corporations in their fight against Sunday closing laws, and by medical associations in their battles against provincial regulations affecting doctors.

Environmental lawyer David Boyd, however, now warns that

corporations are not only able to exploit the Charter's "freedom of association" and "freedom of expression" clauses to evade laws and regulations that restrict their right to engage in commercial activities. They can also take advantage of the sections of the Charter dealing with "life, liberty and security." In 1991, for example, the courts ruled in *R. v. Wholesale Travel Group Inc.* that corporations could explicitly make use of these Charter clauses (s.7) as a basis for asserting their rights and freedoms.

Moreover, as political commentator William Greider notes, corporations have capacities which ordinary citizens do not possess when it comes to enacting business firms' legal rights as artificial "persons" and "citizens" under the law. Corporations, unlike human beings, can potentially live forever. They can exist in many places at once. They can alter their identities and become different "persons." They can sell themselves to new owners. Above all, corporations possess economic and political resources which citizens, for the most part, could never hope to accumulate. Indeed, big business has managed to persuade the courts to turn a blind eye towards these inequalities and differences. As "citizens," large corporations compete on equal terms with small businesses and individual citizens. In effect, corporations are granted the status of first-class citizenship under the law, while the people at best are relegated to the status of second-class citizenship in this country.

Corporations are able to use their first-class citizenship status to make major gains through both the courts and governments. When corporations, for example, are charged with committing crimes such as dumping toxic wastes or failing to apply adequate environmental safeguards, CEOs are quick to ensure that their companies are treated as "artificial legal entities" by the courts. In doing so, they avoid being held personally accountable for their deeds.

Similarly, profitable corporations in Canada frequently take advantage of their special status as "citizens" by directing their lawyers and accountants to make use of every loophole available to avoid paying their fair share of taxes. Either that, or they utilize the extraordinary device of deferring taxes, a special privilege which is available exclusively to corporations. In doing so, they substantially reduce public revenues and thereby weaken the capacity of governments to regulate their operations. As Greider points out, corporations are "citizens" who regularly break the law with impunity, both in criminal and civil terms.

In recent years, the legal status of corporations as first-class "citizens" with political rights has been extended on a global basis, not only through international law, but more particularly through the establishment of the new free trade regimes. As we have seen, both NAFTA and the WTO are designed to provide legal protections for the rights and freedoms of transnational corporations. The national treatment clauses in NAFTA, which guarantee that foreign investors have the same rights and freedoms as domestic firms, are expected not only to be entrenched but even expanded under the new WTO.

What this means, in effect, is that transnational corporations are poised to become the only entities recognized as global "citizens" with guaranteed political rights throughout the world. Wherever they go—Citizen Exxon or Citizen Ford, Citizen IBM or Citizen GE, Citizen Mitsubishi or Citizen Shell, Citizen Pepsi or Citizen McDonald's—their political rights as investors will be constitutionally guaranteed under the new free trade regimes.

Indeed, NAFTA and the WTO are designed to be the economic constitutions of the new world order. Here in Canada, if a conflict should arise between a particular piece of federal or provincial legislation and the investor rights of a foreign-based transnational corporation under free trade, the legislative authority of NAFTA or the WTO would supersede our own legislation.

The tragic irony is that corporations are being granted first-class citizenship rights at a time when people in this country and elsewhere in the world are losing many of their basic rights as citizens. Whether it be full employment, health care, social assistance, environmental safeguards, adequate housing, child care, old age pensions, public broadcasting, consumer protection, or a host of related concerns, Canadians see some of their basic rights as citizens being severely weakened, if not removed altogether. The problem here is not only that the rights of corporations now supersede those of citizens in many areas. Nor is it that corporations and people are increasingly being divided into first-class and second-class citizens. The tragedy is that corporations have become "citizens" while people are being stripped of their citizenship and relegated to the status of "consumers."

Political Machine

By consolidating their citizenship status, corporations have established a legal base from which they can play an increasingly active political role in redirecting the affairs of state. There is, of course, nothing new in big business playing an influential role in public policy-making in Canada. From the Hudson's Bay Company and the

Bank of Montreal before and after Confederation to the latter-day family empires of the Bronfmans, the Irvings, the Westons, the Thomsons and the Blacks of contemporary Canadian politics, corporations have played a crucial and often decisive role at various times in determining the economic and social policy directions of this country.

What is new today is that big business has become much more strategic and dominant in its political activities. As we have seen, the BCNI has provided the corporations with a powerful mechanism for influencing politics and governance. By pooling and targeting their financial capacities and professional skills, says Greider, corporations have begun to think and act, both individually and collectively, as a "political machine."

First, corporations have learned how they can more effectively translate their considerable assets into political clout. Obviously, cabinet ministers in Ottawa and the provincial capitals cannot easily disregard the policy proposals and demands of CEOs from corporations representing major sectors of the Canadian economy, such as the Big Three automakers (General Motors, Ford, and Chrysler) with combined annual sales in 1995 of $62.7 billion, or the Big Five national banks (Royal, C.I.B.C., Montreal, Nova Scotia, and Toronto Dominion) with 1995 revenues totalling $61.4 billion, or computer and telecommunication companies (B.C.E. Inc., Northern Telecom, IBM Canada, Bell Canada) with $54.2 billion in 1995 revenues, to name but a few. And when the 160-member BCNI, with combined assets of $1.5 trillion, throws its full weight behind specific policy demands, the impact can be overpowering.

More recently, however, CEOs are claiming to represent a constituency base as well as raw economic power. In advocating their policy demands, CEOs increasingly claim to represent the interests of hundreds of thousands of workers, shareholders, customers and suppliers whose livelihood allegedly depends on "their" corporation. Given today's global economy, which enables corporations to pack up and shift production wherever they can exploit the cheapest labour and lowest taxes, this claim to a constituency base is clearly spurious, but it still serves to maximize their political influence.

Second, corporations have devised diverse ways of developing and promoting a political platform calling for massive changes in public policy. The BCNI's 1994 ten-point program advocating an overhaul of Canada's fiscal, economic, social and trade policies, which the Chrétien government has scrupulously followed, is a prime example of this kind of corporate political platform. But BCNI chief

Tom d'Aquino, knowing full well that big business is vulnerable to the charge of representing vested interests, has been careful to ensure that a more diversified strategy is pursued in promoting its political platform.

As we have seen, this is where corporate think tanks like the C.D. Howe and the Fraser institutes come into the picture. Even though the Howe is mainly funded by BCNI member corporations, it has the reputation of being an independent academic institute that can produce detailed studies on specific policy issues. That these studies happen to concur with and reinforce the big business platform is of course entirely coincidental. In the absence of government-sponsored policy think tanks like the Economic Council and the Science Council (which were abolished by the Mulroney government), the Howe has gained manoeuvring room in influencing the Ottawa bureaucracy.

At the same time, the Fraser Institute has played a more ideological role, gradually changing people's attitudes and cultural values by targeting and discrediting sacred cows (e.g., social programs) and applying shock treatment (e.g., debt terrorism). In short, while different agencies and tactics have been deployed, what is important is that the élites have been singing from the same corporate song book.

Third, corporations have learned to make more effective use of their political donations as an insurance policy to guarantee that their platform is not only adopted by the major parties but is implemented by whatever party forms a government. Traditionally, Corporate Canada has been even-handed in its donations to the two major governing parties, the Liberals and the Conservatives. But in 1994 the Liberals received three times more from corporations than the Conservatives and 12 times more than the Reform party. In 1993, no less than 56 per cent of all donations made to the Liberal election campaign came from corporations. It is now generally conceded that no candidate for the leadership of the Liberal party would stand a chance without substantial funding from the corporations. Moreover, increasing business donations to the electoral campaigns of key politicians and cabinet ministers has opened up charges that corporations are simply buying candidates.

In any case, this corporate insurance policy has certainly paid off, most notably perhaps in Paul Martin's policy reversal on debt reduction and job creation. The one exception where corporate donations to the Liberals may have failed to deliver the expected policy results is in the case of the tobacco industry. In 1994, tobacco companies like Imasco and Rothmans were among the major corporate contributors to the Liberal coffers. Although they were handed a substantial tax cut as part of an effort to curb cross-border cigarette smuggling, the proposed tobacco legislation introduced by Health Minister David Dingwall at the end of 1996, calling for a crackdown on tobacco advertising, was a major setback for these companies. (However, this legislation may eventually prove to be a diversionary tactic aimed at "proving" that the Liberals are not totally in the pockets of big business.)

Fourth, corporations have strengthened their political platform by developing more sophisticated lobby machinery. In addition to the BCNI, which has direct and immediate access to cabinet ministers and senior bureaucrats, corporations have hired their own professional lobbyists, such as Hill & Knowlton and Government Policy Consultants Inc. Today there are well over 450 such lobby firms in Ottawa, serving mainly corporate clients, compared with a few dozen back in the early 1980s. Wining and dining politicians and senior bureaucrats on behalf of corporate clients, these lobby firms have become a strategic instrument for big business in directly shaping public policy, both in drafting legislation and spending public revenues.

What's more, this corporate lobbying is subsidized by the taxpayer, since corporations can deduct their lobbying expenses from their taxable income. At the same time, corporations have established sophisticated lobbying operations in key foreign capitals like Washington, D.C. During the late 1980s, for example, Japanese corporations were spending an estimated $100 million a year on political lobbying in the U.S. to modify and in some cases to rewrite U.S. legislation. Some 55 public relations, law and lobby firms are also employed by Canadian corporations and government agencies in Washington to actively promote their interests in the U.S.

Fifth, corporations are making extensive use of political advertising and citizens' front groups to reach a broader public and build support for their platform. As we have seen, one of the major weapons in the corporate arsenal is the use of advertising to carry a political message. An increasing portion of the estimated $150 billion spent on corporate advertising in the world each year is earmarked for political advertising. Yet there are few, if any, effective regulations on such advertising by corporations. Instead of providing information on specific policy issues and proposals for public debate, this kind of political advertising tends to be a form of propaganda designed to promote particular corporate interests.

Although much of this business propaganda comes to us across the air waves from the U.S., there are numerous Canadian examples. One of the more recent was the series of Bank of Montreal ads using black and white scenes of jobless and hungry protesters from the Depression and depicting the B of M as "the bank that cares."

At the same time, corporations have also been active in forming and/or financing their own citizens' front groups to build public support for their issues and policy demands. Although the BCNI maintains an arms-length distance from business-financed organizations like the National Citizens' Coalition and the Canadian Taxpayers' Association, the fact remains that the activities of these groups promote some of the main planks in the BCNI's political platform. Meanwhile, corporations in industries ranging from forestry, tobacco and phamaceuticals, to oil, nuclear energy and telecommunications have been known to organize and finance their own citizens' groups to undercut community-based public interest groups opposed to their projects.

Corporate State

As we have seen, big business utilized these and related components in building its own political machine in this country. Stage by stage, this political machine has been strategically employed by Corporate Canada in carrying out its "coup d'état in slow motion" and its mission to dismantle the Keynesian social welfare state. But this certainly did not mean that the state would have no role to play after the counter-revolution. In advanced capitalist economies such as Canada's, governments have always been used by corporations to create the conditions needed for the accumulation of capital and the maximization of profits.

During the 19th and early part of the 20th century, the country was largely run as a laissez faire state in which government played a minimal role in the economy, thereby allowing corporations and businesses to operate with few regulations and restrictions. Following the Great Depression, a compromise between capital and labour gave rise to a new model of government—what we have been calling the social welfare state—which was based on Keynesian theories and intervened more directly in the running of the economy.

Although the social welfare state was used by big business to serve its interests in accumulating capital and profits, it was also structured in such a way that it could be modified by countervailing powers exercised by labour unions, consumer groups and social organizations. As a result, it was often compelled to play a much more active role in regulating the operations of business and corporations over the past 50 years or so. Now that the social welfare state is being dismantled, another radical overhaul of government is in the works.

At first glance, it certainly seems like the rapid expansion of transnational corporate power has eclipsed that of nation states. After all, there has been a massive transfer of power from the public to the private sector, out of the hands of national governments and into the hands of transnational corporations. Says long-time observer Richard Barnet, transnational corporations have become the "lords of the global economy." What's more, adds political scientist Robert Cox, transnational corporations are not only "bypassing nation states" but the state itself is now compelled to act as a kind of "transmission belt from the global to the national economy."

Whereas the Keynesian model of governance tended to act as a "buffer," defending the domestic needs of its own people against the negative impacts of foreign capital and other external forces, Cox argues that power within the state today is becoming much more concentrated in those agencies which are in closest touch with the global economy. Meanwhile, those agencies of government which service the domestic needs of people are increasingly relegated to a subordinate role in this realignment of power. By functioning as a "transmission belt," Cox implies that national governments are rendered virtually powerless and redundant by transnational corporations in the new global economy.

Canadian political scientist Leo Panitch has a slightly different take. Acknowledging the growing concentration of power in the hands of transnational corporations within the new global economy, Panitch says that the capacity of national governments to control corporations and capital in the past has been overestimated. There is a tendency, he says, to ignore the fact that governments have cooperated with corporations in carrying out strategies for privatization, deregulation and free trade. Economic globalization, he points out, "is also a process that takes place in, through, and under the aegis of states; it is encoded by them and in important respects even authored by them." The state, in other words, is by no means neutral. In Panitch's view, transnational capital is not so much "bypassing" national governments as it is "reorganizing" the state to serve its own agenda. While agreeing with Cox that this entails a shift in power within government structures, Panitch argues that the concentration and centralization of state powers that is taking place is "the necessary condition of and accompaniment to global market discipline." And government social ministries such as health, education, welfare and labour "are not so much being subordinated as they are being restructured."

In short, national governments are being retooled to further advance the interests of transnational capital. But for Panitch, the extent to which national governments are "reorganized" and "restructured" in response to the demands of economic globalization still depends a great deal on the struggle between social forces within each nation state. In preparing government budgets, for example, do Ottawa and the provinces understand themselves to be primarily accountable to international finance? "Or are they accountable to international finance because they are accountable to Bay Street?" Panitch's point is well taken, especially in light of the pressures that finance brokers from Bay Street put on Wall Street bond-rating agencies like Moody's to downgrade Ottawa's credit rate, and the way in which Paul Martin and the finance department manipulated this downgrading to mobilize public support for his 1995 deficit-slashing budget.

But if the role and powers of the state are being reorganized to further advance the interests of transnational corporations, then what kind of state is being created as a replacement for the Keynesian model of government?

At this point, what seems to be emerging is a corporate state that is primarily designed to create the conditions necessary for profitable transnational investment and competition. This, in turn, calls for a more authoritarian model of government. For if the central task of this new corporate state is to facilitate profitable investment and competition, this in effect means that all of the major sectors of a national economy and society—fiscal, monetary, industrial, resource, service, social, cultural, agricultural, trade, transportation, environment, entertainment, communications—need to be reorganized to serve these ends.

While the driving force behind this agenda is the power of domestic and transnational capital, corporations realize that only governments have the authority and legitimacy to restructure the country's economy and society. The state, therefore, has a strategic role to play, not only in reorganizing the main sectors, but also in disciplining the population to make the necessary adjustments to this new system of corporate rule. To do so, certain powers need to be concentrated and centralized in the hands of the national government, while others need to be devolved and decentralized in the hands of provincial governments and agencies.

Just as the Keynesian state was largely organized around the theme of social welfare, so it can be argued that the new corporate state is being organized around a common theme: *investor security.* The prime focus is on security for profitable investment. For the state, the name of the game is to provide a secure place and climate for profitable transnational investment and competition. In other words, security for investors, but not citizens.

As we have seen, Ottawa and the provinces are getting out of the business of ensuring that the basic economic and social needs of Canadians are adequately met, and instead are getting into the business of ensuring that corporations have the conditions they need to become more profitable and competitive. This is what investor security means as an organizing principle for governments today. The priority is on providing *security* for corporations, not for citizens, whose lot has become one of growing *insecurity* (unless, of course, we mean corporate "citizens"). If the property and investments of corporations should be seriously threatened by workers or communities, then the state would likely be obliged to invoke police or even military action to defend the rights of investors with armed force.

In order to make this corporate security state operational, government bureaucracies are not only being downsized, but are also being retooled to take on these new priorities. In Ottawa and the provinces, as well as in most other industrialized countries, Ted Gaebler and David Osborne's *Reinventing Government* has become the textbook for revamping the public service. Gaebler and Osborne provide a blueprint showing how the public sector can be reorganized to function like a business. Ten operating principles are outlined for making government departments more entrepreneurial, competitive and market-oriented. The public sector, they argue, must learn to "do more with less" and to develop a capacity to earn more than it spends.

In recent years, Gaebler's and Osborne's prescriptions have been touted by political leaders of all stripes: from Bill Clinton to Newt Gingrich in the U.S.; from Paul Martin to Ralph Klein and Bob Rae here in Canada. As a result, the cross-fertilization between the public and private sectors (which has always existed in Canada) has rapidly accelerated in recent years, with deputy ministers and CEOs exchanging their positions as if they were walking through a set of revolving doors.

Although a radical overhaul of the public service along these lines was to be expected if Ottawa was going to be able to function in its new role as a corporate security state, it may have gone too far.

Recent trends show a rapid exodus of senior government bureaucrats in search of more lucrative positions in the private sector. But
being on the "wrong side of the fence" may have become more than
a salary issue. As Guelph University's John McMurtry put it: "Where
government expenditures do not serve to increase the profit
maximization of large corporations or rich investors, they are attacked
until they do."

Market Federalism

In order for the corporate state to function in Canada, however,
the federal system and the so-called economic union also had to be
overhauled. Once again, the BCNI led the way by sponsoring conferences on constitutional change, campaigning for a more decentralized Canada and advocating a radical reorganization of federal
and provincial powers. According to the BCNI's vision of federalism, Ottawa would have exclusive powers over fiscal and monetary
policy, international trade and national defence, all of which are key
to promoting investor security interests. Full responsibility for mining, forestry, tourism and housing would be turned over to the provinces, along with regional development, municipal affairs, recrea-
tion and sports.

The provinces would also be given most of the responsibility
for fisheries, agriculture, environment, culture, communication, industrial production and export promotion. At the same time, labour
training, social housing, child care and student loans would be handed
over to the provinces. In effect, the BCNI wants the national government to consolidate its powers over macro-economic policy, where
it can create a favourable climate for profitable transnational investment and competition, while shedding its powers and responsibilities for programs and services where it has been obligated in the past
to provide and maintain national standards. It is much easier for corporations to deal directly with the provinces, playing one off against
another, rather than being restricted by national rules and standards
set by Ottawa.

The BCNI's proposals for constitutional change are designed to
build on the model of market federalism which came into being with
the signing of the Internal Trade Agreement (ITA) between Ottawa
and the provinces in June, 1994. The objectives of the ITA were to
eliminate trade barriers between the provinces and to create a free
market union that would complement Canada's external commitments
under the FTA and NAFTA. But, in doing so, the ITA gave Ottawa

sweeping powers to impose a free market model and "corporate friendly policies" on all political jurisdictions in Canada. Specifically, the legislation authorizes the federal cabinet to "suspend rights or privileges granted by the Government of Canada to the provinces under the Agreement or any federal law...to modify or suspend the application of any federal law with respect to the province... [and] to take any other measures" it considers necessary to enforce the free market disciplines outlined in the ITA.

Accordingly, any provincial policy or legislation (such as labour, environmental, local procurement policies) perceived to be in conflict with the spirit of the ITA could be targeted by Ottawa or a corporation and struck down. While social programs are exempt, Ottawa can still use its equalization payments as a form of blackmail to enforce a more competitive model with respect to "have" and "have-not" provinces. In effect, the ITA contains powers to enforce free market disciplines similar to what is being developed on an international scale through the WTO.

Meanwhile, the Chrétien government tried to reinforce market federalism by introducing its Regulatory Efficiency Act. Under its proposed legislation, corporations would be allowed to bypass health, safety and environmental regulations. Instead of Parliament, cabinet ministers and government bureaucrats would be given the powers to grant companies dispensations from specific pieces of regulatory legislation. By doing so, as the Canadian Centre for Policy Alternatives points out, the proposed act would partially abrogate a 300-year-old British parliamentary tradition wherein the exercise of dispensation powers by the Crown instead of the Commons was declared illegal under the Bill of Rights. Moreover, there would have been no obligation to inform the public of any intention to grant dispensation to a particular corporation, only those parties who would have been directly affected.

With this legislation, Ottawa would have guaranteed corporations an effective escape hatch from the rule of law. That's why the BCNI's d'Aquino has repeatedly urged the Chrétien government to ignore the bill's "fear-mongering" opponents by ensuring its quick passage. Over the past two years, no fewer than three versions of such a bill (Bills C-62, C-84, and C-25) have been introduced, only to die on the Order Paper when the various Parliamentary sessions expired. Still, the Chrétien government seems determined to get a bill of this kind passed to grant regulatory exemptions to corporations, and it will no doubt be given a high priority in the first post-election session of the House of Commons.

Provincial governments, too, have wasted little time adjusting to the new disciplines of market federalism. In Ontario, Mike Harris unveiled the cornerstone of his Common Sense Revolution by introducing the Savings and Reconstruction Act in December 1995, calling for amendments to 43 separate pieces of legislation on the province's statute books. Much of this omnibus legislation was designed to transfer power into the hands of corporations and provide a more favourable climate for business to compete and make profitable investments.

The measures included an overhaul of parts of the province's labour code, the reduction of restrictions for toxic waste disposal on the mining industry, the weakening of environmental regulations affecting the forest industry, and the opening up of the door to private investment in Ontario's health care system by allowing U.S. for-profit corporations to establish facilities for services ranging from cataract surgery to abortions and kidney dialysis.

In Alberta, Ralph Klein's government made similar moves with its own sweeping changes in its regulatory system in favour of increased corporate investment. When, for example, Ottawa began downsizing the federal environment ministry and transferring responsibilities to the provinces, the Klein government responded by shutting down its own regulatory agencies, including the Environment Council of Alberta, the Water Resources Commission, and the Alberta Environment Trust Fund.

At the same time, the new market federalism has triggered a fundamental shakeup in the spending powers of both federal and provincial governments. According to a study conducted by Marjorie Cohen and associates at Simon Fraser University, federal budget measures like the shift to block funding and the Canada Health and Transfer Act have resulted in massive cutbacks in transfer payments to the provinces and particularly to people. Federal-to-provincial transfer payments under both the Mulroney and Chretien governments have been slashed by at least $37 billion.

Indeed, Ottawa used to account for 60 per cent of all government economic activity in Canada. Now it is responsible for only 40 per cent. And if the Conference Board of Canada's forecasts are accurate, Ottawa will account for only 30 per cent of all government spending by the year 2000, making this country one of the most decentralized federations in the world (even in the U.S., Washington accounts for 61 per cent of all government spending).

Although the provinces' spending powers for social programs and public services have increased, the new system of market federalism includes its own built-in disciplinary measures. As the CEO for the National Bank, André Bérard, pointed out, the real objective of decentralization is "to give the power to spend to those who don't have the power to borrow."

In fact, spearheaded by Alberta and Ontario, the provinces have drastically curtailed their own spending powers. In Ralph Klein's Alberta, with almost a billion dollars a year cut out of government spending, all departments were told to slash 20 per cent from their operating budgets in 1994. The Klein cuts included: 12.4 per cent in public education; 18 per cent in health care; 18.3 per cent in social services; 30 per cent in environmental protection; and 48 per cent in municipal services such as firefighting and police.

Not to be outdone, the Harris government's chainsaw in Ontario sliced a whopping $8 billion out of program spending, including a cut of almost 22 per cent from social assistance in the province. With the added promise of a 30 per cent tax cut, the program rollback would become permanent regardless of whether Ontario's public revenues increased in the future. In varying ways, every other province has followed with its own restructuring of program spending. Even before Ottawa killed the Canada Assistance Program, for example, New Brunswick had already introduced its own workfare program. While Quebec was the last to fall into line, the Parti Québécois government under Lucien Bouchard has seemingly bought into the BCNI's vision of market federalism by bringing forward its own restructuring program that includes deep cuts in program spending.

Indeed, provincial governments appear to be reorganizing themselves in such a way that they can function along the lines of the new corporate security state. Despite the rapid pace by which federal responsibilities and programs have been decentralized over the last three years, provincial government have managed to drastically reduce both overall spending and their regulatory measures on corporate activities in most of these areas.

In order to bring about the sweeping changes required, several provincial governments have found it necessary to consolidate and centralize their own powers. In the case of Ontario, for example, the 1996 Savings and Reconstruction Act served to centralize power in the hands of the cabinet at Queen's Park, giving certain ministers unprecedented authority to make sweeping changes in health care, public education, environmental protection and municipal affairs. And the Harris government's 1997 omnibus legislation calling for the amalgamation of municipalities into mega-cities may be the cutting edge of a whole new and more centralized system of municipalities under provincial authority within the corporate state.

The proposal, for example, to take public education off the property tax base and replace it with welfare and social assistance would not only serve to consolidate a great deal of provincial control over education, but would put the future of low-income people on an even more precarious footing.

Meanwhile, there has also been a massive transfer of wealth and power from the public to the private sector which has, in turn, altered the power dynamics of this market federalism. In addition to the transfers that take place through the sale of public sector institutions and enterprises, and the removal of regulatory measures over the operations of corporations in particular industries, there are the direct transfers between governments and banks paid in the form of interest on loans. Between 1988 and 1995, reports economist Jim Stanford, the federal government increased its debt loans to Canadian banks by over 500 per cent, from $15 billion to $80 billion. As a result, Ottawa now pays the Big Five banks close to $7 billion dollars annually in interest payments on these risk-free loans. In other words, the record-breaking profits racked up by the banks in recent years are largely due to a direct transfer of wealth from citizens to bankers in the form of interest payments on government debt loans.

Says Stanford, "The banks and other financial institutions are cashing in on our deficit...the 'debt' of Canadian taxpayers has become an 'asset' of the commercial banks [which, in turn,] can be recycled through the banking system to regenerate even more profit-making loans for the banks."

Adds Winnipeg journalist Frances Russell, Ottawa ends up acting as a "debt collector" for affluent investors.

Class Politics

This massive transfer of wealth—from public to private, from citizens to investors—reveals a new kind of class politics as a driving force behind the emerging corporate state. As Ed Finn of the Canadian Centre for Policy Alternatives points out, it is important to look at these wealth transfers in terms of the formation of an economic oligarchy in this country. Drawing upon the recent work of American sociologist Michael Lind, Finn notes that middle- and low-income earners are not only being taxed proportionately much more than the rich, "but they are being taxed to repay the rich."

In the U.S., argues Lind, the transfer of wealth from ordinary taxpayers to rich Americans through interest payments on the debt is "without precedent in history." This wealth transfer, says Lind, is fuelling the establishment of an economic oligarchy in the U.S. which controls the country's politics.

Here in Canada, says Finn, wealth transfers through interest payments, where nearly 40 cents out of every federal tax dollar goes to service the national debt, are even greater than in the U.S. While we like to think that economic oligarchies are the product of Latin American dictatorships, says Lind, we had better take a closer look at "the overclass" which is controlling money and power in our own society.

While myths portraying Canada as a classless society abound, it is evident that a Canadian overclass—an economic oligarchy—exists for those who want to see it. In 1992, the OECD reported that the top one per cent of the Canadian population owned 25 per cent of the country's assets (compared with 18 per cent in Britain and 42 per cent in the U.S.). The combined wealth of the 50 richest Canadians amounts to $39 billion. The top 50 include eight individuals and families who are billionaires. Leading the pack is newspaper magnate Kenneth Thomson with $8.2 billion, followed by the Irving Oil family at $7.5 billion, Charles Bronfman at Seagrams with $2.9 billion, the Eaton family at $1.7 billion, telecommunications magnate Ted Rogers with $1.4 billion, giant food retailer W. Gaylor Weston at $1.3 billion, the McCain brothers of New Brunswick with $1.2 billion, and Paul Desmarais of Power Corp. with $1 billion. The accumulated wealth of each of the remaining top 50 club members ranges between $145 million to just under $1 billion.

According to an analysis of Statistics Canada data, wealth transfers from middle- to upper-income Canadians over the past 20 years have deeply polarized class divisions in this country. Between 1973 and 1993, reports a CCPA study, the share of national income in Canada rose sharply for the wealthiest 30 per cent over that of the lowest 50 per cent of Canadians. In 1993 alone, the top 30 per cent of Canadian families took home an extra $14.3 billion over and above what they would have done in 1973 *had their share remained the same* and not increased over the 20-year period. Most of this added wealth transfer, the study shows, came from the bottom 50 per cent.

What's more, these class divisions have accelerated over the past six years. Between 1987 and 1993, the share of national income of the richest 30 per cent rose three to five times faster than it did during the previous 14 years, thereby transferring an extra $7.3 billion more into their hands than would have been the case had their share remained at the 1987 rate. Meanwhile, the data show that the bottom half of Canadian families lost income at the same rate. By 1993, their annual share of national income was $7.3 billion less than it would have been at the 1987 rate.

More recently, the annual income of the CEOs from Canada's largest corporations has been skyrocketing. According to a survey of 268 Canadian corporations by the KPMG management consulting firm, the average CEO salary rose "only" 8 per cent in 1995, but their total compensation package (including bonuses and incentives) rose by an average of 32 per cent since 1993. The 100 highest-paid CEOs each received packages totalling more than $1.4 million in 1995. Topping the list was Frank Stronach of Magna International with a $ 47 million compensation package. But these figures do not tell the whole story.

Many top CEOs also receive dividend income as major share-holders. Take, for example, newspaper mogul Ken Thomson. His shares in the Thomson Corporation generated a whopping $296 million in dividend income in 1995. Paul Desmarais Sr. received $55 million in dividend income along with his compensation package of $5.65 million. Other corporate leaders who enjoyed multi-million-dollar compensation packages in 1995 include: Galen Weston ($22 million); Laurent Beaudoin of Bombardier ($19.1 million); Conrad Black ($18.4 million); and the Billes family of Canadian Tire ($7 million). Black, incidentally, reportedly handed himself a gift of nearly $70 million one day this year in the form of a special dividend in Hollinger Inc. shares.

In the meantime, real wage levels of workers, says Andrew Jackson of the Canadian Labour Congress, have not only barely kept pace with the cost of living over the past 15 years but, compared with their bosses, workers' wages have fallen way behind.

Indeed, workers' wages were only a fraction of the pay packages received by their bosses in 1995. At Magna International, for example, Frank Stronach's compensation package of $47 million was more than 1,100 times the average wage of $37,006 earned by a Magna worker that year. At the Cott Corporation, Gerald Pencer's CEO package of $13 million was 927 times that of the average employee's wage of $14,023. Paul Desmarais of Power Corporation takes home a pay package that is 249 times that paid to his workers, which averaged $22,714 in 1995. The CEO of Maple Foods, Brent Ballentyne, who received a 1995 pay package of $3.58 million, was paid 256 times the $14,023 that his average employee received that year.

In the same vein, Richard Thomson's CEO package at the Toronto Dominion Bank was 230 times the average wage of the bank's tellers; Edgar Bronfman took home 180 times what the average worker at Seagrams did in 1995; Gerald Schwartz of the ONEX Corporation received a compensation package that was 159 time the average wage of the people who run the projectors in its theatres; and Purdy Crawford's pay package at Imasco was 100 times what workers were paid on average in the firm's tobacco plants.

In short, these are some of the dynamics of class politics that are spearheading the drive towards corporate rule today in this county. (For the latest figures on the Top 50 CEO compensation packages for 1996, see Appendix IV.) As New York University economist Edward Wolf, who has studied wealth distribution in North America for 25 years, puts it: "We are becoming an oligarchy like so many Latin American countries where economic and political power are concentrated in the hands of a small élite."

The Top 50 club of the richest Canadian families, coupled with the 100 or so CEOs who run the country's largest corporations, constitute the central core of this oligarchy in Canada. For the most part, they are also members of the BCNI. They know that having political power is key to the accumulation of wealth. They have been successful in building a political machine to take control over the levers of governance in both Ottawa and the provinces. Through this political machine, they have effectively restructured the role and powers of the state and the federation to serve their basic interests.

Not only is the state now obligated to reorganize the whole national system in order to secure a free market environment for profitable investment and competition, but it must also ensure an efficient transfer of wealth from the majority of Canadians into the hands of corporations and investors. And while this oligarchy continues to siphon off wealth and power, it employs what Lind calls a "divide and rule" strategy of holding the majority at bay by pitting one group of Canadians against another in "a zero sum struggle for the share of declining wage increases."

Manufactured Consent

At the same time, big business had other weapons in its arsenal to keep the majority of Canadians misinformed and powerless. To pull off a political coup of this magnitude and to engineer a restructuring of the Canadian state and federation without provoking a major uprising meant that the corporate élite had to have an effective means for controlling public discussion and debate in this country. After all, in advanced capitalist societies, social control is traditionally maintained not by military forces but through cultural institutions that shape people's attitudes, behaviour and values: education, entertainment, and especially the media. As Noam Chomsky has repeatedly demonstrated, public consent is often "manufactured" for those who govern and rule in democratic societies.

In recent years, Canada's media have become increasingly dominated by corporate moguls like Conrad Black, Ken Thomson, Paul Desmarais and Ted Rogers. Instead of keeping Canadians well informed about major public issues and stimulating debate from diverse political perspectives, the mainline media in this country have increasingly become a mouthpiece for the corporate agenda.

As media analyst James Winter of Windsor University explains, corporate ownership of Canada's major daily newspapers has become more and more concentrated in fewer hands over the past half century. In the late 1950s, the country's two largest newspaper chains, Southam and Thomson, owned 25 per cent of daily circulation. By 1970, the Special Senate Committee on Media Concentration was expressing alarm that their control had grown to 45 per cent. In 1980, the Kent Royal Commission on Newspapers reported that 57 per cent of daily circulation was concentrated in the hands of three major chains. Fifteen years later, Southam and Thomson controlled 67 per cent of the dailies, with the Toronto Star owning another 10 per cent. On top of this, Paul Desmarais owned four newspapers in Quebec and the Irvings controlled all of New Brunswick's newspapers.

Then came Conrad Black. Noted for being one of Canada's most outspoken CEOs on the ideology of corporate libertarianism, Black had already begun buying up a string of dailies, mainly in small towns and communities, where it soon became clear that he intended to exert influence over editorial content. Then in 1996 Black's Hollinger corporation seized control of the Southam chain and thereby suddenly became the majority owner of nearly 60 per cent of all daily newspaper circulation in the country.

When the deals are competed, Conrad Black, through Hollinger Inc., will own and control 64 out of the 104 daily newspapers in Canada, reaching 2.3 million households across the country. His empire includes all the dailies in Saskatchewan, Newfoundland and P.E.I., plus two-thirds of all the daily newspapers in Ontario. His Southam stable alone includes the *Vancouver Sun, Calgary Herald, Ottawa Citizen* and the *Montreal Gazette*. Moreover, through Southam, Black had effectively gained control over Canadian Press which provides news services to small-town papers and radio stations across the country in both official languages.

Through case studies, Winter shows that those who own and control the media today exert a great deal of influence over news content. This influence is exerted, he says, not only through hiring and firing practices, but also by the placement and the editing of news stories. While the examples are taken from the print media, the same patterns of control and influence can be found in radio and television broadcasting as well.

When former Toronto newspaper publisher John Basset was asked by a television interviewer: "Is it true that you use your own newspaper to push your own political views?", he replied, "Of course, why else would you own a newspaper?" More recently, Conrad Black's own right-hand man at Hollinger Inc., David Radler, succinctly described what ownership means in terms of exercising control over newspaper content when he said: "The buck stops with the ownership. I am responsible for meeting the payroll, therefore I will ultimately determine what the newspapers say and how they're going to be run." Under these circumstances, journalists who, after all, are themselves workers with individual and family responsibilities, have little recourse but to fall into line or join the ranks of the unemployed.

The corporate political views of the media moguls especially affects how the major news stories dealing with the economy are handled. Following the great free trade debate in 1988, for example, studies have showed that the pro-business free trade position promoted by the media, and the limited coverage given free trade opponents, were largely determined by those who owned and controlled most of the newspaper and broadcast media. Similarly, even though the Chrétien government was elected on the promise of jobs! jobs! jobs!, most of the Canadian media downplayed the rash of corporate downsizing during the mid-1990s while big business was making record profits. Instead, says Winter, media reports of massive layoffs and rising profits were often presented "without explanation, or attributed to mysterious and irresistible market forces such as globalization and international competitiveness."

Perhaps the greatest hoax promoted by the media moguls in recent years has been the notion that Canada's debt woes were caused by overspending on social programs. Not only did the media propagate this myth, but they almost totally ignored the real causes disclosed by non-business studies (including Statistics Canada), such as the Bank of Canada's persistently high interest rate policies and the massive drain on public revenues due to lower corporate tax rates and high unemployment.

Clearly, corporate domination of the country's major media industries has had a direct influence on policy decisions in Ottawa regarding communications and public broadcasting. In 1994, for example, Rogers Communications requested the Canadian Radio-Television and Telecommunication Commission (CRTC) to approve its $3.4 billion dollar acquisition of MacLean Hunter (which publishes MacLean's magazine). To consolidate their political influence, Rogers and one of its affiliates contributed a total of $100,000 to the Liberal party coffers that year, and the CRTC approval was promptly granted. A year later, the Chrétien cabinet took the unprecedented step of overturning a CRTC decision not to grant a license for direct-to-home satellite service to a particular Quebec-based corporation. The applicant was a company run by Chrétien's own son-in-law, André Desmarais, son of Paul Desmarais.

Today, one can only predict that similar powerful influences in the media industry are working overtime behind the scenes in Ottawa to ensure that the Chrétien government introduces measures to privatize the Canadian Broadcasting Corporation. All the hype about how "costly, inefficient and wasteful" the CBC is serves only one purpose, and that is the corporate takeover of public broadcasting in this country. While the CBC has often aped its private sector counterparts in helping to "manufacture consent" for the corporate agenda, it has also provided an important outlet for dissenting views. Its loss would be a crippling blow to democracy in this country.

In the long run, the real test of the power and influence of a corporate-controlled media is whether it can reshape the basic attitudes and values of the people and stifle their awareness of rising class divisions. At first glance, it seems like the Blacks, the Thomsons and the Desmarais have been highly successful. After all, we have certainly seen what appears to be a significant "cultural shift to the right" in the attitudes and values of Canadians. Values such as fairness, equality and sharing seem to have been swept away by a tidal wave of market values like competitiveness, profitability and efficiency. This value shift comes through in the meaner and tougher attitudes that, according to public opinion surveys, Canadians now have towards the poor, the unemployed, and immigrants. It is also evident in their apparent readiness to accept the erosion of universal social programs, along with workfare, two-tiered health care, and a minimal role on behalf of government in the future.

Nevertheless, an extensive survey of Canadian attitudes and values conducted by Ekos Research in 1994 (and updated in 1995) concluded that there was a fundamental difference between the perspective of the economic and political élites, on the one hand, and the general public on the other. While the élites were obsessed with controlling the deficit, for example, the public wanted more action on jobs and related social concerns. While the élites wanted the priority to be put on "competitiveness, prosperity, and minimal government," average citizens tended to rank these values towards the bottom of their list.

Indeed, the Ekos study revealed a growing distrust of the élites on the part of citizens in general. In the case of the deficit, half of the respondents said they believed that a crisis had been manufactured by government and big business.

Perhaps the manufacturing of public consent itself has not gone quite as deep as Corporate Canada would like. But the media is not the only cultural institution through which big business is able to shape people's values and mindsets. Public and post-secondary education have also become prime targets for corporate takeover. All over the country, deficit-driven provincial governments have been slashing education budgets, contracting out educational services, and exploring ways of privatizing pieces of the public education system. Cash-starved schools are increasingly turning to corporations to supply them with the technology, curriculum and food services they can no longer afford to buy. Coca Cola, McDonald's, Pepsi-Cola, Burger King, IBM, General Electric, Bell Canada and AT&T are a few of the brand name corporations which are more than ready to provide these services in exchange for the right to advertise their products in a captive youth market.

As education activist Jim Turk explains, corporations moving into the education field these days have three strategic objectives in mind. The first is to capture the youth market and a new generation of consumers. The second is to make the delivery of education more dependent on their corporate funds and products. The third is eventually to change the curriculum and the content of education programming in the schools. Says Turk: "The third objective is part of the corporate strategy of creating a more docile and subservient work force."

With massive cutbacks in federal funding for post-secondary education kicking in now, corporations are lining up at the doors of some universities to provide donations, equipment and services in exchange for new marketing opportunities. Northern Telecom, for example, recently made an $8 million grant to the University of Toronto for the establishment of a new telecommunications institute which will be overseen by a joint university-industry advisory council and where the company's spokesman vows "to get the best bang for our buck." York University's Atkinson College says that corporations donating $10,000 or more will have courses named after them, while Simon Fraser University has allowed companies to buy space over the urinals in men's washrooms on campus for advertising.

Once business firms get a stranglehold on the education system in this country, they will have gained control over one of the major levers for manufacturing consent. After all, corporations have more to sell than their brand names when they enter the education market. The commercialization of the classroom, as Maude Barlow and Heather-jane Robertson have shown, also has a great deal to do with producing a generation of children who will be the entrepreneurs, consumers and workers in tomorrow's economy. That's why programs like "Consumer Kids" in Toronto offer corporate executives workshops on "Marketing in the School System" and "How to Grow Your Customers From Childhood."

Gaining a measure of control over curriculum and educational materials, as well as access to new marketing opportunities in schools, colleges and universities is of strategic importance to the long-term interests of big business in this country. Yet, to give up on democratically-run education is to give up on democracy itself.

Democracy Sabotaged

In the final analysis, however, we are now living under a system of corporate rule that is dealing death blows to democracy in this country. What the Trilateral Commission targeted as "excess democracy" 20 years ago has all but been wiped out. Not only have citizens' rights been subverted in favour of investors' rights, but our society is rapidly moving in the direction where virtually only corporations can be said to have full citizenship status. The state, both at federal and provincial levels, has been restructured to primarily serve corporate demands for capital accumulation by securing a safe haven for profitable investment and competition.

Given the mastery which big business now has over the public policy-making apparatus in Ottawa, elected Members of Parliament have been reduced to a role of simply rubberstamping the decisions already made by cabinet in the interests of the big business shadow cabinet. When it comes to the major fiscal, economic, trade, social and environmental issues of the day, citizens' organizations which collectively represent the majority of Canadians on these issues are summarily dismissed in Ottawa as "special interest groups" and deprived of any effective voice in the corridors of power.

The agents of corporate rule have dealt a heavy blow to the very heart of democracy: civil society. As de Toqueville observed almost two centuries ago, civil society comprises the thousands of voluntary associations made up of citizens concerned about public policy issues. By occupying public space between big business and big government, they constitute the independent sector of society which is the lifeblood of democracy. In a democratic society, it is their role to guard against the tyranny of both the state and the market. But the core elements of civil society in Canada have been grievously weakened by the corporate takeover.

Labour unions, for example, representing 36 per cent of Canadian workers and having supported and pioneered progressive social change for most of the past 60 years, have had their bargaining powers undermined by broken government contracts, while their public image has been continuously assaulted by big business. Women's organizations, which have brought so much passion and vision to the struggle for social equality in this country, have been among the victims of government cutbacks. Environment groups, some of whom have readily put their bodies on the line to stop the onslaught of corporate power, have also been weakened by government cutbacks and attacks by big business. The mainline churches who, along with other religious bodies, have sometimes rallied the nation around a moral vision of social justice, have found their voices being silenced by big money, by the infiltration of right-wing Christian fundamentalism, and by a sharp decline in membership.

To be sure, civil society in Canada is not yet on its death bed. Despite the setbacks, there are still signs of democratic life stirring in labour, women's, environmental, and even religious movements across the country. So, too, in the nationalist movement where the fight for democratic control is coming alive again. But the new system of corporate rule makes it extremely difficult for these citizens' movements to participate effectively in the process of democratic social change. Business representatives now play a dominant role on almost all major government advisory groups, task forces, and commissions. Public access to information about government policymaking has been curtailed, not only by a substantially weakened access to information law, but also by cutbacks at StatsCanada as well as the shutdown of several key public policy research institutes.

More importantly, it is difficult for citizens' movements to know what to do in fighting for social change when the driving forces behind so much of government policy-making today are corporations.

Even if citizens' movements were to focus their sights on corporations as targets for social change, their efforts would be hampered by recent legislation reducing requirements of corporations to disclose information about their operations to Ottawa.

Ironically, a few powerful global investors like George Soros have recently come to the conclusion that fundamental democratic values and traditions are now threatened by the expansion of corporate power. "Although I have made a fortune in the finance markets," wrote Soros in the February 1997 issue of *Atlantic* magazine, "I now fear that the untrammelled intensification of laissez-faire capitalism and the spread of market values into all areas of life is endangering our open and democratic society."

Drawing upon the theory of an "open society" developed by economist-philosopher Karl Popper in the early part of this century, Soros calls for a rethinking of this ideal, which he says "can no longer be defined in terms of the Communist menace." Whereas Popper maintained that the extreme right (fascism) and the extreme left (communism) both suffered from the same problem, namely their reliance on the power of the state to repress the individual, Soros argues that the ideal of an open society today is "threatened from the opposite direction—from excessive individualism. Too much competition," he says,"and too little cooperation can cause intolerable inequities and instability." "The survival of the fittest," he warns, cannot be the guiding principle of an open and civilized society.

From another angle, Ed Finn maintains that we are living today in a plutocracy more so than a democracy. A plutocracy, he says, was the kind of system that existed in ancient Rome where those who ruled held both political and economic power at the same time. But, whereas the plutocrats in ancient Rome were politicians who were also the owners of most of the land, wealth, and slaves, the plutocrats in Canada are "the unelected and unaccountable corporate executives, bankers and money traders who now set the political agenda for all governments of all stripes." The politicians, he says, do their bidding. "The policies favoured and the laws enacted are those that enhance the wealth and power of the plutocracy."

To prevent popular uprisings, Finn notes that the Roman emperors used the formula of "bread and circuses" as the means for keeping the people well fed and entertained. While the modern equivalent of bread and circuses may take the form of food banks and television or sports events, he argues that the political process itself serves the same purpose. Politicians have become merely puppets whose strings are being pulled by the corporations. Like wrestling matches, says Finn, the politicians' antics on Parliament Hill provide Canadians with entertainment rather than genuine democratic governance.

Regardless of the imagery, Canadians must come to grips with the tragic fact that we are increasingly living under a corporate tyranny rather than a true democracy. Although corporations have always been willing to "tame anarchic democracy," political philosopher Benjamin Barber reminds us, they have also had "no problem tolerating tyranny itself." After all, corporations are themselves highly authoritarian and hierarchical institutions. The list of dictatorships around the world, says Barber, which corporations strengthen and legitimize with their investments, is extensive.

There is something insidious, however, about the corporate tyranny that oppresses our lives today. We are left with the illusion that all of this is simply a matter of "free choice" and "free will." The corporate state, after all, is grounded in the free market. Like democracy itself, the market offers people a free choice. But, as Barber says, quoting de Toqueville: "The body is left free but the soul is enslaved. Ideology of choice," he says, "liberates the body but totally constricts the soul. You choose, in effect, not to choose."

5. Citizens' Agenda

It's the corporations,
STUPID!

...You have to ask your-
self these days: how come
people aren't up in arms?
Where's the fight-back?
Do people really want to
live in a world that's
ruled by big corpora-
tions? Seems to me like
everyone has given up!

...That's not quite true.
Look at what's been go-
ing on in Ontario, where
200,000 people took to
the streets and pretty well shut down the entire city of Toronto. They
were protesting against the Harris government's dismantling of pub-
lic programs and services. Now, that's what I call mass resistance!

...Yeah, but you have to realize all that opposition was aimed at
the Tory government, as if only the government was to blame. You
know as well as I do that getting rid of Harris and his gang isn't
going to change anything. We'll still be living under corporate rule.
Whatever party is elected these days, big business still runs the show.

...Sure makes you wonder how much value people put on de-
mocracy. It's hard to believe Canadians are always ready to go to
war to fight for democracy in other countries, but don't want to stand
up for their democratic rights at home.

...Yeah, most Canadians these days seem to be sleepwalking
through this social and economic nightmare. There has to be some
way to wake them up! If people keep passively accepting corporate
rule, everything our parents and grandparents fought for will be
lost.

... Reminds me of that slogan Bill Clinton used in his first elec-
tion campaign: "It's the economy, stupid!" That sure got people's
attention. Maybe our slogan should be: "It's the corporations,
stupid!"

Citizens' Movements

THERE IS A FLIP SIDE to the story of the counter-revolution
that has been unfolding in this country over the past two decades. This has to do with the popular resistance that was mobilized by citizens' movements to the corporate agenda. Throughout the 1980s and the early 1990s, a dynamic movement of resistance took shape and form. A vibrant network of labour unions, women's groups, nationalist associations, religious organizations, environmental groups, farmers' associations, cultural
groups, professional organizations, international agencies, sen-
iors' groups, and a variety of community associations came together to fight some common battles around a variety of economic, social and environmental policy issues.

When the membership base of these citizen movements was
counted, their combined total accounted for the vast majority of
Canadians. What's more, the resistance mounted by these citizens' movements around key policy struggles like free trade were
effective in at least slowing down the momentum of the big business agenda at certain strategic moments. Without this popular
resistance, the counter-revolution we are experiencing today
would have been entrenched on a much deeper and more widespread scale.

The backbone of this broadly-based citizens' movement has
been, to a large extent, the country's labour unions, in both the
public and private sectors. The Canadian Labour Congress, the
largest labour central, represents over 2.5 million workers in almost every major sector of Canada's economy—automotive,
mining, steel, forestry, petroleum, hydro, food processing, railway, electrical, communications, pulp and paper, newspaper,
broadcasting, education, health care, culture, social services,
postal and retail services, along with federal, provincial and
municipal governments. The CLC has played a pivotal role over
the past ten years in providing much of the organizational resources required for social movement building.

Affiliates such as the Canadian Auto Workers, the United
Steel Workers, the Canadian Union of Public Employees, the
Communications, Energy and Paperworkers' Union, the Canadian Union of Postal Workers, the National Union of Public and
General Employees, and the Public Service Alliance of Canada
have also been key players from time to time in this process. So,
too, has the Confédération des syndicats nationaux, which repre-

sents a majority of the non-CLC affiliates in Quebec.

While labour unions have generally formed the backbone, the sparkplug for this resistance movement has often been generated by various social organizations. The Council of Canadians developed campaigns for mobilizing citizens on the basis of a socially progressive nationalism in this country. The National Action Committee on the Status of Women often provided creative leadership in designing campaigns, as well as reaching out to the majority of the population through more than 600 women's groups. Organizations like the National Farmers' Union made certain that the movement related to rural as well as urban Canada. Greenpeace and the range of constituencies that make up the Canadian Environmental Network were active in putting ecological priorities on the national agenda. Through bodies like the Ecumenical Coalition for Economic Justice, key sectors of the national churches (Anglican, Catholic, United, Presbyterian, and Lutheran) became actively engaged. Networks of teachers' associations and nurses' unions provided leadership on public education and health care issues, while international development agencies like Oxfam, CUSO and Inter Pares were instrumental in developing alliances in Third World countries, as well as addressing foreign policy concerns.

By 1988, these labour and social organizations had coalesced to form a broadly-based national coalition. At first called the Pro-Canada Network, it soon became known as the Action Canada Network. The ACN emerged as the vehicle through which labour unions and social organizations could develop common analysis, strategies, and campaigns for tackling the massive restructuring of economic and social policies. The ACN's sister organization, the Canadian Centre for Policy Alternatives, coordinated work on much of the research and analysis needed for the movement's activities and published numerous background documents on major economic and social policy issues. Provincial coalitions affiliated with the ACN were organized to develop campaign strategies on regional issues, as well as to coordinate campaign activities on national issues across the country. In Quebec, the Solidarité populaire Québec was set up as a national coalition which, in turn, developed a bi-national working relationship with the ACN. Three times a year, the member organizations of the ACN came together in a national assembly to hammer out agreements on common campaign strategies. In addition, through another sister organization, Common Frontiers, the ACN devel-

oped alliances with similar coalitions in other countries, primarily the United States and Mexico.

During this period, resistance campaigns were mobilized on
a nation-wide basis. While the Mulroney government managed
to win the 1988 free trade election, the movement used creative
popular education strategies in mobilizing 53 per cent of the population to vote against the U.S.-Canada deal. Campaigns were
mounted against the slashing of program spending in the federal
budgets of 1989, 1990 and 1991. In 1990, the movement waged
a vigorous battle with the Mulroney government over the implementation of the Goods and Services Tax, which came close to
being scuttled by a vote in the Senate. Single-issue campaigns
were also organized by member groups against the massive cutbacks in unemployment insurance, Medicare, the Canadian National Railway, and public broadcasting. By 1993, public opposition to NAFTA reached the point where it became the dominant
theme of a mass rally of over 100,000 people on Parliament Hill.

While all of this resistance contributed to the unprecedented
rout of the Mulroney Tories in the 1993 election, it wasn't long
before the Chrétien government became the target of a new round
of fightback campaigns. In 1994, the remnants of naive optimism
led the movement to participate in the Chrétien government's
social policy reform process, but by the time Paul Martin was
ready to bring down his infamous 1995 budget, the battle lines
had been drawn once again. Thereafter, the Canada Health and
Social Transfer (CHST) became the prime focal point for resistance, with single-issue campaigns being organized against the gut-
ting of the Canada Assistance Program, the weakening of Medicare,
and the proposed privatization of the Canada Pension Plan.

As early as 1991, however, there were signs that this movement of popular resistance was being demobilized. As the recession of the early 1990s deepened, right-wing values and attitudes
towards the poor and the unemployed began to harden. A split
between labour and women's groups erupted over the debate on
the Charlottetown constitutional accord, which found the CLC
lined up with the economic and political élites on the one side
and the NAC with the Reform Party and other populist forces on
the other side. Moreover, after a series of intense campaigns resulting in defeats, including some near misses, many activists
had reached the "burn-out" stage. The commitment to resistance
inside labour unions, women's groups and the churches began to
erode. When it became clear that the New Democratic Party

(largely due to the party's performance in power in Ontario, Saskatchewan, and British Columbia) could no longer mobilize its traditional base of support, there was a significant swing in political allegiance by 1993 that further contributed to the demobilization of popular resistance.

Although the election of the ultra-right Mike Harris government has provided a catalyst for the revival of popular resistance in Ontario, through the successful Days of Action mobilization, it remains unclear whether this new burst of solidarity is being geared toward a radical reversal of the "Common Sense Revolution," or merely a changing of the guard at Queen's Park.

New Politics

A closer look reveals a more fundamental strategic problem. As we have seen, the BCNI and its big business allies had already consolidated their stranglehold in Ottawa and most of the provinces in almost all areas of economic, social and environmental policy-making. The emergence of the corporate security state has, in effect, substantially transformed the nature and role of government in the interests of big business. While the citizens' movement described above often defined its resistance campaigns in terms of challenging the corporate agenda, the strategies and tactics employed did not necessarily reflect the analysis. In other words, the movement's campaign strategies were primarily aimed at governments *per se*, leaving unscathed the corporate power structure that is driving the public policy-making process in the first place.

When it comes to mobilizing resistance to the Chrétien regime in Ottawa, or the Harris and Klein regimes or their counterparts in the other provinces—on such issues as job creation, health care, social assistance, or environmental protection—there is a natural tendency to fall back into the trap of focusing people's opposition against governments alone without targeting the corporate powers that lie behind them and their agendas.

In turn, this strategic problem is further hampered by the fact that the BCNI, along with the C.D. Howe and Fraser Institutes, have also made government and the state the central targets of their campaigns. As we have seen, through their relentless propaganda over the past 20 years or so, they have successfully labelled government intervention and regulation as Public Enemy No. 1. At key points, spurred on by the Reform Party, they have effectively whipped up anti-government attitudes, almost to a frenzy. By doing so, they not only created a negative image of government, but they have also been able to camouflage the powerful role that corporations play behind the scenes in setting the terms and conditions for public policy-making in this country.

As a result, citizens' movements found themselves increasingly locked into a defensive position. Instead of going on the offensive, resistance campaigns—as their name implies—were more or less geared towards defending the status quo: the social welfare state. Despite the fact that most of the movements involved in these campaigns found the social welfare state to be inadequate, and in some cases degrading and punitive, the political dynamics of corporate rule compelled them to adopt a basically defensive posture. To compound their problem, the piecemmeal dismantling of the welfare state was accompanied by an erosion of their access to the public policy-making apparatus. For citizens' movements today, the core of this strategic problem lies in a dependency on conventional approaches to democratic social change. Here, the prime target for social change is government policies. The name of the game is to either advocate changes in government policy and practices, or to change the party in power by electing a new government. This approach, of course, is based on two erroneous assumptions: that the welfare state is still essentially intact, and that it is still democratically elected governments who rule.

The realities of the corporate state call for a quite different strategic approach. It is simply no longer sufficient to focus strategies for social change on government policies and programs alone. Nor should citizens' movements suddenly shift their targets from governments to corporations themselves. Concentrating solely on tackling the corporations while losing sight of the state would be unrealistic. Yes, the real target for social change today must be the system of corporate rule itself. But this means putting strategic priority on *both* corporations and governments. Together, they constitute the corporate state which dictates the direction and content of public policies affecting our economic, social and environmental future.

All of this, of course, signals the need for a new politics for citizens' movements. To develop a new politics, however, requires some strategic planning. Once again, it is important to recall that it took big business and its right-wing allies fully 20 years to mobilize the forces needed to dismantle the Keynesian welfare state. If citizens' movements on the democratic left today are serious about confronting and rolling back this counter-revolution, then it is imperative to dig in for the long haul. This calls for both long-term and short-term strategic planning. Looking ahead over the next 10 to 20 years, the long- range task is to develop strategic plans for dismantling the mechanisms of corporate rule in this country and rebuilding institutions for democratic control over our economic, social and environmental future.

Before digging in for the long haul, however, the need for strategic planning and action in the short run must be addressed. Over the next five years or so, the energies of citizens' movements need to be focused on creating a climate for the new politics. During this period, the primary task will be to develop campaign strategies designed to publicly expose the corporate powers that lie behind policy-making both in Ottawa and in provincial capitals across the country.

In order to create a climate for a new politics, creative steps are needed to enable Canadians to focus their public anger and demands for social change on the big business side of the corporate/government alliance. Just as big business and its allies have generated a negative set of public attitudes and expectations towards government, so citizens' movements need to target the role of corporations. Over the next five years, the prime objective should be to make the corporate powers that are dominating government policy-making in Ottawa and elsewhere "Public Enemy No.1," rather than government alone.

This will require campaign strategies designed to publicly expose the big business side of the corporate/government regime in Ottawa and the provinces. Unless the corporate face that now hides behind government decision-making is exposed, citizens' movements will continue to be put on the defensive. Indeed, the only way to go on the offensive now is to publicly target the corporate players that dominate our political life and threaten our democratic future. This does not mean that labour unions, social organizations or community groups need to put aside the issues and struggles that are of immediate vital concern to their constituencies. On the contrary, no matter what issues are of prime concern to citizens' groups today—unemployment, health care, toxic wastes, child care, job security, social housing, workfare, unemployment insurance, public education, social security, water exports, clearcut logging, public broadcasting, student loans and many more—there are bound to be key corporate players who are directly influencing, if not dictating, public policy decisions on these issues.

To develop a new politics along these lines over the next five years, citizens' movements will need to refine their methods and capacities for democratic social change. Here, the prime task is three-fold: *targeting, unmasking, and profiling* the key corporate players that are the driving forces behind economic, social and environmental policy-making at both national and provincial levels. Creative methods and strategies will be required for all three.

At first glance, this will undoubtedly appear to be a difficult undertaking. After all, some of the country's most powerful corporations, let alone their CEOs, are not household names in the same sense as most of Canada's leading politicians are. Yet, once citizens' movements pick the corporate targets related to their issue priorities, gather the data available on them, and probe further into their internal operations and connections, the more they will be able to make these faceless corporations and their CEOs publicly visible. In short, what Canadian politics needs now is a heavy dose of corporate literacy. And if social organizations, labour unions and community groups are going to take the lead in cultivating this kind of corporate literacy in our political life, then they will need to equip themselves for that undertaking.

Before turning our attention to what citizens' movements can do to move in this direction, it is crucial to keep in mind that big business and its allies are also doing their own strategic planning. The Fraser Institute, for example, recently outlined a five-year plan, "Towards the New Millenium," which sets new targets for expanding its monthly magazine, its "media penetration" program and book production. Michael Walker also plans to make the Fraser's Economic Freedom Index "the most utilized index of economic freedom in the world" by hosting annual Economic Freedom Forums in 10 countries, establishing an annual Economic Freedom Award at the World Economic Forum in Davos, Switzerland, and enlisting the help of transnational corporations for this program.

On the home front, the Fraser plans to: "become Canada's leading source of information on private health care;" lobby for provincial "right to work" legislation; promote a "private property, market-based solution" to environmental problems; develop an index on "the increasing costs posed by government tax and regulatory activities;" provide an "alternative" to the Vanier Institute on the role of the family in society; and launch a new project on "law and markets" designed to reform Canada's legal system to promote economic growth, including perhaps the privatization of criminal justice.

To muster an effective counter-offensive, the democratic left must therefore develop a new politics. At the outset, it is imperative that citizens' movements ground their new approach in a solid foundation that reflects Canada's political and cultural heritage.

Popular Sovereignty

One of the major challenges for citizens' movements in developing a new politics along these lines is to consolidate a basis for action. Appealing to democratic rights as the foundation for citizen action has become more and more difficult in recent years. Not only have "citizen rights" in a democratic society been superseded by "investor rights" in the new global economy, but the very role and meaning of the term "citizen" has been changed and distorted. Concerted campaigns waged by the Fraser Institute and the Reform Party have, in effect, reduced the role of "citizens" to that of "taxpayers" and "consumers" in our political culture.

In the new market economy, the priority is on individual rather than collective rights. To an increasing degree, citizens have been stripped of their political rights and social entitlements in a democratic society. Instead, it is corporations which have gained political and collective rights in the new global order. If citizens' movements, therefore, are going to develop a new politics, then conscious steps must be taken to retrieve and reclaim fundamental democratic rights as a basis of action.

Over the past two centuries, peoples all over the world have fought for the recognition of sovereign democratic and human rights. They include the right to adequate food, clothing, and shelter; the right to employment, education and health care; the right to a clean environment, social equality, cultural diversity and public services. Of central importance is the right to self-determination and the ability to effectively participate in decisions affecting these rights. Today, these basic democratic rights are enshrined in international covenants such as the Universal Declaration of Human Rights, the United Nations Covenant on Economic, Social and Cultural Rights, and the Covenant on Civil and Political Rights. To these must be added the sovereign rights of the Earth itself, its natural systems and diverse species, which were enshrined in the Earth Charter at the Rio Summit on the Environment and Sustainable Development. Today, however, these sovereign rights of peoples and the Earth are in danger of being tossed into the dust bin of history. Increasingly, they are not only being undermined and eroded in the new market culture, but also hijacked in this new age of corporate tyranny.

Taken together, these are the communal rights that people are entitled to by virtue of being citizens of a democratic society. They constitute the core of what is called popular sovereignty. What is involved here is a kind of sovereignty from the ground up. It is out of a strong sense of democratic rights based on popular sovereignty that citizens' movements are able to actively resist forms of tyranny and oppression. For Canadians, this is not some kind of abstract theory. It is deeply rooted in the history of social movements in this country.

Take, for example, the popular movements that led the 1837 rebellions in Upper and Lower Canada. According to historian Stanley B. Ryerson, Upper Canada (now mainly Ontario) was ruled 160 years ago by the Family Compact, composed of large landowners, bankers and merchants who, along with the high clergy of the Anglican Church, had direct ties with London-based capitalists and British colonial authorities. As one of the popular movement leaders, William Lyon Mackenzie, described the situation at the time: "This family connection rules Upper Canada according to its own good pleasure and has no efficient check from this country to guard against its acts of tyranny and oppression."

At the same time, Lower Canada (now mainly Quebec) was ruled by a feudal system of seigneurial tenure where large tracts of land were granted to the Catholic Church and corporations such as the British American Land Company. The revolutionary democrats of Lower Canada, known as the Patriotes, led by people like Joseph Louis Papineau, described the seigneurial tenure system then as "the frightful picture of feudal oppression."

Mounting popular resistance to the Family Compact's model of corporate rule in Upper Canada during the 1830s, Mackenzie declared that "the whole of the revenues of Upper Canada are in reality at their mercy; they are the Paymasters, Receivers, Auditors, Kings, Lords and Commons.

"The farmer toils, the merchant toils, the labourer toils," he exclaimed, "and the Family Compact reap the fruits of their exertions." Declaring the sovereign rights of the people, Mackenzie and his compatriots organized a broadly-based coalition to fight the abuses of colonial compact rule. After being elected mayor of Toronto (a surprise blow to the Compact) in 1834, Mackenzie set up a committee of grievances to hear about the demands of the people. When the committee issued its report of popular demands, top priority was placed on setting up a form of "responsible government," since "no such system...to protect from Executive usurpation of popular rights can be found in Upper Canada."

In 1837, under Mackenzie's leadership, a People's Convention was organized for Upper Canada which was to assume power with the backing of a mass demonstration in Toronto. But a military offensive launched by the Compact soon crushed the popular movement for "responsible government" before it had a chance to build momentum.

Similarly, the Patriotes in Lower Canada blasted the system of land monopoly and seigneurial tenure where "capital ... is swallowed up in the treasury of our lofty masters and overlords, the Canada Land Companies." At their Assembly in 1834, the Patriotes adopted 92 resolutions calling for an end to colonial rule and the adoption of their own form of responsible government based on democratic rights. Rejecting the British model of government, the Patriotes advocated the idea of a popular assembly as a form of governance. As Papineau put it: "We demand political institutions in conformity with the conditions of society in which we are living."

The resistance led by Papineau began with a mass boycott against British goods, reaching a climax in 1837 when 5,000 people from the six counties of the Richelieu gathered for a mass rally. The event set the stage for a provisional people's government. In the armed struggle that followed, the Patriotes were initially successful in routing the British forces. In 1838, the Patriote movement issued a Declaration of Independence from Great Britain calling for the establishment of a "patriotic and responsible government." While the Patriotes organized in camps along the Richelieu river in the summer of 1838, Ryerson records that the British military forces were determined not only to defeat the hated "rebels" but to exterminate them.

Yet the movements led by Papineau and Mackenzie were largely based on popular sovereignty and aimed at dismantling structures of corporate rule in their times. So, too, were the per-

haps better known Métis rebellions in Manitoba and Saskatchewan led by Louis Riel following Confederation. In 1869, the
Métis people declared sovereign rights over the Red River Val-
ley, set up their own provisional government, and issued a "List
of Rights" as a platform of demands in opposition to a deal being
made between Ottawa and the Hudson's Bay Company. In short,
a huge real estate transaction had been struck between Ottawa
and London covering the vast land mass of the Northwest in which
the Hudson's Bay Company would be paid large sums of money
for Indian lands it did not own in the first place.

There are other moments in our history, ranging from the
Winnipeg General Strike of 1919 through the Cape Breton coal
miners' strikes and the western farmers' protests against eastern
tariffs in the 1920s, where popular resistance against excessive
forms of corporate power was rooted in the sovereign rights of
people. And not only men, but often women like Agnes MacPhail,
played key leadership roles in the struggles of farmers and workers for basic democratic rights against corporations which had
the government by the throat.

Today, these sovereign rights need to be reclaimed from our
history and political culture as a common basis for citizen action. It is on the basis of popular sovereignty that citizens (a)
express their common dreams and aspirations as members of a
political community; (b) claim their right to have control over
their economic, social and ecological future; (c) determine priorities, standards and conditions that must be met by corporations operating in the community; (d) insist the government exercise its moral and political obligations to ensure that corporations fully meet these standards and conditions before being allowed to operate; and (e) take whatever forms of action are necessary to see that these basic communal rights are upheld.

In short, these are some of the foundations stones on which a
citizens' agenda needs to be grounded. It is only by reclaiming
popular sovereignty as a basis of action that citizens' movements
can begin to rebuild their capacities to challenge the realities of
corporate rule.

Corporate Campaigns

For more than two decades, citizens' movements have waged
some impressive campaigns of resistance on an international scale
to curb the power wielded by corporations. Throughout the 1970s

and '80s, a world-wide boycott and lobbying campaign was organized against Nestlé (which controls half of the global baby food business) for its use of notorious sales practices to promote infant formula as a substitute for breast feeding by mothers in Third World countries. During the same period, shareholder campaigns were organized in Europe and North America to put a stop to any new bank loans and investments to the apartheid regime in South Africa.

Similar shareholder campaigns in the U.S. and Canada were mounted against banks and corporations doing business with the bloodthirsty dictatorship of General Pinochet in Chile.

In 1984, Union Carbide became the target of multi-million-dollar libel lawsuits and public campaigns when toxic gas releases at its plant in Bhopal, India, caused thousands of deaths and injuries. More recently, Shell Oil became the target of a global boycott when it—along with a handful of other top oil corporations—devastated the environment in southern Nigeria, destroyed the farming and fishing livelihood of the local peoples like the Ogoni, leading to severe human rights abuses by the Nigerian government (which receives 80 per cent of its revenues from oil, half from Shell alone).

Closer to home, numerous citizen campaigns have been mobilized against the conduct of corporations in both the U.S. and Canada. In 1976, for example, the Amalgamated Clothing and Textile Workers, using strategic skills developed by Ray Rogers, organized a sophisticated campaign against the J.P. Stevens Co. for exploiting its cotton mill workers, by targeting the interlocking directorships of companies that finance, supply and do business with that giant textile corporation. Later, the union-organized Janitors for Justice movement in the U.S. combined direct action strategies (e.g., traffic blockades) and community organizing to build public pressure against real estate companies.

Among the many corporate campaigns initiated by the U.S. environmental movement, the campaign organized by the Rain Forest Action Network against Mitsubishi for its destructive logging practices in old growth forest regions has gained world-wide attention. Here in Canada, labour unions have used diverse forms of economic leverage to tackle corporate power, ranging from the Canadian Auto Workers' successful bargaining and strike campaigns against General Motors and Ford to the United Steel Workers' strategy of worker ownership through the buy-out of Algoma Steel. Similarly, UNITE has waged a vigorous campaign on behalf of textile and clothing workers here and in Central America to persuade the GAP clothing chain to adopt a code of conduct in its practices.

The churches have also organized shareholder action campaigns to challenge a variety of banks and corporations concerning social, environmental and human rights abuses. More recently, creative public campaigns have also been waged by environmental groups like Greenpeace. In the case of Clayquot Sound on Victoria Island, for example, a civil disobedience campaign coupled with international pressures on suppliers was partially effective in forcing the B.C. government to curb the logging operations of MacMillan Bloedel in old growth forest areas.

Citizens' movements like the Council of Canadians have also begun to move in this direction by launching a legal challenge and public action campaign against Conrad Black's takeover of Canadian newspapers through his Hollinger corporation. And of course the anti-smoking movement has waged a series of successful campaigns against the major tobacco companies in Canada, as well as in the United States.

Taken together, these campaigns indicate what citizens' movements can do when they decide to focus their energies on the role of corporate power in society. In particular, case studies of these and related campaigns reveal the various kinds of strategic and tactical tools that can be used for intervention: litigation, boycotts, strikes, shareholder action, direct action, and economic leverage aimed at interlocking directorships.

Each of these campaign strategies, however, has shortcomings as well as strengths when it comes to the task of dismantling systems of corporate rule. For the most part, these corporate campaigns are focused on single issues. They are primarily designed to address the specific abuses and violations of individual corporations. While this issue-focused approach to corporate misconduct has proven in many cases to generate active public participation, it also tends to divert people's attention away from the more systemic and political dimensions of corporate rule. What's more, by concentrating on the abusive practices of a particular corporation, there is a tendency to ignore the deeper dimensions of corporate power.

The nature of corporations, for example, their mandate and role, their rights and freedoms, and who gives them their authority are seldom addressed. Making individual corporations more "socially responsible" and "democratically accountable" will not get at the root causes of corporate rule. Nor will campaigns based exclusively on boycott actions which have a tendency to reduce "citizens" to the role of "consumers" in society. While consumer boycotts can certainly be important strategic tools, citizens' movements must learn to use them in such a way as to avoid being sucked into the vortex of marketplace politics.

The realities of corporate rule today call for a new style of corporate campaign on the part of citizens' movements. This does not mean tossing out the strategies and tactics that have been developed over the past two decades or more. What is called for, however, is a reorientation of citizen-based campaign strategies for tackling the structures of corporate rule today. This reorientation needs to be based on several assumptions.

First, corporations (be they domestic or foreign-owned) have become dominant players in almost every aspect of public life in this country. This is the case whether we are talking about the traditional areas of corporate dominance in the private sector such as finance, manufacturing, agriculture and resource industries, or the emerging areas of corporate takeover in the public sector such as education, health care, social security, water, transportation and communications. Hence, the stage is set for citizen-based corporate campaign activity at all levels of our public life.

Second, the nature of the corporation as a political machine needs to become the target of citizen-based campaigns. This, of course, refers to the increasingly powerful role corporations now play in determining and controlling public policy-making through everything from corporate think tanks, election financing, political advertising, and exclusive lobbying machinery to the direct role they play in policy decisions of governments and the special status they now enjoy as "citizens" with constitutionally protected political rights.

Third, citizen-based corporate campaigns need to be firmly grounded in the ideal of popular sovereignty. Just as ancestral movements led by Mackenzie, Papineau, Riel, MacPhail and others were rooted in a vision of popular sovereignty, so citizens' movements today must retrieve and reclaim fundamental democratic rights as their basis for action.

To develop a new style of corporate campaigns along these lines of orientation will of course take time. Yet there are some signs beginning to emerge. In India, for example, citizens' movements have organized campaigns to have corporations like Cargill and Kentucky Fried Chicken thrown out of the country altogether, on grounds that they are having a destructive influence on the livelihood and culture of people in that country. In the U.S., citizens' groups in several states have attempted to have the charters of corporations like Weyerhauser in the State of Oregon and Waste Management Inc. in Pennsylvania actually revoked, on grounds that they have violated the mandates they were given by a sovereign people under the law through their state legislatures.

While these campaigns are not necessarily designed to tackle the nature of corporations as political machines, they do go beyond addressing particular abuses to dismantling the operations of corporations that are playing a destructive role in society. Moreover, they are doing so from the standpoint of the basic democratic rights of citizens and their claim to popular sovereignty. What needs to be done here in Canada is to develop a style of campaign designed to tackle the corporate political machines that are the driving forces behind public policy-making that directly affects people's economic, social and ecological future in this country and around the world.

In the short run, citizens' movements have an opportunity to develop this new style of corporate campaign over the next five years. During this period, the strategic purpose is to create the climate for a new politics by focusing public attention on the enormous power wielded by corporations and asserting our sovereign democratic rights as citizens. The prime objective would be to develop citizen-based campaigns aimed at corporations which, in key sectors of Canada's economy, are operating as political machines, directing and controlling public policy-making on a variety of fronts. The task is to *target, unmask,* and *profile* these corporate political machines that are determining our economic, social and ecological future. It now appears, looking over the political landscape in this country, that citizens' movements have a chance to develop corporate campaigns simultaneously on at least three battlefields over the next five years.

Battlefield # 1

The first major battlefield for developing citizen-based corporate campaigns has to do with control over our *economic* future. This is the arena of macro-economic policy where major decisions will be made about what road Ottawa takes on key issues like debt reduction and job creation. To play on this field means dealing with a variety of policy struggles around finance, trade, investment and taxation issues. Understandably, many citizens' movements tend to shy away from tackling policy issues in this arena. But this is where big business has gained a stranglehold on economic policy-making at federal and provincial levels. While the Chrétien government can be expected to try and paint a social liberal face on both its debt reduction and job creation strategies, it should not be forgotten that the business Liberals are still very much in the driver's seat in Ottawa.

More importantly, the BCNI and the corporate political machinery in key sectors of the Canadian economy will be busy setting the terms and conditions of what Ottawa can and cannot do on these fronts. Over the next five years, a concerted and sustained campaign strategy needs to be aimed at targeting, unmasking and profiling the main corporate players directing government strategies on debt reduction and job creation at both federal and provincial levels.

Debt Reduction: As Ottawa heads towards its zero deficit target in 1999, the big policy debate will focus on what to do with a surplus in government revenues that some analysts predict could reach $90 billion. Almost certainly, the political machine of the finance sector will be revving up its engines to ensure that the bulk of these revenue surpluses go towards paying down the debt and reducing taxes, rather than restoring social program spending. The key players in this financial political machine include, of course, the Royal Bank of Canada, the C.I.B.C., the Bank of Nova Scotia, the Bank of Montreal and the Toronto Dominion Bank, along with their corresponding investment houses, RBC Dominion Securities, Wood Gundy, Scotia McLeod, and Toronto Dominion Securities, plus insurance companies like Great West Life. As we have seen, these institutions have all profited immensely from government debt woes. What is needed is a well-orchestrated and sustained campaign designed to publicly expose how these financial institutions will continue to profit if Ottawa makes debt reduction its ongoing priority rather than renewed social program spending.

Such a campaign could show how the banks would continue to reap windfall profits on risk-free loans (already averaging between $6 and $7 billion in interest payments a year) by taking over more of Ottawa's debt load allowed under the recent deregulation of Canada's bank laws. It could also show how these same financial institutions have been by far the biggest contributors to the federal Liberal party's coffers, both in and out of election years, and how they use political advertising to sell their policy agenda. While the target of such a campaign could be a particular bank and its investment house, the strategy should aim to unmask and expose the entire financial sector and its political machinery.

Job Creation: With official jobless figures stuck close to the 10 per cent mark, coupled with structural problems of underemployment as well as hidden unemployment, the public pressures on Ottawa to come up with a job creation plan are bound to escalate. What big business wants to ensure is that Ottawa does not develop some sort of industrial strategy for job creation. Here, the financial sector and its political machine will continue to insist that the Bank of Canada "stay the course" by keeping inflation in check through maintaining high real interest rates, rather than making job creation a priority by sustaining a policy of lower interest rates. This pressure, in turn, will likely be reinforced by the nation's top corporate downsizers and their political machinery. Led by Canadian Pacific, the big corporate downsizers include auto-makers like General Motors and Ford Motor Co.; resource companies like Alcan, Abitibi-Price, Domtar, Noranda, and Stone Consolidated; plus retail and manufacturing firms like Imasco, K-Mart, Provigo and Sears.

What is needed is a concerted public campaign that targets two or three of the country's leading corporate downsizers, plus one or two banks. The objective would be to profile how these corporate targets function as a political machine to prevent Canada from developing an adequate job creation strategy. Such a campaign could be designed to show: how profitable corporations have been allowed to engage in massive downsizing; how the tax system rewards this kind of corporate downsizing; how the banks further stifle job creation by failing to provide adequate loans to small businesses; how the free trade deals are used to restrict Ottawa's options; and how most foreign investment these days goes into the purchase of existing companies (often triggering huge layoffs) rather than into job-producing industries.

These are two of the major policy battles that will continue to dominate decision-making about the economy in the next few years. It is imperative that labour unions, together with social organizations and community groups, design and implement campaigns aimed at exposing the corporate political machines which are not only driving the policy decisions in Ottawa and the provinces along these lines, but which are also in a position to directly profit from them. At the same time, several other policy struggles are also emerging on this battlefield over the next five years. Strategic actions on these fronts could fortify corporate campaigns waged on debt reduction and job creation. For example:

Trade Missions: Now that Canada has become one of the world's foremost cheerleaders for free trade, Ottawa's involvement in trade negotiations and trade missions will undoubtedly continue to accelerate over the next five years. Corporate Canada has high stakes involved in trade negotiations that will continue to take place around both the expansion of NAFTA under the Summit of the Americas and the development of APEC as a free trade regime on the Pacific Rim. It is crucial that campaign strategies developed by citizens' movements on these two major trade fronts focus their energies on targeting and exposing the role of the BCNI and/or specific corporate players who are the driving forces behind these trade agendas and their negative impacts on jobs and wages, social security, health care and the environment. The APEC Leaders' Summit to be held in Vancouver in November, 1997 provides an opportunity to develop such a campaign strategy.

Similarly, a more concerted plan of action could be developed around the annual high-profile trade missions organized by Ottawa, highlighting the ways in which the prime minister and the premiers have become pimps for big business in terms of selling their products.

Financial Speculation: One of the major policy battles that is likely to heat up over the next few years will be the continuing rapid growth of unregulated financial transactions which fuel the casino economy. It is now estimated that over $27 trillion in financial transactions are cleared each year through Canada's banking system. These financial transactions include everything from the sale of stocks and bonds and money market trades to options, futures and derivative contracts. Most of these financial transactions, as we have seen, are for speculative rather than productive purposes. Yet, unlike goods and services which are now regularly taxed under the GST, these transactions are tax free in Canada.

A campaign strategy around financial speculation would be an important step in creating a climate for the new politics. Such a campaign could be aimed at identifying and unmasking those wealthy individuals and profitable corporations who make a killing every day from speculative financial transactions. The connection between these financial transactions and Canada's debt and jobs crisis should also be highlighted.

Corporate Taxes: In recent years, steps have been taken by citizens' movements to draw attention to the fact that many profitable corporations in Canada do not pay their fair share of taxes. Still, the struggle on this battlefront could be intensified. Clearly, the whole issue of corporate taxation is a key factor, not only as a major cause of the country's debt problems, but also as a cause of unemployment, particularly when corporations are rewarded for downsizing through tax credits and write-offs. A well-organized public awareness campaign highlighting the inequities of the corporate tax system, including the use of transfer pricing and offshore tax havens, would be timely. An ad campaign, for example, could be developed to expose Canada's top 15 corporate tax deferees in 1996—Seagram Co., Bell Canada, BCE Inc., Canadian Pacific, Imperial Oil, Alcan Aluminum, Pan-Canadian Petroleum, Chrysler Canada, Shell Canada, Petro-Canada, Noranda, Norcen Energy Resources, Anderson Exploration, Home Oil Co., Alberta Energy Co., Westcoast Energy, Suncor, IPL Energy, Thomson Corp., and Dofasco. *(See Appendix IV charts.)* Such a campaign could be designed to offset the growing demands of big business and its right-wing allies for still more drastic tax cuts.

Investment Treaties: Over the next two years, a flurry of negotiations will be taking place with a view to establishing an international investment treaty. While the OECD plans for a "high standard" Multilateral Agreement on Investments (MAI) have been temporarily postponed, the United States still expects to have the MAI adopted no later than May 1998. If the MAI continues to be stalled, then efforts will likely be made to have such a global investment treaty established through the World Trade Organization. In either case, the Canadian government will almost surely continue to be one of the main cheerleaders for the MAI, so a concerted campaign to expose it as a corporate rule treaty will be urgently needed.

After eight years of first-hand experience with investment codes under the FTA and NAFTA, Canadians are painfully aware of how these mechanisms enhance the rights and powers of transnational corporations. The MAI, however, if it is enacted, would have a much more devastating impact on our economy and society. It would in effect clamp a straitjacket around the federal and provincial governments, seriously hobbling their ability to take policy initiatives on job creation, health care, culture, education, the environment, and even the constitution. *(See Appendix V.)* A campaign targeting the MAI would expose these and other major threats it poses to our economic, social and political well-being, as well as exposing the major players in Corporate Canada who are promoting this corporate rule treaty.

These are some of the main policy struggles that will be fought out on this battlefield over the next few years. They are battles in which Corporate Canada has a major vested interest in keeping its political machinery well oiled and ready to play a decisive role in controlling the direction of economic policy-making in Ottawa. What happens here will also affect what takes place on the other two battlefields.

Battlefield # 2

The second battlefield for developing citizen-based corporate campaigns has to do with the fight for control over our *social* future. This is the arena where the struggle over Canada's social programs and public services is unfolding. It is on this battlefield that corporations, both domestic and foreign-owned, are on the offensive to take over programs and services previously provided by the public sector, especially in health care and education. Given the major shortfalls in the financing of health care and education, caused largely by the federal Liberals' CHST, provincial governments have been rapidly introducing privatization measures such as contracting-out, delisting, user fees, etc.

Once a government privatizes a public service, including parts of our health care, education and water systems, it is obligated under NAFTA to open the contracts to bids by U.S. corporations. As U.S. consulting firms like Lehman Brothers report, health care and education have become prime targets for corporate investment and takeover. Just as private insurance, hospital, pharmaceutical and medical product companies took control of the health care market in the U.S., says Lehman Brothers, becoming "the gatekeepers of the health care dollar" and "dictat[ing] the direction of health care spending" in the U.S. during the 1970s and '80s, so the privatization of Canada's health care system makes it ripe for private sector investment in the 1990s. Now, moving into the new millennium, Lehman Brothers has targeted the education sector, providing corporations with a road map of the market and investment opportunities opening up through increased privatization. Borrowing a phrase from the Canadian Union of Public Employees, the question is: "who's cashing in" on this privatization?

Over the next five years, citizen-based campaigns need to be mounted which are designed to unmask and profile the main corporate political machines in the service sector that are planning the takeover of Canada's health and education systems.

Health Care: Canada's public health care system is an annual $72 billion dollar enterprise. Today, private U.S. health care corporations are planning their strategies for global expansion, starting with Britain but with an eye on the Canadian market as well. Several management consulting firms have been hired to promote the privatization of health care in Canada, including the world's largest, KPMG, whose Toronto office is headed by the same people who masterminded the drive to privatize hospitals in London, England.

While a national campaign has been mounted to save Medicare in this country, steps also need to be taken to see that the debate over the health care responsibilities of Ottawa and the provinces does not become a smoke-screen for the corporate plays being made behind the scenes to cash in on piecemeal privatization. What is needed is a shift in campaign strategies towards unmasking the corporate invasion of our public health care system.

Here, there is no shortage of corporate political machines at work—whether it be U.S.-based hospital chains such as Columbia/HCA, Tenet Healthcare, and Kaiser Permenante manoeuvring to set up for-profit hospitals in the future, or their partners in new Canadian-based for-profit health care corporations like MDS; or private insurance companies like Sun Life, Manulife, Liberty Mutual, and Great West Life taking advantage of delisting by provincial health plans to open up new markets; or the Home Maintenance Organizations (HMOs) which have mushroomed as an industry in the U.S. over the past decade, led by corporations like Kaiser Permanente and Aetna Health Care Inc.; or the host of patent drug companies, led by the Pharmaceutical Manufacturers' Association of Canada, which are fiercely lobbying for a further extension on their monopoly patent protection period, leading to another big increase in drug prices.

A corporate campaign on several of these flanks could be a major step in laying the grounds for a new politics.

Public Education: Canada's public education system now represents an estimated $60 billion a year market. In most provinces, massive government cutbacks to public and post-secondary education have induced school boards, colleges and universities to enter into business "partnerships" with corporations. Over 20,000 business-school partnerships have been formed across Canada. Cash-strapped school boards, unable to afford adequate supplies or technical equipment to meet their education needs, are entering into "partnerships" with technology and communication corporations like AT&T Canada, Bell Canada, General Electric, Hewlett Packard, IBM Canada, Northern Telecom, UNITEL, and YNN.

Similarly, school boards lacking funds for school lunch programs or cafeteria services are forming "partnerships" with food and beverage companies like Burger King, Coca Cola, McDonald's, Pepsi-Cola and Pizza Hut. In exchange, these corporations are allowed to openly advertise their products to a new generation of consumers in schools where kids spend 40 per cent of each day. Colleges and universities are also forming similar "partnerships," including the naming of courses after corporations which make a substantial donation.

As a result, schools and universities are emerging as an increasingly important battleground for the struggle against corporate rule. What is needed are some strategically planned campaigns highlighting the big business takeover of our education system and unmasking the operations of specific corporate political machines at work. Such campaigns could be organized in strategically selected schools and universities by cadres of concerned students, teachers and parents. Public campaigns could also be designed to support needy schools, colleges or universities in negotiating clear terms and conditions for regulating the activities of sponsoring companies for specific projects and holding them accountable.

While health care and public education may be the main events on this battlefield, they are by no means the only ones. Several other social programs and public services are also being privatized and therefore subject to corporate takeovers. It will also be important for citizens' groups involved in these issues to target the main corporate players and their political machines and to develop strategic actions on these fronts where possible during the next five years.

Public Pensions: The stage has been set for the privatization of the Canada Pension Plan. Backed by key elements of big business, the C.D. Howe Institute along with the Earnscliffe Strategy Group (the prominent public relations firm with close ties to the Finance Department) have been waging a relentless campaign to convince Canadians that private pension plans in the form of RRSPs would be preferable to the CPP. As a result, Ottawa is now proposing that the multi-billion dollar CPP Fund be managed by private sector investment firms.

Over the next ten years, the CPP Investment Fund is expected to balloon from $40 billion today to approximately $120 billion. Such a block of capital would be worth as much as the seven largest mutual fund companies combined. Morover, these CPP funds will be invested not only in provincial government bonds, as in the past, but in a mix of private and public equities and bonds. This includes investment overseas as well as here in Canada, thereby signalling that the 20 per cent limit on foreign investments by private sector pension plans may soon be lifted as well.

As the debate over the future of Canada's public pension system continues, campaign strategies need to take aim at those corporations that will be cashing in on these privatization measures: the national banks and their investment houses.

News Media: As we have seen, increasing corporate concentration and control of the news media poses a severe threat to the future of democracy in Canada. That's why the Campaign for Press and Broadcasting Freedom launched by an alliance of labour unions and social organizations is an important initiative. By targeting Conrad Black's Hollinger corporation, which controls close to 60 per cent of all newspapers in Canada, this campaign will increase the awareness of Canadians about the dangers of allowing the editorial content and quality of news coverage to be dominated, not only by one big corporation, but by a corporation that is run by a man who harbours deeply rooted right-wing ideological views on the major issues of the day.

The fight to save the CBC through this and related campaigns, however, needs to shift in a similar direction. As a strategic part of the public campaign pressure on Ottawa to restore full funding for the CBC, concerted steps could be taken to identify and target those corporations that have a vested interest in having the CBC privatized and ripened for a corporate takeover.

Social Housing: Through recent budgets, Paul Martin terminated the federal government's role in providing social housing for low- and moderate-income groups, thereby leaving the housing market to private developers. After dismantling the Canada Housing and Mortgage Corporation, Ottawa passed federally funded co-operatives onto the provinces where, as in the case of Ontario, subsidies were to be eliminated and management of the cooperatives were to be turned over to the municipalities. As a result, big private developers like Bramelea, Minto, Tridel, Centara, Menkes, Camrost, and dozens of local companies will be in a position to take full control of the housing market in Canada.

In developing their fightback campaigns, citizens' groups concerned about social housing need to target and expose the big developers who will be cashing in on these moves, their own political machinery, including their alliances with major real estate corporations and the banks that finance their operations. For the most part, these campaigns will have their greatest impact in local communities.

Workfare: There are also vested corporate interests at stake in the transition from welfare to workfare programs, following the demise of the Canada Assistance Plan, that need to be uncovered and profiled. While provincial governments claim to be stamping out "welfare cheaters" as they drastically cut back on their social assistance programs, the list of "corporate cheaters" in the tax system continues to grow. Once again, the top 15 corporate tax deferees *(see Appendix IV chart)* could be used to dramatize the hypocrisy of such claims, as well as the outright theft of public revenues that results from such an unfair tax system. At the same time, campaign strategies against poverty could target and profile select corporations that are cashing in on government workfare programs.

After all, workfare functions as a "cash cow" for business. It serves both to provide a pool of cheap labour and to subsidize employers. It has also proven to be an effective mechanism for keeping wages down and profits up. As a recent Quebec survey shows, 50 per cent of the companies involved in workfare programs admitted they would have had to hire these people at full wages if the provincial program did not exist. The public spotlight needs to be turned on the corporate players who are promoting workfare at provincial and community levels.

This is just a sample of the kinds of corporate campaigns that could be waged in the ongoing struggle against the dismantling of social programs and public services over the next few years. Many others could be added, including the growing pressure to privatize postal services, dismantle agricultural marketing boards, and contract out numerous public services. In the U.S., a major campaign is now under way to privatize and corporatize social security programs in several states—a campaign that could well spill over into Canada. By publicly targeting and exposing the corporate players who are cashing in on these and related schemes, citizens' movements have a chance to start going on the offensive once again.

Battlefield # 3

The third battlefield for citizens' movements in carrying out corporate campaigns is the environmental arena and the fight for control over our *ecological* future. While Canada is a region of the planet that is rich in its biodiversity (i.e., diverse natural resources, plant, wildlife, and fresh waterways), environmentalists now claim that this heritage is being seriously threatened by climate changes due to global warming caused by the unbridled release of greenhouse gases like carbon dioxide into the atmosphere. The main source of this ecological turbulence being generated by the emission of greenhouse gases is the burning of fossil fuels (i.e., coal, oil, natural gas) and the rapid depletion of the Earth's forests.

In Canada, the country's major petroleum companies and forest developers have been the driving forces behind Ottawa's resource policies which are largely designed to promote the rapid exploitation and export of our oil, natural gas and timber. As we have seen, it was the oil industry lobby which most fervently promoted a free trade agreement with the U.S. that would remove any restrictions on the production and export of fossil fuels. It was also the major oil corporations, along with forestry and mining companies, which successfully lobbied Ottawa for a set of natural resource policies that were much more deregulated, privatized and decentralized.

Over the next five years, the corporate stranglehold on this country's energy and forestry production policies which threaten our ecological future, could become a major battlefront for citizens' movements.

Forestry Development: Although Canada's forests, which account for 10 per cent of the world's reserves, are considered to be the northern "lung" of the planet, the fact is that one acre of timber is being cut down every 12 seconds in this country. The shift to clearcut logging practices by the big forestry companies, which now account for over 90 per cent of all logging in this country, has dramatically accelerated the erosion of our forest reserves. Despite provincial reforestation projects (which the U.S. lumber industry contends is an "unfair trade subsidy"), there has been a five-fold increase in areas classified as "not satisfactorily restocked."

What's more, the new technologies being used for clearcut logging have substantially reduced the number of people working in the logging industry. Canada's leading corporations in forest and pulp and paper production—MacMillan Bloedel, Avenor Inc., Abitibi-Price, Domtar Inc., Noranda Forest, Cascades Inc., Fletcher Challenge, Canfor Corp., Repap Enterprises, and Stone-Consolidated Corp.—play a powerful role in determining forest management policies in both Ottawa and provincial capitals. So, too, do foreign-based transnationals like Mitsubishi, Daishawa Paper and Louisiana Pacific. These are the corporate political machines of the forestry sector. While several of these corporations have been the targets of environmental campaigns (e.g., MacMillan Bloedel in the Clayquot Sound campaign), greater public awareness would come from a nationally coordinated campaign that identifies a couple of the key players and shows how they maintain a stranglehold over forest management policies. To be effective, however, such a corporate campaign needs to be based on an alliance between workers and environmentalists.

Energy Production: Now that Ottawa has deregulated and decentralized much of the energy industry in Canada, the prospects of new oil and gas megaprojects, hydro power developments, and even large-scale water export schemes stress the urgency of developing corporate campaigns on these fronts. As Canada's conventional supplies of oil and gas are depleted, the push by the industry's leading players—Imperial Oil, Amoco, Shell, Petro-

Canada, Pan Canadian, Chevron, Occidental, Norcen Energy, Total Petroleum, Husky Oil—to develop frontier reserves in ecologically fragile regions like the Canadian north and offshore areas is expected to accelerate in response to increased U.S. export demands.

The environmental stakes are raised even higher when corporate players involved in pipeline construction and tanker transportation are added to the equation. Similarly, the country's main electrical power utilities—Ontario Hydro, Hydro-Quebec, B.C. Hydro, Canadian Utilities, TransAlta Corp., as well as other provincial hydro corporations—are planning expansion projects to meet domestic and export demands. Leading the way will be Hydro Quebec with Phase Two of the James Bay project where more massive damming and flooding of rivers threatens to destroy wildlife as well as native communities. In addition, plans for large-scale fresh water exports to thirsty regions of the U.S. which have been on the drawing board for years (including the $100 billion Grand Canal scheme backed by powerful U.S. corporations like Bechtel) may well be reactivated.

While it is quite possible that corporate campaigns will be launched on all three of these energy fronts over the next five years, it is crucial that such campaigns be designed to publicize not only the environmental consequences of these megaprojects but also how these corporate political machines have seized virtually complete control over energy policy-making in this country.

In developing campaigns on either the forestry or the energy fronts, it will be important to highlight the strategic linkages between the main corporate players in each sector and how they function as a political machine (including their role in the BCNI) in determining the priorities and direction of natural resource policies in this country. Meanwhile, struggles emerging in other resource industries could also become the focal point for coordinated corporate campaign activities.

Mining Practices: Canada's leading mining corporations—Alcan Aluminum, Inco Ltd., Cominco, Noranda Mines, Falconbridge Ltd., Barrick Gold, Placer Dome, Rio Algom—have been on the firing line with environmentalist groups over the past two decades, mainly over the dumping of mine tailings and chemical wastes into river systems. As provinces like Ontario continue to deregulate to the point where mining companies are given virtually a free ticket and are almost left to regulate themselves, this battlefront may start heating up again. Certainly Inco's plans for the development of the huge Voisey Bay nickel deposit in Newfoundland will be prominent on the environmental watch. Canadian mining companies (which Ottawa has strongly promoted on its Team Canada missions) have also become notorious for their overseas operations. In Chile, for example, one-third of the workers in Barrick Gold's El Indio Mine are chronically sick with silicosis, pneumonia, bronchitis, kidney failure, arsenic poisoning, and lung and testicular cancer. In the Philippines, Placer Dome caused an environmental disaster when it spilled tons of copper-bearing mine waste into a river system. And, before it became the centre of "the biggest scam in mining history" in developing the Bussang gold deposit in Indonesia, Bre-X was in partnership with Freeport, which has had a notorious record for enviromental and human rights abuses over the past 30 years in that country. (Many Canadian mining companies operating overseas are registered with the Vancouver Stock Exchange, which is well known for its lax rules on stock activities.)

Despite these and many similar incidents, Ottawa continues to turn a blind eye. What is needed is a public campaign that systematically targets and exposes this network of mining corporations and their power in Ottawa.

Waste Management: With lower standards than the U.S. for the disposal of toxic and nuclear wastes, Canada has become a dumping ground for American chemical and metal companies. At one point, four-fifths of all toxic wastes dumped by U.S. corporations ended up in Canada. For example, Tricil, a waste disposal company in Sarnia, disposes of between 80 and 90 per cent of all U.S. toxic wastes. The Canadian shield has been identified as a possible site for the storage of nuclear wastes.

Chemical giants like Dupont use their massive lobbying apparatus to ensure that Ottawa maintains its lower toxic waste disposal standards, while agri-chemical giants like Cargill make sure that Canada's pesticide control standards are harmonized with lower U.S. levels under free trade. Meanwhile, Ottawa tries to find a way of getting rid of 50,000 PCBs generated in the past, largely by chemical corporations. Urgently needed is a campaign to target and expose the big chemical and metal corporations that have successfully turned Canada into a toxic wasteland.

Genetic Engineering: Canada also has one of the largest bio-tech-nology industries in the world, one that is leading the way in experimenting with genetically engineered forms of food pro-duction. With the exception of the U.S., there are more geneti-cally engineered crops tested in this country than anywhere else in the world. In recent years, chemical and pharmaceutical gi-ants like Monsanto and Eli Lilly have spent millions of dollars lobbying the Ottawa bureaucracy to accept the use of bovine growth hormone (BGH), a performance-enhancing drug to in-crease the milk production of cows. Despite studies warning about potentially negative health effects from the use of BGH, Monsanto is known to have used some ruthless tactics in its lobbying cam-paign on Parliament Hill, including reports about the use of fraudulent documents and a bribe offer to Health Canada offi-cials. In the next few years, bio-tech corporations involved in genetic engineering affecting the food chain could increasingly become the targets of corporate campaigns launched by citizens' movements.

Water Privatization: One of the new frontiers of corporate take-over on the environmental front is in the field of fresh water sup-plies, water delivery and sewage systems. Billed in business cir-cles as "the national mega-industry of the next decade," water systems are expected to attract tens of billions of dollars in in-vestment. In October 1996, the Harris government announced it was going to privatize the Ontario Clean Water Agency, a Crown corporation (the largest such in North America) which holds long-term contracts with municipalities in the province to provide water and sewage treatment services.

In almost every other province, water privateers have been making deals with governments involving the sale and export of fresh water resources. In Ontario and Quebec, for example, pri-vate sector consortiums have been put together that include some of the largest transnational corporations in this field (e.g., the Bechtel Corp. in the U.S., France's giant water privatizer Lyonnaise des Eaux, and Britain's North-West Water), along with several Canadian firms (e.g., Westcoast Energy, TransCanada Pipelines, Nova Corp., IPL Energy, and financial institutions like CIBC's Wood Gundy and Newcourt Credit Group).

Increasingly, cash-strapped municipal governments are turn-ing to consortiums like these to take over their water supply sys-tems, sewage lines, and waste treatment facilities. What this calls for in response are some well-organized community-based citizens' campaigns that target these water privatizers and point out that water resources are a public asset that must not be handed over to profit-making corporations.

Political Capacities

In the final analysis, we cannot simply assume that citizens' movements are prepared to develop and implement corporate campaigns on any of these three main battlefields. The fact remains that most of the progressive labour unions in this country, let alone the public interest groups, social organizations, environmental networks, religious associations and community organizations, are not yet equipped to become actively involved in targeting and tackling the mechanisms of corporate rule.

The problem here is not only a lack of financial resources. If that were the case, ways could be found to overcome it. First and foremost, the main problem has to do with the fact that most citizens' movements today are wedded to conventional methods of fighting for democratic social change. We cannot begin to tackle the structures of corporate rule through strategic methods that are fixated on governments alone as the prime target for social change. Instead, we must develop the capacity to target corporations as the driving forces behind the new corporate state. To do so, citizens' movements will need to refine and sharpen their political tools.

A useful starting point would be the kind of political education that needs to be done with the membership and constituencies of citizens' movements. Whether we are a labour union, a women's association, an environmental organization, a public interest group, a church or religious body, or another kind of citizens' organization, some form of political education of our membership is essential to develop the organizational capacities and tools for social change. What is needed are new educational and training opportunities that enable our members to see themselves, their issues and their struggles for social change through a new set of lenses.

In the first instance, this means coming to grips with the fact that we are now living in a new political era, the age of corporate rule, where corporations function as political machines determining government policy and direction. Whatever public issues concern our members can be seen in new ways through this prism.

At the same time, this new set of lenses can help us develop a political self-understanding of ourselves as citizens who have fundamental democratic rights. By becoming more grounded in this kind of popular sovereignty, citizens' movements can strengthen their political capacities to target and tackle the new realities of corporate rule.

From this base, steps can be taken to develop the kinds of political tools needed to organize corporate campaigns. Once activists review their issue priorities and their struggles for social change through the prism of corporate rule, then they are in a position to identify the major corporate players in their sector and select the ones that should become the targets of their campaign. In selecting campaign targets, it is important to focus on those corporations that are actually operating political machines in determining the direction of public policies. In other words, the targets chosen for campaign strategies in any one of the three main battlefields should be those which best illustrate the dynamics of corporate rule in relation to the particular policy struggle(s) in which a citizens' movement is engaged.

The task then is to develop a profile of the targeted corporation(s) as a political machine. This calls for some initial research into such factors as: the basic strategic objective of the corporation(s) involved in this policy struggle; the specific policy agenda they are demanding; the government departments they are lobbying; their working relationship with minister(s) and senior bureaucrats; the kind of resources and machinery they are using for lobbying; the types of political advertising they are deploying to build public support for their positions; and the financial contributions they have made to political parties and election campaigns.

In addition, strategic points of leverage need to be researched and identified. This entails gathering information and intelligence on, for example: the ownership of the corporation and the composition of its board of directors; the type of charter or certificate of authority it has been granted to operate and under what jurisdiction (federal or provincial); the kind of financing the corporation requires and the specific sources of that financing (what banks, brokers, investment houses, etc.); the type of suppliers the corporation needs and the names of those suppliers; the main business customers that purchase the corporation's products or services; the previous legal history of the corporation in terms of its record on labour, environmental, consumer, and human rights practices; and the personality and public relations record of the corporation's CEO and other key figures.

While at first glance gathering this kind of data and intelligence may seem to be an onerous task for most citizens' organizations, in fact much of this information is fairly accessible. Our citizens' guide to corporate research, supplied in Appendix I, identifies some basic tools and sources that can be used for gathering this kind of information.

Armed with these kinds of political tools, citizens' movements are in a position to develop their own campaign strategies and tactics. In the short run, the strategic objective is to target, unmask, and profile key corporations as political machines within the system of corporate rule. By doing so, the intent is to begin building popular resistance and thus create a political climate for the long-range objective of dismantling the mechanisms of corporate rule and creating new institutions for democratic control.

In developing campaign strategies for the short run, the variety of tactical options available range from charter challenges and court injunctions to consumer boycotts and labour strikes, to political lobbying and direct action or related forms of civil disobedience. The tactics chosen will, of course, depend on the political capacities of the citizens' groups organizing the campaign, as well as the strategic points of leverage identified for the target corporation(s). In any case, campaigns based on multi-level strategies employing a variety of tactics are likely to be more effective.

Moreover, in order to build popular resistance among Canadians, it is important to make use of creative tactics for popular education and theatre, appealing to peoples' sense of humour, fun and play where possible. Our citizens' guide to corporate campaigns, outlined in Appendix II, contains some suggestions and tips.

Whatever corporate campaigns are organized by citizens' movements on any of these battlefields over the next five years or so, it is crucial that they be done with a view to building alliances and coalitions. No one citizens' organization, regardless of how much economic clout or political power it may have, is equipped to tackle a major corporation and its political machinery effectively on its own. The help and involvement of other organizational allies and their constituencies are essential. Building a broadly-based citizens' movement to combat corporate rule in the long run means cultivating and sustaining strategic alliances in the short run. Coalition building, in other words, is a political aptitude that citizen activists need to develop as an essential ingredient of their corporate campaign work.

What this means, in effect, is that in cases where tensions have flared up in the past (e.g., between environmentalists and loggers), special skills may have to be applied in order to mobilize and rebuild alliances that have a chance of being sustained for the long haul.

Finally, citizens' movements are going to have to consider making some strategic investments in the fields of media and communications if they are going to have any real chance of creating a climate of public opinion for the new politics. As long as Conrad Black and his big business allies own and control the major newspapers and radio and television outlets in this country, the task of tackling—let alone dismantling—the system of corporate rule will prove overwhelmingly difficult. One significant source of capital is people's pension funds. Ed Finn estimates that unionized workers' pension funds in Canada now total nearly $400 billion. If, for example, even 5 per cent of these pension funds were earmarked for social investment purposes, it would be possible to purchase a string of newspapers, TV and radio stations in strategic locations throughout the country. And if a plan were developed whereby journalists and media personnel with socially progressive credentials were deployed in strategic positions within these newly-acquired communication centres, it could have a profound impact on the political understanding, motivation and resources of citizens' movements.

Obviously, such a plan of action would have to be carefully worked out and thoroughly discussed within the labour movement itself. For the most part, unionized pension funds are controlled by trustees appointed by corporate employers. The strategic question now is how do unions regain control over what are really deferred wages earned by workers. As Finn points out: "In a society where clout and influence are measured by the size of the financial club you carry, a policy of letting employers, banks, trust and insurance companies control the biggest accumulation of union members' money—and use it frequently for anti-union purposes—is a policy that keeps the balance of power in labour-management relations tilted decisively in management's favour."

Although workers understandably want to be assured that they will get a good return on the investment of their pension funds, there is no reason why this would not be the case. After all, most newspapers, radio and television stations are profitable enterprises that would generate reasonable returns on investment. Although workers should not be turned into investors, the fact is that, unless steps are taken to ensure that workers' pension funds are invested, at least in part, for socially productive purposes, they will continue to be used for investments that are counter-productive to the struggles of working people in this country.

The issue here is how do workers gain enough control over their own pension funds where they can redirect a portion for investment in socially productive enterprises that will also bring them a reasonable return. By moving in this direction, the cornerstones for building a citizens' movement for the long haul can be put in place. ◖◗

6. Democratic Control

Looks like we'd better dig in for the long haul!

...Guess what? Yesterday, I was at a day-long regional meeting of community groups where people were really worked up about the corporate takeover of health care and education. We're going to meet again in a couple of weeks to pick our targets and plan our research.

...Looks like some action may finally be heating up. When I went by the union office the other day, they said the national was calling a special strategy session to organize a campaign against corporate downsizing.

...That's great. And I hear about other plans to tackle the banks on interest charges, and the forest companies on all their clear-cutting. But people still want to know where all these protests are going to take us. I mean, we can probably expose what these corporations are doing, but what will that really accomplish? Sooner or later we have to find a political outlet—a government that will work for us, not big business.

...Fat chance! I mean, the record speaks for itself. No matter how concerned with our problems a party may sound in opposition, it always converts to the corporate agenda when it forms the government. The corporations run the country now, no matter what bunch of politicians we favour with our votes.

...Which proves that we need to do more than elect a party on the basis of its election promises. Unless a party is firmly and openly committed to dismantling corporate rule and makes that its first priority, our elections will be meaningless. They won't change anything.

...Right! But most people still don't know that. They still think the way to change things for the better is through the political process. Until they become aware of how that process has been hijacked by big business, we won't be able to regain the democratic control of our country, our economy, and our future.

Political Movement

THE NEW POLITICS OF CITIZENS' movements cannot be based solely on mobilizing resistance to the structures of corporate rule. While the politics of resistance is a critical component of a citizens' agenda, people's actions also need to be anchored by a sense of hope for the future. If people are going to commit themselves to a resistance movement, they need to know that they are fighting for something.

An alternative vision of the future, in other words, is an essential part of any struggle for democratic social change. Yet the public is constantly being fed a heavy dose of TINA—There Is No Alternative—by the country's business and political élites. This, of course, is simply a form of intellectual terrorism. There *are* alternative options which should be a vital part of public discussion and debate in a democratic society.

The strategy of selling TINA is based on the politics of fear, which in the end is anti-democratic. But what this means, in effect, is that people not only need to know that alternatives exist; they must also believe these alternatives are viable and achievable if they are going to commit themselves to a prolonged struggle to make them a reality.

In order to build popular support around a program for social change, therefore, people must be given a sense of hope through a vision of the future, coupled with a sense of confidence that this vision can be realized. In short, to combat the politics of fear we must build a movement that effectively combines a politics of resistance with a politics of hope.

We must also recognize that citizens' movements are limited in what they can accomplish. They alone cannot, for example, be expected to dismantle the system of corporate rule that exists in this country. Indeed, this is where party politics becomes an essential part of the struggle for democratic social change. It is only by taking over the reins of governance through electoral politics that a program for social change can be implemented. What is often missing in struggles for social change are strategies that reflect the distinctive roles to be played by both citizens' movements and political parties.

Citizens' movements can create a climate conducive to changing the political culture by focusing public debate around issues, values and priorities. In so doing, they can generate a social base and public momentum for change. A political party, on the other hand, has a key role to play in developing and promoting a political platform that reflects the major issues and priorities of this changing political culture. By winning public support and forming the government, a political party is in a position to carry out its platform for social change. What is needed in this country is a political party with a platform and a strategy for dismantling the structures of corporate rule and developing new institutions for democratic control.

A quick glance at the parliamentary rostrum reveals that there is no political party on the national scene these days that clearly fits this bill. Despite its electoral rhetoric, the ruling Liberal party under Jean Chrétien, as we have seen, has become completely dominated by its business wing and is bankrolled primarily by the corporate and wealthy sectors of society. So, too, is the Conservative party today under Jean Charest which, even though it was reduced to a rump group in Parliament, not only adheres to the same corporate agenda as it did under Brian Mulroney, but has moved even further to the right.

As the chief beneficiary of the electoral losses by the national Conservatives, the Reform Party under Preston Manning has been on the vanguard of right-wing politics in Canada, promoting economic and social policies that serve the interests of big business and wealthy individuals. And, while the Bloc Québécois under Lucien Bouchard occasionally displayed some signs of social conscience, sovereigntist politics has become increasingly wedded to a business-dominated agenda, particularly since Bouchard became the premier of Quebec and made deficit-slashing his government's top priority.

This brings us to the New Democratic Party. In terms of its historic roots, the NDP is certainly in the best position of all the political parties in this country to champion this struggle. Its predecessor, the Cooperative Commonwealth Federation, was led by heroic figures like J.S. Woodsworth, Agnes MacPhail and Tommy Douglas, who made the fight against monopoly capitalism one of the cornerstones of the party's platform. Both the CCF and its successor, the NDP, were able to build public support for this platform, culminating in the NDP's 1972 campaign against "corporate welfare bums" under David Lewis.

While the forms of monopoly capitalism have certainly changed since the heyday of the CCF, the logic of the system has remained the same. But, as long-time party observer James Laxer has shown, the NDP of the 1990s has shifted course. Indeed, the performance of NDP provincial governments during this decade has demonstrated the extent to which the party has been willing to embrace elements of the corporate agenda in order to win support from the business community.

At the same time, the party has also been weakened by problematic working relations with the women's movement, the labour movement, and broader-based coalitions. But, perhaps most significantly, the NDP has not yet devised a comprehensive platform and strategy for challenging the corporate political machines and instituting new forms of democratic control.

Even if the federal NDP with Alexa McDonough at the helm is able to restore its original purpose and vision, it is imperative that steps be taken to rebuild the democratic left as a political movement into the new millennium. In doing so, it is important to take stock of what resources and capacities we have. For example, many of the counterparts to the corporate agenda and the political right are already in place. The Canadian Labour Congress is the natural countervailing force to the BCNI. The Canadian Centre for Policy Alternatives with its network of researchers and educators is the obvious counterpart of the C.D. Howe and Fraser Institutes. Organizations like the Council of Canadians have emerged as counterpoints to the National Citizens' Coalition. But if these organizations are to function effectively as democratic-left challengers of the corporate agenda, their resources need to be consolidated and strategically coordinated.

Beyond these key coordinates looms a broad range of significant citizens' movements, including the National Action Committee on the Status of Women, the Canadian Federation of Students, the social justice constituencies of the mainline churches, the Canadian Health Coalition, environmental networks like Greenpeace, the Canadian Environmental Law Association and the Sierra Club, plus international development organizations like Inter Pares, OXFAM and CUSO. The question is whether or not these and related social movements can be re-energized to form a broadly-based common front and political movement committed to the task of reclaiming democratic control by challenging the structures of corporate rule.

All of this, of course, requires some long-term strategic planning over the next five, ten and even 15 years. Here, special attention needs to be given to the task of developing a political platform with a social vision that can revitalize a left-wing form of populism in this country. One of the major keys will be a new generation of youth leaders emerging from the ranks of the student, labour and environmental movements who have a gut-felt need to fight for their basic democratic rights as citizens in an age of corporate tyranny.

At this point, the corporate campaigns waged by citizens' movements could have a vital role to play. For it is by working in the trenches on the battlefields against the corporate political machines that this new generation of youth can acquire some first-hand training and experience in exercising their leadership skills. It is also out of the struggles waged around these corporate campaigns that some of the basic elements of a platform for revitalizing the democratic left will emerge.

Indeed, the time is ripe! All across the country today there are increasing signs that the politics of insecurity are alive and well. Stubbornly high levels of joblessness, massive layoffs from corporate downsizing (including governments), along with the dramatic shift from full-time to part-time employment, have created a climate of growing *economic insecurity* for many Canadians. The relentless wave of cutbacks in government funding for heath care, public education, social assistance, post-secondary education, and unemployment insurance has greatly heightened levels of *social insecurity,* particularly among women. On top of all this, there is an increasing sense of *ecological insecurity* among Canadians, who fear what will happen as governments reduce environmental regulations, cut back on the monitoring and enforcement of pollution standards, and make it easier for mining, forestry, and energy corporations to speedily extract and export our non-renewable natural resources.

The theme running through all of this insecurity is a fear that people are losing control over their economic, social and ecological future. In turn, this fear is intensified by the growing awareness of the extent to which corporations now control their political as well as their economic and social welfare. When deepening class divisions are added, this politics of insecurity becomes a potentially volatile mixture.

In the midst of all this upheaval, however, some rays of hope may be detected. After all, as William Greider explains, the system of corporate rule has been built on shaky foundations, economic as well as political. So much so that its built-in contradictions could intensify to the point where major political cracks may soon appear. Take, for example, the casino economy in which investment has become a game for gamblers and speculators. The trillions of dollars in cyber-money transferred around the world every day have inflated a financial bubble that could well burst if not controlled in the near future by some kind of global financial sector regulation.

Or take the industrial sectors of the economy, which have deployed new technologies to produce a massive supply of goods and services, but cannot sell them because of inadequate consumer demand and purchasing power.

Consider, too, the signs of anxiety and uncertainty now surfacing among some CEOs and their political and academic allies. Until recently, they extolled the merits of unrestricted international competitiveness and foreign investment as the foolproof tools for building a prosperous global economy. Now they are beginning to see that the free market religion is not delivering the economic Utopia its high priests had promised.

Add to these first cracks in the corporate rule structure the rumblings of social unrest generated by the inequality and insecurity it has spawned, and we can find reasons to believe that the reign of the business overlords may not be as absolute and as long-lasting as they intended it to be. Even if it does not collapse from its internal stresses and contradictions, the corporate New World Order is surely vulnerable to community-based resistance focused on its weakest elements.

The challenge now for the democratic left is to seize the opportunity to forge a full-fledged political movement. As we move into the 21st century, the crisis of democracy itself is bound to deepen and intensify under the heels of corporate tyranny. What is needed is a political platform that outlines ways in which the mechanisms of corporate rule could be dismantled and new institutions for democratic control developed. At the core of such a platform could be the call to increase people's control over their economic, social and ecological future.

While this is the task that a political party like the NDP needs to undertake, there is no reason why the process should not be initiated by citizens' movements. Indeed, it is imperative if the politics of resistance is to be complemented by the politics of hope. What follows, therefore, is an attempt to map out some of the pieces of such a platform. It should be emphasized that this is not a blueprint, but rather a set of proposals and strategies that will need to be tested through discussion and debate.

National Reconstruction

At the outset, one of the main questions that needs to be addressed by the democratic left in developing a new political platform for Canadians is how to rebuild our economy and society after the devastation wreaked under corporate rule. Canada, after all, was originally founded on a mixed economy in which both the private and the public sectors were understood to be the engines of economic and social development. These were the foundation stones of the Canadian experiment, as distinct from the exclusively free market economy of the U.S. But now that the big corporations and their political machines have taken a wrecking ball to the public sector, the foundations of the Canadian experiment have been badly damaged.

The signs of the wreckage are all around us today, from plant shutdowns and business bankruptcies to hospital closings and food bank line-ups, to the disappearance of fish stocks and the clearcutting of our forests. Most of all, it is felt in people's growing sense of economic, social and ecological insecurity.

The question of how to rebuild Canada's economy and society from this wreckage must start by forcing the debate over what kind of economic and political model should guide this reconstruction.

As we have seen, Canada's economy and society are dominated today by a corporate model of development. The free market reigns supreme with the private sector the prime engine of economic and social development, largely unfettered by government intervention or regulation. Increasingly, the economy has been reoriented to serve the interests of corporations, both domestic and foreign, for greater profitable investment opportunities.

Driven by the doctrine of international competitiveness, Canada's economy has been redirected to serve primarily the external demands of transnational capital rather than the basic needs of our own people. Through its extensive political machinery, Corporate Canada has been able to ensure that government economic and social policies are redesigned to consolidate this model of development. Despite all the rhetoric about cost-saving efficiencies, however, this corporate model has proven to be enormously wasteful in terms of both human and material resources.

A nation with over two million workers rendered unproductive on a permanent basis, over a third of its production facilities and machinery lying idle, and tens of billions of dollars from people's savings squandered to finance corporate takeovers, mergers and investment abroad, is a nation that is wasting its human and natural resources.

In rebuilding our economy and society today, this corporate model must be clearly and firmly rejected. As economists Sam Gindin and David Robertson have emphasized, there are no halfway measures. Once you accept the rules of the corporate model, you find yourself on a slippery slope from which there is no escape. Instead, Canada needs to adopt an alternative, more democratic model which puts priority on the development of its citizens' capacities to build up the country's economy and society. According to this model, the democratic development of people's basic needs and their productive capacities would be the primary goal of the nation's economy.

A nation's well-being, argue Gindin and Robertson, depends a great deal on the productive insights and capacities of its citizens who are working people. Rather than concentrating on becoming ever more internationally competitive, this model emphasizes the importance of developing the productive skills and resources of its citizens. This is how Canadians will best be able to contribute to the economic, social, and ecological reconstruction of their country and their communities and take control over their own future.

To do so, of course, requires a much more participatory model for developing our economy and society. Obviously, this calls for a dismantling of the system of corporate rule and its mechanisms, including the political machinery used by big corporations to determine and direct the development of economic, social and environmental policies. But it takes more than the removal of these corporate mechanisms of power and control to make the economy more participatory for its citizens. Democratic control implies, as Gindin and Robertson note, that people have equal access to participation in the economy (i.e., democracy as universal) and that they have concrete opportunities to develop their potential as citizens.

By the same token, people cannot participate effectively if their basic needs are not being met, and so this is another important precondition for exercising democratic control. At the same time, new institutional mechanisms need to be designed to encourage and maximize citizen participation in defining development priorities and in planning economic, social and environmental initiatives, especially in local and regional community settings. In effect, these conditions are essential if people are going to be able to exercise their rights in a truly democratic society.

Replacing the corporate model with a more democratic model of development for the rebuilding of our economy and society does not mean a rejection of corporations or even globalization, *per se*. Clearly, corporations and their workers have a vital role to play in the economy. By mobilizing capital and technology to produce goods and services for both domestic and global markets, they spur the creation of economic growth and wealth. What is being rejected is a model of the economy and society in which corporations are allowed to wield their power and wealth in such a way as to dominate, exploit and control the lives of people. More specifically, it is the powerful role that corporate CEOs and their political machines play in determining (if not dictating) the economic, social and environmental priorities and directions of the country.

What our alternative model requires is that corporations and their operations be brought under democratic control. Nor does replacement of the corporate model mean an outright rejection of globalization. Clearly, advances in transportation and communications technology have made global interdependence a fact of life. As a trading nation, Canada will always have a vital interest in negotiating international relationships and access to global markets as part of a national development plan. What is being rejected is an economic model wherein transnational corporations, driven by a doctrine of ever-growing international competitiveness, set the terms and conditions of globalization.

All of which points to the need for a public debate over what kind of model should define the rebuilding of Canada's economy and society. In many ways, the political platform we have been proposing should be designed to stimulate such a debate. At its core, the nature of this debate would be ideological. After all, very different values and assumptions about the nature of our economy and society lie behind the corporate and the democratic models.

The timeliness for such a debate is becoming more and more evident. Not only is the need to develop a plan for national reconstruction becoming more urgent, but the prospect of an expanding surplus in Ottawa's finances at the turn of the century makes this task all the more imperative. The question is whether or not the democratic left will be able to seize the moment by putting forward a plan for national reconstruction that is clearly based on a democratic model rather than a continuation of the corporate rule which has caused so much misery and insecurity in this country.

But more is needed if there is to be a platform that provides a road map for dismantling corporate rule and instituting democratic control.

Democratic State

A key component of any plan for national reconstruction along these lines would have to deal with the question of what to do with the state. As we have seen, the "Keynesian" state, which was the model of governance in this country and throughout the western world for almost half of the 20th century, has been systematically dismantled by big business and its allies and replaced by the corporate state. As long as the primary role of the federal government in this country is seen in terms of reorganizing the entire national system—fiscal, economic, social, cultural, and environmental—to promote profitable investment and competition, there is little hope of being able to bring forward, let alone carry out, a comprehensive program for national reconstruction.

The state, in effect, has been re-invented as the political arm of big business. Some of its powers have been stripped away, while others have been redirected and strengthened to serve corporate interests. It is therefore not enough for a party of the democratic left to take over the pivotal role of opposition, let alone to form the government in Ottawa sometime during the next decade or so, without having some sort of plan for overhauling the roles, responsibilities and powers of government. Otherwise the party will have little or no credibility in advancing a bold platform for democratic social change.

In effect, an alternative platform needs to contain a program and strategy for replacing the corporate state with a democratic model of governance. In keeping with the principles outlined above, the cornerstone of a democratic state would be the defence and promotion of the basic rights and freedoms of citizens. The prime purpose of the state would be to ensure that the economy operates in such a way as to serve the basic needs and develop the productive capacities of its citizens.

This would not simply mean a reinstatement of the old Keynesian model. To be sure, like the Keynesian version, the democratic state would have the powers and tools it needs to intervene in the market on behalf of the public interest. But the way it functioned would differ. For example, given the realities of the new global economy, it makes sense for the democratic state to have the kind of mandate and powers that the present corporate model has used for reorganizing the entire national system. The difference, of course, is that the state would be mandated to reorganize the national system to serve the needs of its citizens rather than its corporations. Moreover, it would have to do so in ways that encouraged and maximized citizen participation.

"The real issue of our time," says Leo Panitch, "is not less state vs. more state, but rather a different kind of state." Citing the Spicer Commission, which conducted cross-country consultations and town hall meetings around issues of constitutional reform in 1991-92, Panitch contends there is substantial evidence that Canadians want to see some fundamental changes in the whole system of government. The Spicer Commission's conclusion was that people wanted more democratic forms of representation, accountability and control over public institutions. This popular demand, according to the Commission, was due in part to people's sense that "traditional Canadian values are being usurped by anonymous market forces and that governments are doing nothing to deal with these."

While this message has been picked up by the Reform party in its platform of right-wing populism, notes Panitch, it is high time that the left developed its own plan for democratizing the state. "A dynamic democracy is not one that represents and freezes current opinion," he says, but "one that encourages the development of human capacities—above all, our collective capacities for creating a social order governed by justice. It is a process of collective development and education through participation."

Any attempt, however, to overhaul the state by democratizing the machinery of government can expect to meet resistance from the senior bureaucracy. The idea that a new progressive-minded government could count on an independent, loyal, dedicated and neutral civil service ready to carry out its wishes, has become pure myth. All the more so, in recent years, as civil servants have been retrained to operate like public entrepreneurs, treating citizens like consumers and turning policies, programs and services into "products" to be bought and sold in the political marketplace.

The CEOs and their political machines would also fiercely

resist any effort to dismantle the mechanisms of the corporate security state. The corporate élite, even more than the senior bureaucracy, have a vested interest in maintaining the status quo. To bring in a democratic model of government, therefore, a concerted plan of action needs to be devised. Otherwise, a progressive government would find its plans being sabotaged by a hostile corporate/bureaucratic alliance.

An agenda for democratizing the state, says political scientist Greg Albo, must begin by "deepening representative democracy and political freedoms" in the Ottawa bureaucracy. This entails three measures. *First,* ministerial staff and new personnel need to be brought onside immediately to ensure that the government's plans for democratic reforms are speedily implemented. Relying on outside consultants will not be sufficient, says Albo, because they are too distant from the trench warfare that will necessarily be waged at the centre.

Second, a central planning and policy review board should be established to coordinate the government's initiatives. This body would be pivotal for "breaking up concentrations of power in the hands of the senior bureaucracy," as well as moving beyond a crisis management mode to developing a capacity for long-term planning.

Third, the administrative bureaucracy would have to be democratized by "loosening rigid operating structures, pushing decision-making authority to lower levels, crossing jurisdictional boundaries, multiplying points of citizen access, and decentralizing services."

To move in this direction, an alternative platform would have to outline some broad steps that could be taken to dismantle the corporate security state and its mechanisms. Here, the prime target would be the political machinery of the corporations. Legislative action, for example, could be taken to: eliminate or substantially restrict all forms of corporate financing for political parties and election campaigns; impose tight rules on big business lobbying operations and ensure greater access by other citizens' organizations to the policy and decision-making processes of government; and prevent corporations from engaging in forms of political advertising to promote policy changes or ideological viewpoints.

Other measures could be taken to restrict the direct influence of corporate think-tanks on the policy-making process in Ottawa. In taking this kind of action, the objective would be to restore democratic control of our political system by dismantling those parts of the corporate political machine which have been used to gain a stranglehold on policy-making in Ottawa and the provinces.

For a democratic state to function in the new global economy, a review of the federal system in terms of its distribution of powers would also have to be undertaken. This is not the same set of issues that have to be dealt with concerning Quebec's political future, which will require special attention in its own right. The issue here is two-fold. On the one hand, there is the question of how to strengthen the Canadian state to, for example, negotiate with powerful transnational corporations (as well as other nation states) so as to ensure that national standards are maintained in the delivery of social programs and public services across the country.

On the other hand, there is the question of what powers should remain in the hands of provincial governments where, for example, the responsibility for delivering most of the social programs and public services now rest, along with that of promoting economic development in their regions. The underlying purpose of the review would be to ensure that powers are centralized and decentralized in ways that ensure the democratic development of people in this country. In turn, a review of federal and provincial powers along these lines would also necessitate the opening up for renegotiation of major pieces of legislation such as the Canada Health and Social Transfer Act and the Internal Trade Agreement.

Developing a democratic state along these lines, however, would be insufficient without introducing measures to increase the capacities of citizens for popular planning and management. Here, Albo proposes three more steps. *First,* "network teams" composed of officials, consultants, unionists and users should be formed around major policy and program areas. These "network teams" could function as a means for increased popular planning in Ottawa and would go a long way towards loosening bureaucratic rigidities.

Second, measures should be introduced to develop an equal relationship between producers and users in the delivery of services. The current model of bureaucratic dependency, whereby users are dependent on producers, could be changed by putting a priority on developing active associations of users and by promoting new bonds of relationship with producers.

Third, new opportunities for popular planning and self-management should be introduced. Frontline workers and user groups, for example, should be encouraged to come up with their own plans for providing and distributing services, and a higher priority should be put on democratizing the workplace.

The challenge here is to design new and imaginative mechanisms for citizen participation in both popular planning and self-management. This does not mean dusting off some of the old models of consultation and re-instituting them. On the contrary, emphasis should be put on setting up elected councils of citizens with a mandate to do popular planning and program management for democratic leaders and administrators. This, says Panitch, will encourage and facilitate authentic citizen participation in popular planning and self-management.

Just as citizens, for example, are elected to school boards to monitor the implementation of education policies, so similar types of institutions could be established for citizen participation in the development and implementation of economic, social, and environmental policies at regional levels. The problem here, notes Panitch, is that one cannot assume an active citizenry at a time when so many people feel a sense of powerlessness and lack a sense of community. It is therefore important that democratic leaders and administrators have the skills required to animate and facilitate citizen participation in these processes.

In addition, social policy analyst Paul Leduc Browne proposes that the democratic state should include a strategy that combines economic and social development by uniting the public sector with the "social economy," which includes non-profit organizations, voluntary associations, cooperatives, mutual insurers, and community economic development enterprises. While only the state, through the public sector, can mobilize and command the resources needed to provide and distribute collective goods in a fair, efficient and equitable manner, there is a vital need to link economic, social and sustainable development initiatives to local community networks and grassroots citizen movements.

To perform this role, the social economy would have to be adequately financed and strengthened without undercutting the public sector. Browne suggests that this could be done through a combination of direct and indirect government grants to the social economy sector, and by setting up non-profit funding agencies at arm's-length from the government. The latter would have boards composed of community stakeholders with a mandate to distribute funds to organizations that serve the community on a non-profit basis. Strengthening the social economy would also ensure that citizens' movements would have the resources they need to be actively involved in struggles for democratic social change.

Political Sovereignty

Any platform outlining a program for national reconstruction and development would have to deal with the question of how to rebuild Canada's sovereign powers as a nation state. As we have seen, the ruthless measures employed to privatize and deregulate Canada's economy throughout the 1980s, reinforced by the new free trade regimes of the FTA and NAFTA towards the end of that decade, followed by increasing dependence on foreign debt financing in the 1990s, have all had profoundly debilitating effects on Canada's national sovereignty. Through these measures, Ottawa (and the provinces as well) effectively surrendered many of the powers and tools required to develop a national plan to meet the economic, social and ecological needs of Canadians. More specifically, these measures have stripped Ottawa and the provinces of most of the tools they once had at their disposal to regulate the activities of corporations, both domestic and foreign, in relation to the country's development needs.

While it is true that nation states like Canada never have had the sovereign powers and tools required to effectively control the operations of transnational corporations in their domain, the problem has become much more acute over the past few decades. It is imperative, therefore, that a plan of action be developed to assert a significant measure of democratic control over corporations in the economy.

At the outset, Ottawa would have to find a way of re-regulating corporate investments, both domestic and foreign. In accordance with the national plan for reconstruction and development, a new and comprehensive set of investment criteria reflecting economic, social and environmental priorities would have to be established. Based on these criteria, performance requirement standards could be set on matters ranging from job content to appropriate technology, from worker safety to pollution limits, from food safety to export quotas on natural resources. Other performance requirements might be developed to meet the goal of increasing people's productive capacities.

Related legislative measures could also be introduced outlining, for example, conditions that must be met regarding plant closures in terms of responsibilities to workers and communities, or conditions calling for more local community control over foreign investment such as "site here - sell here" policies. In any case, what is needed are clear investment criteria with adequate enforcement measures to ensure that corporate investment, both domestic and foreign, is designed to meet the economic, social and environmental goals for national development.

One of the more effective ways that corporations are able to subvert the political sovereignty of nation states like Canada is through the increasing concentration of ownership and control. Through monopolies, mergers and cartels, giant corporations are able to consolidate their control over key sectors of the economy. A recent example, as we have seen, is the ownership and control of close to 60 per cent of Canada's newspapers by Conrad Black of Hollinger Inc., the world's third largest newspaper empire. In order to counter the build-up of these corporate power blocks, steps need to be taken to identify the corporate monopolies in key sectors of the economy which are having an adverse effect on national development priorities, and then take appropriate legislative action to break them up.

In part, this would entail an overhaul of Canada's competition legislation which, as noted before, was virtually written by the BCNI itself. But strong leadership on this front might also involve a rigorous application of anti-trust legislation which has been used before in other countries, including the U.S., to break up powerful corporate monopolies that are not acting in the public interest.

In addition, concerted action should be taken to repatriate Canada's debt holdings from foreign bond holders and to curb capital flows outside the country. As Ottawa's main instrument of monetary policy, the Bank of Canada has the option of entering the money markets and purchasing Treasury bills and longer-term bonds on its own account. In so doing, the Bank of Canada can buy back more of Ottawa's debt load from foreign bondholders, thus diverting back to the public treasury interest payments that would otherwise leave the country. Steps also need to be taken to repatriate the tens of billions of dollars that corporations move offshore every year to avoid paying their fair share of taxes and the social costs of doing business in this country.

While Canada abandoned the use of direct capital controls back in 1951, they are still used by some 11 industrialized countries and 109 developing countries to curb the flight of capital. A variety of tools are available for governments to monitor and control capital outflows. And, just as police forces are now calling for the closer monitoring of global capital flows to restrict the laundering of drug money, so international agreements could be negotiated requiring that capital that crosses borders illegally is returned to the country of origin.

At the same time, there are major obstacles built into trade deals like NAFTA which would undoubtedly be used to block some of these moves to restore Canada's political sovereignty. The investment code of NAFTA, for example, restricts governments from applying performance requirements like job content or appropriate technology provisions. Similarly, NAFTA's energy code prevents the use of export quotas, and the finance code forbids all kinds of capital and foreign exchange controls.

Although these are some of the more contentious clauses, there are other NAFTA-related obstacles to this agenda. In this context, Ottawa would have two options. It could make use of the abrogation clause in NAFTA and inform its partners of Canada's intention to withdraw from the trade agreement altogether, or it could take steps to reopen negotiations on the main contentious clauses. Given the fact that these clauses, in many ways, constitute the centrepiece of NAFTA, it is unlikely the U.S.—or, more precisely, corporate North America—would agree to opening them up for renegotiation. However, it might make more strategic sense to proceed first with an all-out effort at renegotiation and then, if that fails, take steps to invoke the abrogation clause.

There are also ways in which Ottawa (and the provinces) could strengthen political sovereignty by providing concrete opportunities for citizens' movements to exercise popular sovereignty over corporations. Through legislative action, governments could enact a procedure that would allow citizens' movements to review, challenge and amend corporate charters. In the U.S., for example, the authority of citizens to challenge corporate charters has been the law of the land in most states since the early part of the 19th century. The rationale is that, since governments are acting in the name of citizens when they grant corporations the authority to operate in their jurisdiction, then citizens' movements should have the right to participate in the process of evaluating the performances of corporations and recommending whether their licences should be extended, amended or revoked.

Similar procedures could be instituted here in Canada. The criteria used for evaluating corporate performances could essentially be the same as those used for assessing corporate investment plans, which are based on the economic, social and environmental priorities of the national development plan. Utilizing legal processes, citizens' movements could evaluate the track records of targeted corporations in the light of these criteria and, if necessary, petition either to have their charters revoked on the grounds that they violated people's basic democratic rights, or amended to ensure that these violations are not repeated.

If necessary, court injunctions could be used to prevent further harm or the sudden relocation of targeted corporations. What's more, citizens' movements could utilize these procedures to challenge the political machinery used by corporations to dictate government policy-making.

Public Finance

One area where the democratic left has certainly made significant advances in developing a process for citizen participation has been in the field of public finance through what has become known as the Alternative Federal Budget. Using a method originally designed by CHOICES!, a coalition of citizen activists in Manitoba, the Canadian Centre for Policy Alternatives and CHO!CES jointly coordinate an annual process in which citizens' movements from a variety of sectors participate in developing an alternative federal budget for Canada. Through an extensive negotiating process involving both citizens' groups and technical experts on a sector-by-sector basis, program and revenue priorities are set for an alternative policy agenda which, in turn, provides the framework for developing the Alternative Federal Budget (AFB).

By treating Canada's deficit and debt as primarily a revenue problem, not a spending problem, the AFB contains creative proposals for reducing the deficit while at the same time strengthening public investment in the development of human resources through job creation, social programs and environmental safeguards. In particular, the AFB outlines steps that can be taken to increase democratic control, as distinct from corporate control, over the nation's finances.

To begin, concerted action needs to be taken to overhaul the corporate tax system in this country. As we have seen, one of the principal causes of Canada's lingering debt problems has been diminishing public revenues from profitable corporations, which often receive substantial government subsidies while not being required to pay their fair share of taxes. Ottawa could strengthen its public finances considerably by introducing a series of measures to change the corporate tax system, such as: substantially reducing or eliminating tax-delivered subsidies to corporations (e.g., tax write-offs for meals and entertainment, lobbying expenses, etc.) which even the IMF has cited as being excessively generous; adopting a minimum corporate tax to ensure that all profitable corporations pay their fair share of public revenues and have access to fewer favourable tax provisions; applying a tax on excess profits, starting with the Big Six national banks which reported profits in excess of $6 billion in 1996 alone; eliminating the capital gains exemption and the tax credits for dividend income which give special tax treatment to wealthy investors; and introducing a wealth tax which almost every other OECD country already has in place. Through these and related measures, the corporate welfare system in this country could be substantially overhauled.

To curb excessive speculation in financial markets, as well as raise additional public revenues, a financial transactions tax (FTT) should be adopted in Canada. Such a tax would apply not only to stocks, bonds, and money market trades, but also to options, futures and derivative contracts.

Through such a financial transactions tax, Ottawa could at least begin to exercise some control over speculation in money markets in a time when economies are increasingly fuelled by what happens in the financial casino. There is some debate about what the revenue base for an FTT would be in Canada and whether it would be large enough to warrant such a tax, but it is worth noting that several other countries, including Britain, Switzerland and Japan, have already adopted a domestic tax of this kind.

To ensure that investors do not avoid the tax by taking their money offshore, the FTT should be applied to all Canadian residents and their affiliated corporations, no matter where the transactions actually occur. By instituting a domestic financial transactions tax along these lines, Canada would be well placed to play a pivotal role in negotiating an international agreement for the adoption of the "Tobin Tax" on global financial transactions (named after Nobel prize-winning economist James Tobin). Indeed, a modest tax on all international financial transactions would be imperative, for otherwise investors would simply transfer their money to tax havens in other countries.

Regaining control over public finances also requires developing an independent monetary policy. After all, big business has succeeded in having the Bank of Canada put top priority on fighting inflation by maintaining a policy of high interest rates which, in turn, has been a prime cause of our increasing debt loads. Ottawa could immediately instruct the Bank of Canada not only to continue with its more recent lower nominal interest rate policy over the short term, but also to take decisive action to lower real interest rates on a longer-term basis. One of the ways the Bank of Canada can exert influence over longer-run interest rates is to re-enter the money markets itself and purchase on its own account longer-term government bonds as well as Treasury bills.

Lowering real interest rates over the long run is essential if government revenue is going to increase sufficiently to reduce the nation's debt load through lower interest payments. Moving in this direction means restoring the central bank to its proper role in implementing monetary policy. After all, the Bank of Canada was never mandated to fight inflation alone. Its founding legislation, the Bank of Canada Act, stipulates that employment and the financial health of the country should also be among its major responsibilities.

At the same time, the brakes need to be applied to private bank holdings of government debts. As we have already seen, the Big Six national banks have recently been cashing in on Ottawa's "debt crisis" by purchasing risk-free government bonds, thereby adding tens of billions of dollars to the public debt. As proposed above, the Bank of Canada could be called upon to reverse this trend by re-entering the market itself to purchase a much larger proportion of government bonds. In this case, the money "borrowed" from the government's own bank would in effect be interest-free.

To be effective, however, steps would also have to be taken to restore the reserve requirements of the private banks and other financial institutions which were relaxed in 1991. What this means is that the banks, trust companies and other financial institutions would be required by law to keep a portion of their deposits in reserve with the central bank. Restoring these reserve requirements would not only strengthen the capacity of the Bank of Canada to purchase government bonds on money markets, but also to control the overall growth of money supply and thus avert any inflationary trends that might otherwise be triggered by these changes.

All these measures, however, will do little to increase democratic control over the nation's finances if steps are not also taken to make banks and other financial institutions more responsive to the needs of citizens in their local communities. More specifically, mechanisms need to be developed to enable citizens to evaluate the performance of banks and other financial institutions in terms of how well they serve community needs. For example, the charters issued by Parliament permitting the national banks to operate could be assessed and renewed—or rescinded—depending on how well they have performed in relation to such standards as re-investment in the community, provision of home mortgages, and related community needs.

John Dillon suggests that, just as broadcasting licences are renewed on a regular basis by the Canadian Radio-television and Telecommunications Commission (CRTC) in terms of performance standards, a similar system could be developed to evaluate the performance of banks. While the CRTC may not be the best example, given the bureaucratic entanglements that have impaired its effectiveness, there is no reason why an appropriate mechanism could not be designed that would allow concerned citizens' movements to become actively involved in the performance evaluation of financial institutions at community and regional levels. Similar measures should also be devised to ensure that the Bank of Canada is made more directly accountable for its monetary policy, both to Parliament and to regional concerns across the country.

Economic Production

A key component of any alternative platform would, of course, be a plan for national economic reconstruction. In keeping with the development priorities outlined above, the prime goal here would be to develop the capacities of citizens by providing real jobs in strategic sectors of the economy. This is where the shift from the corporate model to the democratic model of economic planning and development comes into play in a more precise and practical way.

The corporate economic strategy adopted by Ottawa, which is based on a "winners and losers" approach of picking certain corporations to excel as world class competitors in global markets (e.g., Northern Telecom), would have to be abandoned. Instead, Ottawa could opt for an economic strategy that organizes and coordinates production networks in key sectors of Canada's economy.

Gindin and Robertson, for example, have proposed that companies could be clustered together to form production networks in each of the major industrial sectors (i.e., manufacturing, resource, agriculture) which in turn would be coordinated with other key sectors of the economy (e.g., finance, service, communications, transportation, and related public services). Through these production networks, plans could be developed for enhancing productivity for both domestic needs and export markets.

By giving priority to the development of people's productive capacities, a much more coordinated approach could be taken towards job creation. Each production network could commit itself to increasing workplace democracy be ensuring that workers are given a role in decisions on production and investment. Wherever possible, emphasis could also be put on promoting a greater degree of worker and community ownership of enterprises.

Obviously, this kind of economic planning and development could not be left in the hands of corporations and banks. On their own, corporations and banks plan their investment decisions solely on the basis of profit maximization, which often results in a major exodus of capital from the country and a corresponding depletion of the resources required to meet economic, social and ecological development priorities at home. Instead, Ottawa (in collaboration with the provinces) would need to take the lead in launching a national economic development plan that would encourage corporations to shape their investment and production decisions. This could be greatly facilitated by a reorganization of the economy along the lines of production networks.

Obtaining the cooperation of key corporations in strategic sectors of the economy would be imperative. While Ottawa would certainly need to hone its negotiating skills in dealing with corporations (both domestic and foreign), it also has strategically important bargaining chips to play. After all, Canada remains one of the world's best long-term investment locations. But, if corporations want access to our natural resources, consumer market, skilled labour, and a relatively safe and stable climate for investment, then they will have to meet certain economic, social and environmental standards and conditions. To move in this direction, however, Ottawa would need to develop new policy tools for asserting democratic control over economic development. Here, the AFB has already outlined a number of options.

To begin, a nation-wide public investment program needs to be developed and implemented as a vehicle for stimulating new job creation. This would be a broadly-based public sector pro-gram involving federal, provincial, territorial and municipal gov-ernments. Priority would be placed on rebuilding the county's social and environmental infrastructure, making use of Canadian-made materials and services.

Through this program, the AFB proposes that capital invest-ments could be made in a range of development priorities—pub-lic transit systems, construction of social and co-op housing, water and sewage systems, waste reduction and recycling, retrofits for public buildings, installation of computers in public libraries and post offices, as well as the provision of community-based, not-for-profit child care and elder care centres and services against violence to women.

New employment opportunities generated by this kind of public investment could be directed toward young people, social assistance recipients and laid-off workers on UI. Employment training programs could be geared to young people at risk, women, visible minorities, persons with disabilities, and Aboriginal peo-ples. The federal portion of the program could be financed from a percentage of new public revenues to be collected through the reorganization of corporate taxation and the introduction of a fi-nancial transactions tax.

A public investment strategy of this kind should also be com-plemented by, and coordinated with, a plan of action to redirect private investment for the purpose of strengthening the produc-tion networks and creating new jobs. Between 1991 and 1993 alone, some $60 billion of private Canadian capital was invested in foreign business ventures, while in the same period billions more were lost by Canadian financial institutions through the fi-nancing of unproductive mergers and real estate speculation.

Steps need to be taken as part of a national economic strat-egy to ensure that a sizeable portion of this Canadian capital stays at home to be re-invested in this country. For these purposes, the AFB has proposed the establishment of an Enterprise Develop-ment Bank to provide low-cost debt or equity capital to Cana-dian-based businesses undertaking new investments. As a new policy instrument, this Enterprise Development Bank could be designed to encourage Canadian businesses to invest in new job-creating industries related to the production networks, by pro-viding capital at lower costs to offset the higher returns they may get for their investment elsewhere in the global market. The Bank itself could be initially financed through revenues generated by the excess profits tax. To prevent profitable corporations from engaging in massive downsizing, a system of tax penalties could also be put in place.

Other policy instruments, such as research and development and the redistribution of work time, could also be designed to support these public and private investment strategies. When it comes to research and development, Canadian corporations have a dismal track record, investing well under half as much as their U.S. counterparts. To close this gap in innovative investments, Ottawa needs to put some teeth into its otherwise relatively generous program of R&D incentives for corporations. This should include a combination of public investments in research and technology diffusion through the National Research Council, several federal government departments, universities and technical institutes, plus a mix of tax and loan measures to stimulate much more private investment by corporations in joint sectoral-based R&D related to the priorities of various production networks.

At the same time, a plan designed to stimulate the redistribution of work time could considerably enhance both the creation of new jobs and the development of people's productive capacities. By setting limits on overtime work in the public sector and encouraging voluntary reduction of overtime in the private sector, more of overall work time can be shifted from the overemployed to the unemployed and underemployed, thereby creating new jobs and a better quality of life. Existing programs like (Un)Employment Insurance might be redesigned to make it possible for workers to take education and training leaves to increase their productive capacities, while pension plans could be improved to encourage early or phased-in retirement, thus opening up more job opportunities for young workers.

This kind of national economic strategy, however, will not be effective unless it is accompanied by policies designed to facilitate greater citizen participation and control. Priority therefore must be given to community economic development (CED) which employs local people to produce goods and services for local needs. In addition to providing state funding for CEDs, local branches of banks and trust companies could be directed to make low-interest loans available for community economic projects, the overall amount being a percentage of all the funds they loan to regular business clients each year.

In many cases, CED plans could be designed in collaboration with the proposed regionally-based production networks, perhaps putting an emphasis on worker-owned or community-owned enterprises. To enhance citizen participation, regional investment and employment boards comprised of elected people could also be established. These elected boards would have a mandate to review all plans and proposals for both public and private investment in their region, to make sure they are designed to increase job creation as well as workers' productive capacities. Appropriate criteria, of course, would have to be set for board elections to achieve adequate representation from the various community sectors.

Social Security

One of the main tasks for the democratic left in outlining a program for national reconstruction is to determine how Canada's shattered social security system could be rebuilt. Big business, by depleting public revenues through tax avoidance and pushing governments to slash program spending, has spearheaded the drive to dismantle much of our social security system. To make matters worse, corporations are now lining up to take over some of the more lucrative parts of our social programs and public services as they are privatized.

Contrary to popular opinion, Canada lags far behind most of the OECD countries when it comes to national social spending. On average, European countries spend 23 per cent of their GDP on their social security systems, while Canada spends less than 14 per cent. In particular, the Chrétien government's CHST has dealt a crushing blow to the system that was put in place over the past 60 years to provide Canadians with a minimal degree of social security.

In outlining a platform of reconstruction in this area, it is important to note that what is called for here is the "social productivity of capital." Corporations, in other words, are being called upon to invest in the social future of Canadians. This is not simply a moral obligation, but a political necessity. For, without social security, big business can hardly expect much in the way of political stability.

At the outset, immediate action would be required to develop a program and strategy aimed at preventing the further privatization and corporate takeover of Canada's social security system. As we have seen, U.S. for-profit health corporations are targeting pieces of Canada's $72 billion annual public health care system for takeover once they become privatized. Similarly, cash-starved schools, colleges and universities are increasingly forming "partnerships" with corporations to maintain their operating revenues in exchange for giving their business partners opportunities to corner and capture the country's youth market, as well as parts of the country's $60 billion a year public education system.

Nor is this the end of it. Bay Street will soon be managing the investment of Canada's public pension funds in the stock market, while Ontario and Nova Scotia are experimenting with allowing private companies to run their jails. To get a handle on these rapidly emerging trends, an independent monitoring agency needs to be established to assess the impact of government funding cuts on all aspects of Canada's social system. This agency would also identify the corporations which are or may be targeting social and public services in Canada, as well as their political machinery, and the mechanisms in the various free trade regimes (FTA, NAFTA, WTO, and the Internal Trade Agreement) that let corporations gain access to these markets. Based on this information, legislative initiatives could be developed to curb further privatization and corporate takeovers.

Obviously, before Ottawa could take such remedial measures, it would have to develop a plan to stop and reverse the financial hemorrhaging of Canada's social security programs. For this purpose, the AFB proposes that a National Social Investment Fund be established as a replacement for the CHST. This National Social Investment Fund would contain several components: a Health Care Fund to restore the levels of federal funding required for a national Medicare program based on the five basic principles of the Canada Health Act; an Income Support Fund designed to replace the Canada Assistance Program which Ottawa scuttled with the CHST; a Post-Secondary Education Fund to restore and enhance federal funding for higher education; a Child Care Fund to finance the establishment of a national child care program in the public sector; a Housing Fund to provide the capital required for the construction of social and co-op housing; a Retirement Income Fund to preserve and improve Old Age Security and Canada Pension Plan benefits for senior citizens; and an Unemployment Insurance Fund that would ensure that unemployed workers receive the benefits they need and have paid for through their UI premiums.

Taken together, all of these programs, comprising the core of Canada's social security system, would be financed under the new National Social Investment Fund out of existing public revenues already allocated for these programs, plus additional revenues collected from both the overhaul of corporate taxes and the new financial transactions tax.

As outlined by the AFB, the National Social Investment Fund would be designed to bring Canada's funding commitments for social security in this country up to European standards over a five-year period. This strategy, in turn, could be made financially viable and implemented without adding to the country's debt burden, provided that the kinds of proposals spelled out earlier for reorganizing Canada's public finances were carried out as well. By restoring and enhancing its federal funding base for these basic programs, Ottawa would then be in a position to ensure that national standards for social security are maintained by all provinces across the country.

Rebuilding the federal funding base for these programs would also serve to ease financial pressures on the provinces, allowing them to restore adequate funding for the programs in their jurisdiction, such as public education and welfare, which are also key components of the overall system of social security in Canada. But rebuilding these social security programs also means making them more universal and effective. In the case of Medicare, for example, the AFB proposes that the program be expanded to include a national drug plan, which would help to make overall health care more cost-effective. And, when it comes to health care delivery at the community level, greater priority would be put on the establishment of community health clinics.

At the same time, rebuilding Canada's social security system by reasserting democratic control over corporate power in our economy requires a concerted attack on poverty and class divisions. Continuing high unemployment, coupled with the dismantling of social programs and the massive transfer of wealth caused by our current regressive tax system, has greatly contributed to a shameful increase in poverty in Canada in recent years. Our society has been divided into two solitudes: one composed of relatively affluent, upwardly mobile people with full-time, secure forms of employment; the other composed of relatively poor people with part-time, insecure forms of employment, or no jobs at all. And the gap between the two solitudes is widening.

The Income Support Fund outlined in the AFB would serve as a necessary stopgap measure. Integrated with the provisions for job creation, training, health care, social housing, child care, pension reforms for senior citizens, a higher minimum wage and other measures, a frontal attack could be mounted against the new realities of poverty. The AFB outlines specific targets for the reduction of both poverty and unemployment. To carry out these programs, however, requires a well-integrated set of economic and social policy tools, along with a multi-pronged strategy.

Still more would have to be done to overcome the deepening class divisions resulting from the massive transfers of wealth taking place across the country. The two solitudes reflect the realities of an "overclass" and an "underclass" in Canadian society. An alternative platform could, of course, contain steps to make the personal income tax system more progressive by increasing the rates applicable to very high incomes. Just restoring upper-income rates from 29 to 34 per cent, the level they were at before the Mulroney government's tax reforms in the mid-1980s, would help put the brakes on the transfers of wealth.

But perhaps a more symbolic and effective way would be to introduce a "solidarity" wage. As previously noted, there is now an astronomical gap between the compensation packages paid to CEOs in many corporations and the average wages paid to their employees, often at a ratio reaching well over a 100 to 1. As a society, Canada could establish a solidarity wage ratio of no more than, say, 20 to 1. While it may be difficult to legislate a solidarity wage along these lines, measures could be taken to reduce or deny tax deduction eligibility to corporations which pay their CEOs salaries that exceed this ratio.

In any case, Canada's social security system cannot simply be rebuilt without also strengthening the links between the public sector and the social economy. As indicated earlier, new measures could be developed to ensure that state funding is provided for community-based networks of citizen activities that serve people's social development needs—ranging from women's shelters and community kitchens to cultural and youth drop-in centres to local anti-poverty groups.

At the same time, regionally-based social security boards composed of elected citizens could be established with a mandate to evaluate and improve the delivery of programs in their jurisdiction. In particular, these regional boards could monitor the delivery of social programs to guarantee that national standards are being maintained, as well as keeping an eye on attempts by private for-profit corporations to take over social programs or public services in their region. On the basis of these and related activities, such regional boards would be in a position to make concrete proposals to both provincial and federal governments for improvements in the delivery of social programs.

Sustainable Development

Any alternative platform for rebuilding Canada's economy and society must include a plan of action for sustainable development. For some environmentalists, the term "sustainable development" is a contradiction in terms. After all, how can one talk about sustaining development when, in effect, most of the Earth's environmental problems can be traced back to our current model of industrial development? If the goal is to move towards a greener economy in the future, what should be the terms and conditions for a model of development that is both sustainable and ecologically progressive?

Once again, the distinctions between a corporate model and a more democratic model of development come into play. For it is precisely the corporate model of "development" that has been primarily responsible for the patterns of unlimited industrial expansion and economic growth that have brought the planet close to the brink of ecological disaster.

An economic model based on democratic control would have to be designed to reverse these trends by promoting the kinds of development that are sustainable. Among other things, this means promoting economic production that reduces the use of materials, resources and energy, and transmits waste from one process as material input for other processes of production. While fossil fuels and other non-renewable resources will continue to be used for economic production, decisive steps must be taken to bring about a targeted reduction of their use and a transition to more renewable resources in the long term. This can only be achieved in an economy where corporate power is brought under democratic control.

For Ottawa to embark on an effective strategy for sustainable development along these lines, it would have to start by restoring its own capacities to monitor and enforce environmental standards across the country. As already noted, a 33 per cent cut at Environment Canada, including a quarter of its staff, plus 40 per cent staff reductions in the Canadian Forestry Service and similar cutbacks in Natural Resources, Fisheries and Oceans and the National Parks division of Heritage Canada have substantially weakened the federal government's ability to monitor, let alone enforce, national environmental standards.

An alternative platform could include a strategy that is not only designed to restore funding levels, but also reorganize the work of Environment Canada to coordinate with Natural Resources and other federal departments to effectively monitor and enforce environmental standards. This reorganization should also be undertaken with a view to the longer-term plan of moving toward sustainable development. For example, environmental regulatory regimes would have to be strengthened through a variety of new (and old) policy tools, including those designed to ensure that the market absorbs most of the ecological (and social) costs of production.

In restoring the staffing capacity at Environment Canada and other federal departments, priority could be put on providing new jobs for youth in this field. The funding required for these purposes could come directly from a series of new green taxes designed to stimulate greater environmental responsibility (see below). Indeed, most of these changes could be financed through additional revenues from a modest increase in gas consumption taxes designed to curb the use of fossil fuels by motor vehicles.

In developing a national plan of action for sustainable development, top priority would be put on tackling the problem of global warming by meeting Canada's commitments for carbon dioxide emission reductions made at the 1992 Rio Earth Summit. Not only has Canada failed to make significant progress in reducing its fossil fuel emissions to meet the agreed-upon target levels by the year 2000, but at current rates of emissions this country will exceed these limits by 10 percent, and by 34 per cent in the year 2020.

The causes of greenhouse gas emissions are shared by several sectors, with oil and gas corporations being largely responsible for 35 per cent, non-energy industries (including forestry corporations) being accountable for another 40 per cent, and households picking up the remaining 25 per cent. What is needed is a concerted attack on all three fronts, starting with reductions in fossil fuel emissions.

The AFB proposes a series of measures, including the imposition of a national atmospheric user fee on corporations involved in the emission of carbon dioxide. The user fee would be applied to each tonne of carbon contained in energy sources utilized for production. The AFB also proposes that fuel economy standards be raised on all motor vehicles and that financial support be given to research into both the use of non-fossil fuels such as hydrogen and ethanol, and the use of electric motor vehicles.

At the same time, government action on greenhouse gas emissions would need to be reinforced by action on conservation, renewable energy use and waste management. If Canada is going to live up to its responsibilities in addressing the problems of global warming and climate change, then a national forestry conservation plan of action is imperative, especially in preserving the boreal forest regions.

While responsibility for Canada's forests is largely a matter of provincial jurisdiction, this is a case where a new federal-provincial conservation agreement is urgently needed, as well as new alliances between forestry workers and environmentalists in building truly sustainable communities for the future.

Strategies are also needed to greatly increase Canada's use of alternate energy sources, such as electricity from wind, solar, biomass, and fuel cells. Although Canada's current use of alternate energy sources is only 6 per cent of total energy use, the AFB proposes that a target of 15 per cent be established for the year 2010, with Ottawa providing funds and tax incentives to stimulate the transition to alternatives by industries and households.

These measures, in turn, could be strengthened by new programs designed to provide subsidies for both inner-city rail and urban mass transportation as a substitute for dependence on motor vehicles, as well as the housing retrofit program outlined above in the strategies for job creation.

To encourage better waste management practices, the AFB proposes a variety of tax measures, including a hazardous product input tax on such products as mercury and a levy on the disposal of hazardous wastes. To ensure that resource extraction sites are properly rehabilitated after they have been mined, resource corporations could be required to post bonds or pay a levy to cover the costs of clean-up and rehabilitation.

However, for Ottawa to effectively carry out a plan for greening the country's economy along these lines, it would first have to develop some new tools for dealing with corporations in both the resource and industrial sectors. The program priorities of the Natural Resources department, for example, would have to be reoriented to better reflect this kind of environmental agenda and the demands for sustainable development, rather than primarily the directives of the petroleum, mining and forestry corporations. To get a better handle on these matters, an independent agency could be established to monitor the operations of the major corporate players and their political machines, and to design tools that could be used for more effective enforcement of environmental priorities.

Such an agency could, for example, scrutinize and unmask the "greenwashing" activities of certain corporations who pretend to be environmentally friendly but engage in environmentally destructive practices. It could also monitor and track the overseas operations of Canadian mining companies and devise tools that could be used by Ottawa to ensure that they maintain environmental standards for sustainable development abroad. Such an agency could also be used to ascertain whether the new free trade regimes (NAFTA, APEC, WTO) are being used by corporations (both domestic and foreign) to avoid environmental safeguards and, if so, to propose what corrective action should be taken.

Together, these policy options and strategies are aimed at facilitating the transition of Canada's economy towards sustainable development, based on a democratic rather than a corporate model. To carry out this transformation, however, a road map is required with program targets and schedules that would have to be met over a five-to-ten-year period. Also needed would be direct citizen participation in monitoring and evaluating government and industry progress toward these targets.

Sustainable development boards, therefore, could be established on a regional basis. In some ways, they would be similar to the conservation boards that were set up and had a significant impact on environmental policy directions in some provinces during the 1970s and 1980s. Composed of elected citizens concerned about ecological issues, these boards would have a mandate to review and assess plans for industrial and resource development in their region in terms of meeting environmental standards. Procedures would of course have to be devised with due process for adjudicating cases that fail to meet such standards. Steps would also have to be taken to provide some state funding for this sector of the social economy through the mechanisms outlined previously.

* * *

In the final analysis, all of the major components of this alternative platform—political sovereignty, public finances, economic production, social security, sustainable development—would serve as building blocks for re-tooling the state to serve the basic development needs and democratic rights of its citizens. Once again, it is important to keep in mind that this is meant to be a long-term plan of action that could well take the next 10 to 15 and perhaps 20 years to accomplish. After all, we are still enmeshed in the whirlwind of a counter-revolution which is radically "reinventing" the role and priorities of the state in such a way that citizens have less and less control over their economic, social and environmental future.

Inescapably, the task of national reconstruction will therefore be a long and arduous struggle. It will require a revitalization of political will and a restoration of public confidence. This is why concerned citizens must commit the time and energy needed to rebuild the political movement on the democratic left in this country. If an alternative platform embodying the basic components outlined above is to become the focal point for such a revitalization, then it must be crafted and inspired by the kind of vision that will revitalize people's energies, restore their confidence, and give them hope that they can once again control their own destiny.

In preparing to carry out this kind of plan for national reconstruction, it is crucial that conscious steps be taken to build and cultivate international alliances. For the most part, the various policy platforms outlined above could not possibly be undertaken by any one national government without simultaneously developing strategic alliances with corresponding movements and governments in other countries. After all, the global managers are making sure that this new era of corporate rule is world-wide in scope.

The task of dismantling some of the dominant mechanisms of corporate rule in trade regimes like NAFTA and the WTO, or financial institutions like the World Bank and the IMF—which is essential if this kind of national reconstruction is to be carried out—demands that top priority be put on developing international strategies and alliances.

At the same time, it should be clearly understood that dismantling the corporate security state and pursuing a national reconstruction program along these lines would almost certainly provoke retaliatory measures. Corporate Canada and the transnational corporations that have vested interests at stake in the Canadian economy are not likely to stand idly by while their powers, privileges and profits are under attack. Nor would the U.S. government and the governments of the other G-7 nations.

Special attention, therefore, would have to be given in advance to the task of developing a viable transition strategy. Along with counter-measures that Ottawa could take to offset the expected retaliatory actions, this strategy would have to include ways of preparing Canadians for some of the shock waves that might ensue. A major component of this plan would be the building of strategic alliances, not only with key sectors and groups in this country, but also with citizens' movements and like-minded governments in other countries which offer the best hope of building solidarity links for the long haul.

This could also, in turn, be one of the ways of developing a new foreign policy and redesigning both international aid and trade strategies. While this may seem, at first glance, to be a difficult (if not impossible) undertaking in today's global economy, significant and encouraging counter-trends are bound to develop in the near future. Already, progressive labour and social movements in Canada have forged their own international solidarity links which could be helpful in identifying and assessing such progressive trends in other countries. ◖◗

Postscript

FOR MANY, THE PLAN OF action outlined in the last two chapters may seem like a daunting, if not a hopeless task. After all, transnational corporations have come to dominate virtually every facet of our lives—where we work, what we eat, what we buy, how we're entertained, how we vote. Now this constellation of powerful economic forces has moved into the very centre of our history where, as corporate political machines, they are shaping the destinies of peoples and nations throughout the planet.

So how can Canadians be expected to resist this kind and degree of corporate domination? Is it really possible that citizens' movements can challenge, let alone dismantle, mechanisms of corporate rule in this country? What chance, if any, is there of developing and implementing new institutions for democratic control like those we have been discussing?

The answers to these questions lie in how we understand the nature of the *silent coup* that has taken place, and whether we are prepared to confront it for what it is. The corporate takeover has been described here as a political coup d'état. While it has not been a conventional military operation, it does have certain military characteristics. The corporate political machines we have been discussing operate like modern, high-tech armies of occupation. We can see this, for example, in the way they move into hitherto unoccupied territory (e.g., health care, education, social security, public services), mobilize their ground troops (i.e., workers, suppliers, customers, and shareholders), or deploy their political "artillery" (e.g., think tanks, lobbyists, legal firms, public relations experts, party donations, and political advertising).

Ironically, this is the image that long-time peace activist and noted scholar Ursula Franklin has been using recently to describe what is happening in this country. Franklin maintains that the collapse of the Cold War did not mean the end of war or the use of military tactics. Instead, the military war-making apparatus has been shifted to the economic arenas, such as trade and finance. What we have now, she says, is an "economic war" against people. The new "enemy" is people, and the new territories of occupation are "the commons," by which she means those not-for-profit public spaces that we "hold in common" in a democratic society, including education, health care, culture and the environment. In Franklin's view, we are now in effect living under a military-style occupation in this country, with "puppet governments" who are running the country on behalf of the corporations and their "armies of marketeers."

The question then arises: how do people learn to build a resistance movement while living under conditions of military occupation? Says Franklin: just like the people of France under the Nazi occupation during World War II, we also find ourselves in a position of being "collaborators" with the agents of corporate occupation today. We also want to protect our families and on many occasions may find ourselves collaborating with our occupiers in order to survive. But just as the French began to develop strategies of resistance under Nazi occupation, so must we.

As Franklin puts it, we need to develop strategies to slow down the advance of the occupation and block it wherever we can. And while our corporate occupiers today do not wear uniforms and therefore cannot be so easily identified, we must find ways to make them recognizable and expose their operations.

In effect, this is the task that we have already set ourselves in our strategic discussions about *identifying, unmasking* and *exposing* the major corporate players and their political machines that now control public policy-making in Ottawa and the provinces (Chapter 5). But if people are going to start developing resistance strategies along these lines, the raison d'être of their resistance must be clear. Those engaged in the resistance movement against the Nazi occupation knew that they were fighting for the democratic rights and freedom of their people. So we, too, must become conscious of the corporate oppression that is trampling on the democratic rights and freedoms of people in this country today. If we are going to be build a resistance movement for the long haul, then we must consciously make a decision to commit ourselves to fight for our democratic rights and freedoms.

This is what it means to *confront* the big business takeover of Canada. There will, of course, be many who will deny that we are actually living under corporate rule. So, if we are going to build resistance to this corporate occupation and its puppet governments, we must enable people to look at the present political reality through a new set of lenses. They need to see and understand how their democratic rights and freedoms as citizens have been hijacked. Essentially, this is what Mackenzie, Papineau, Riel and McPhail did in organizing their own democratic movements of resistance against corporate domination in their times. Unless people become aware that they now live under corporate rule, they will not feel the urge to fight for their basic dignity as persons and their democratic rights as citizens. They will continue to live in a state of denial.

Around the world today, there are encouraging signs that popular resistance against corporate occupation and oppression is building. People are organizing to fight for their democratic rights and freedoms—from the farmers in India who succeeded in having Kentucky Fried Chicken run out of their country, to the peasants of Mexico who formed El Barzón and turned it into a mass movement challenging the banks and financial institutions; from the struggle of workers in the streets of South Korea against corporate-driven state repression of workers' rights, to the mobilization of public service workers in France against deficit- driven social spending cuts; from the protests of workers and communities in Chile against the exploitative practices of foreign-based mining corporations, to the struggles against INTEL and other electronic companies by environment and economic justice groups in New Mexico; from the mobilization of mass protests in Europe against the adoption of a single currency being promoted by big business interests, to the mass blockades that were organized in opposition to the APEC leaders' summit in the Philippines.

Here in Canada, there are also signs that citizens' groups are beginning to identify and target the corporate takeover and occupation—whether it's local parents and teachers opposing business-school "partnerships," or health care activists targeting for-profit corporations taking over hospitals or other medical services; whether it's public demands for government action to stop the corporate concentration of media ownership and control in Canada, or the campaign to prevent the privatization of the CBC; whether it's organizing community protests against the big six chartered banks for their failure to reinvest their huge profits locally, or publicly castigating the top five corporations who have been the county's major job-killers, or developing a local campaign strategy to keep Wal-Mart out of the community; whether it's mobilizing a blockade against clear-cut logging by one of the forest giants, or raising public awareness about plans to privatize and export fresh water resources, or defending a wetland area from being developed for industrial purposes; whether it's publicly exposing the corporate players and strategies that lie behind global institutions like the WTO, the World Bank and the IMF, or the new trade regimes like NAFTA and APEC; or whether it's developing and advocating alternative budget plans designed to curb corporate power and provide opportunities for increasing democratic participation.

While much remains to be done to link and integrate these and other diverse campaigns into a coherent movement along the lines described in Chapters 5 and 6, these are nonetheless important and inspirational signs of popular resistance.

In building this kind of resistance, however, it is crucial that people develop a sense of self-confidence. All this discussion of corporate power can have a paralyzing effect. As the history of democratic struggles shows us, there is nothing inherently inevitable about the emerging system of corporate rule. Nor are these corporate political machines invincible. Both the system and the corporations have their Achilles heel. Whether it's the growing fear that the financial bubble being inflated through the casino economy will burst, or the prospects of a series of looming ecological disasters, or mounting social unrest on the part of workers and citizens around the world—cracks are beginning to show in this global corporate fortress. The key is to be ready to seize the moment when these cracks begin to widen, to be in a position to leverage the kind of changes that are needed. The same holds true in mounting campaigns against specific corporations as political machines. The question is whether citizens' movements can learn from one another about the most effective ways of identifying and taking advantage of the vulnerabilities of corporations in challenging their power.

At the same time, it is crucial that public space be provided for citizen activists who are engaged in corporate campaigns to come together, both to develop a common understanding about the system of corporate rule and to design common strategies for taking democratic control. Under any military occupation, the people involved in resistance need to meet, share experiences, exchange intelligence, improve communication links, strengthen their commitments, and develop common or complementary strategies.

Over the next five years, it is important that steps be taken to convene strategic planning events where citizen activists who are engaged in organizing corporate campaigns around issues in the three battlefields identified in Chapter 5 can come together with other activists and policy analysts from key sectors of the community to work on the two-fold objective outlined above.

While it is imperative that space be provided for groups to do this kind of strategic planning, it is also important to organize conferences, seminars and teach-ins to do some broader public education, as well as internal political education with particular organizations and their constituencies.

Finally, the resistance against corporate rule and the fight for democratic control must become a global movement in the new millennium. After all, the corporate armies of occupation are on the move all over the world. The extent to which political space is opened up to confront corporate power and institute democratic control depends on the degree to which citizens' movements through popular struggles are able to mobilize countervailing force, both here and elsewhere.

Over the next five years, steps should be taken to develop and strengthen bonds of solidarity between labour and social movements involved in the resistance by organizing strategic planning events along the lines proposed above, on both continental and global bases. Indeed, the key to the future lies in building a political movement on the democratic left around this agenda, not only in Canada but throughout the world.

Let us hope that, out of this process, a new citizens' politics will begin to emerge at the dawn of the 21st century.

Chapter Notes

1. Corporate Canada

IN TRACING THE THEMES AND events portraying the emergence of big business as a dominant political force over the past 20 years, I found several background sources to be very helpful. James Laxer's *Canada's Economic Strategy* (Toronto: McClelland & Stewart, 1981) describes some of the reactions and strategies of Corporate Canada in the late 1970s and early 1980s. The organization, program and strategy of the Business Council on National Issues is documented by David Langille in a seminal article, "The BCNI and the Canadian State," *Studies in Political Economy* (autumn, 1987). Stephen Clarkson's *Canada and the Reagan Challenge* (Toronto: James Lorimer & Co., 1985) provides some insights on the role and strategies of big business during the battles around the National Energy Program and the Anti-Inflation Program during the latter stages of the Trudeau government. John Calvert's *Government Limited: The Corporate Takeover of the Public Sector* (Ottawa: Canadian Centre for Policy Alternatives, 1984) provides an original and detailed analysis of some of the themes and issues taken up in this chapter and subsequent ones. Ron Graham's *One Eyed Kings* (Toronto: Totem Books, 1986) provides a detailed and lucid account of the interface between big business during the Trudeau and Clark governments. Maude Barlow's and Bruce Campbell's *Straight Through The Heart* (Toronto: Harper Collins, 1996) contains some helpful information and data on the role of the BCNI and its member corporations during the Mulroney government. Several other works shed light on the relevant aspects of the free trade battle: Linda McQuaig's *The Quick and the Dead* (Toronto: Penguin Books, 1991); Duncan Cameron and Mel Watkins (eds.), *Canada Under Free Trade* (Toronto: James Lorimer & Co., 1993); John Warnock's *Free Trade and the New Right Agenda* (Vancouver: New Star Books, 1987); and Maude Barlow's *Parcel of Rogues* (Toronto: Key Porter, 1990). For an analysis of the resurgence of right-wing populism in relation to big business interests, see Murray Dobbin's *Preston Manning and the Reform Party* (Toronto: James Lorimer & Co., 1991). And my previous book, *Behind The Mitre: The Moral Crisis in the Canadian Catholic Church* (Toronto: Harper Collins, 1995) contains a summary version of several of the themes discussed in this chapter.

In terms of quotations and statistics used in this chapter, several were taken from Laxer's *Canada's Economic Strategy*, op.cit.: Powis (pp.38, 41, 42); Twaits (pp. 38, 39, 40, 41); Friedman (p. 28); Reisman (pp. 30, 31, 32, 33); MacLaren (p.35). Information and quotes related to the Fraser Institute, the National Citizens' Coalition and the Canadian Taxpayers' Association were cited in Murray Dobbin's "The New Right and How Things Got This Bad," Council of Canadians, AGM Discussion Paper, 1995. Data and quotes related to the NEP, FIRA and the AIB can be found in Stephen Clarkson's *Canada and the Reagan Challenge*, op.cit. Information of the BCNI's program, task forces and strategy was initially outlined in David Langille's "The BCNI and the Canadian State," op.cit. and Murray Dobbin's "Thomas d'Aquino: The De Facto PM," *The Canadian Forum*, November, 1992. Data on the deficit, debt and interest rates were taken from Bruce Campbell's research published in *Straight Through The Heart*, op.cit., chapter 2. The data on foreign ownership came from David Robinson's research presented in a Council of Canadians' factsheet, "Who Owns Canada: Foreign Ownership and Corporate Power." The stats on corporate layoffs since the signing of the FTA were originally published by the *CCPA Monitor* (Canadian Centre for Policy Alternatives, Vol.2, No.5, October, 1995). Information on the role of the corporate lobby groups in Ottawa can be found in John Sawatsky's *The Insiders: Power, Money and Secrets in Ottawa* (Toronto: McClelland & Stewart, 1989). See also, Stevie Cameron's *On The Take*. The reference to the top 25 most powerful CEOs in Canada comes from the list published by the *Globe & Mail's Report on Business Magazine,* July, 1996.

2. Global Managers

A variety of important books have served as background resources for this chapter. David Korten's *When Corporations Rule the World* (San Francisco: Kumarian Press Inc. and Berrett-Koehler Publishers, Inc., 1995) provides a more in-depth look at the main themes of this chapter. William Grieder's *One World, Ready or Not* (New York: Simon & Schuster, 1997) gives us a detailed picture that vividly portrays what the global managers are up to in what he calls "the manic logic of global capitalism." His previous book, *Who Will Tell The People* (New York: Simon & Schuster, 1992) has also been a pivotal source for much of the analysis that lies behind this book. Patricia Marchak's *The Integrated Circus: The New Right and the Restructuring of Global Markets* (Montreal and Kingston: McGill - Queen's University Press, 1993) contains some important background information and analysis of the Trilateralists and libertarian movements. Richard Barnet and John Cavanagh's *Global Dreams: Imperial Corporations and the New World Order* (New York: Simon & Schuster, 1994) traces the global movement and expansion of transnational corporations. Jerry Mander and Edward Goldsmith's (eds.) *The Case Against The Global Economy* (San Francisco: Sierra Club Books, 1996) contains a valuable collection of articles on corporate power and economic globalization by writers and activists around the world. Vandana Shiva's *Monocultures of the Mind: Perspectives on Biodiversity and Biotechnology* (London: Zed Press, 1993) provides a classic analysis of the new corporate technologies. Kenichi Ohamae's *The Borderless World: Power and Strategy in an Interlinked Economy (*New York: Harper-Business, 1990) gives some insight into the mindset of the new global managers. Jeremy Rifkin's *The End of Work: The Decline of the Global Labor Force and the Dawn of the Post-Market Era* (New York: G.P. Putnam's Sons, 1995) is particularly useful for its analysis of the jobless world economy. Many of the themes addressed in this chapter were also taken up in a workbook I prepared for the International Forum on Globalization on *The Emergence of Corporate Rule: And What Can Be Done About It* (San Francisco: IFG White Paper, No.1, 1997).

The description of Akio Morita at the outset of this chapter is presented in more detail in Barnet and Cavanagh's *Global Dreams,* and the quotes outlining his vision of a deregulated global market was presented by him in his *Atlantic Monthly* article on "Toward a New World Economic Order," in June, 1993 (88, 92-3). The stats comparing global corporations and nation states, plus the top 200 corporations, are taken from a report prepared by Sara Anderson and John Cavanagh at the Institute for Policy Studies, October 1996, Washington, D.C. The data on the worldwide deregulation of investment between 1991 and 1994 were cited in the *World Investment Report 1995* on "Transnational Corporations and Competitiveness." The quotes from Ohmae are from his book *The Borderless World*, op.cit. The material on the Trilateral Commission here is largely found in Patricia Marchak's *The Integrated Circus*, op.cit (pp. 93-114), while the quotes on democratic governance were cited in the Trilateral document prepared by M. Crozier, S Huntington, J Watanuki on *The Crisis of Democracy: Report on the Governability of Democracies to the Trilateral Commission* (New York: New York University Press, 1975).

Information on the U.S. Business Round Table can be found in Korten, *When Corporations Rule The World* op.cit. (pp.144-5) and on the European Round Table of Industrialists, see A. Doherty and O. Hoedeman, "Misshaping Europe: The European Round Table of Industrialists," in *The Ecologist*, 24(4), 135-141. Korten op.cit. provides information on the citizen front groups of corporations in the U.S. (pp. 143, 146). See also M. Magalli and A Friedman, *Masks of Deception: Corporate Front Groups in America* (Washington, D.C.: Essential Information, 1991). The World Economic Forum quote is from Madelaine Drohan, *Globe and Mail*, February 5, 1996. Information on the Forum's structure was cited in *The Economist* (April 19, 1997), and the quotes from Huntington were cited in a column by Tony Hall in *Canadian Forum*, (May, 1997). The series of quotations from Frederich. Hayek and his corporate libertarian followers (i.e., Harris, Seldon, Gilder and Kristol) were cited in Marchak, op.cit. pp. 96-102, including the quote from Marchak herself (p. 95).

The analysis of transnational regimes here is based on an earlier version which I developed in my article "The Mechanisms of Corporate Rule" published in Jerry Mander's and Edward Goldsmith's *The Case Against The Global Economy* op.cit. (pp. 297-309), which has been updated and revised with data from the 1996 *Global Fortune 500 Report*. On intellectual property rights, see Vandana Shiva's *Biopiracy: The Plunder of Nature and Knowledge* (Boston: South End Press 1997.) In terms of the casino economy, the quotes from Keynes were cited in John Dillon's *Turning The Tide: Confronting The Money Traders* (Ottawa: Canadian Centre for Policy Alternatives, 1996) as are the stats comparing daily financial transactions and central bank reserves. The "Big Bang" on the London Stock Exchange is described by Richard Barnet and John Cavanagh in "Electronic Money and the Casino Economy" published in Mander and Goldsmith, op.cit.

(p. 360-374). A vivid account of George Soros's bet with John Major and other incidents can be found in William Greider's *One World, Ready or Not*, op.cit.. Walden Bello's analysis of structural adjustment programs is found in his article "Structural Adjustment Programs: "'Success' for Whom?", published in Mander and Goldsmith op.cit. (pp. 285-296) which includes the stats cited later on poverty and debt payments in the South. For an excellent analysis of structural adjustment by a Canadian, see John Mihevic's *The Market Tells Them So: The World Bank and Economic Fundamentalism in Africa* (Penang and Accra: Third World Network, 1995) Jonathan Cahn's quote comes from his article, "Challenging the New Imperial Authority: The World Bank and the Democratization of Development," *Harvard Human Rights Journal* 6,1993 (p.160). The Carla Hills quote was cited in Korten, op.cit. (p.123). The analysis of the WTO here (including the opposition mounted in various countries) is largely based on Ralph Nader and Lori Wallach's article, "GATT, NAFTA and The Subversion of the Democratic Process" in Mander and Goldsmith, op.cit. (pp. 92-108). Martin Khor has published numerous articles on the WTO from the perspective of the Third World Network in their magazine *Third World Resurgence*, which he edits. For an analysis of the MAI and the WTO, see Martin Khor's "The WTO and the Proposed Multilateral Investment Agreement: Implications for Developing Countries and Proposed Positions," published by the Third World Network, 228 Macalister Road, 10400 Penang, Malaysia. The Herman Daly quote was cited in Nader and Wallach, op.cit. (p.95). On the build-up of corporate armies in Africa, see Elizabeth Rubin, "An Army of One's Own," *Harper's Magazine*, February 1997.

3. National Surrender

This chapter owes a debt a gratitude to the work done by Maude Barlow and Bruce Campbell in their book *Straight Through The Heart: How The Liberals Abandoned the Just Society* (Toronto: Harper Collins, 1995). The paperback edition published in 1996 includes more updated information. Barlow and Campbell trace the story of how the business Liberals gained and secured power in the party under Chrétien's leadership and how the four M's who held the initial round of economic ministries—Martin, MacLaren, Manley, and Massé—worked to consolidate the big business interests at the centre of the party's agenda. Linda McQuaig's *Shooting The Hippo: Death by Deficit and Other Canadian Myths* (Toronto: Viking, 1995) provides some valuable insights on debt and deficit issues. Edward Greenspon and Anthony Wilson-Smith's *Double Vision: The Inside Story of the Liberals in Power* (Toronto: Doubleday Canada Ltd., 1996) offers additional insider information on what took place behind the scenes, particularly in relation to the two key figures, Jean Chrétien and Paul Martin. In addition to these books, there were numerous magazine and newspaper articles that provided further information tips to fill in the gaps. In particular, Edward Greenspon of the *Globe and Mail* and Mark Kennedy of the *Ottawa Citizen* wrote a number of articles that were useful for background purposes in relation to this chapter.

The distinctions between "business" and "social" Liberals is outlined by Duncan Cameron in an article on "Political Discourse in the Eighties" in Alan Gagnon and Brian Tanguay (ed.), *Canadian Parties in Transition* (Scarborough: Nelson Canada, 1989) pp.64-82. For Barlow's and Campbell's version, see *Straight Through The Heart,* op.cit. pp. 8-9. The BCNI's platform was outlined in its document, "A Ten Point Growth and Employment Strategy for Canada" (1994). Data on corporate financing for the 1993 Liberal campaign is found in Barlow and Campbell, op.cit. p. 57, while data on 1994 corporate donations to the Liberals based on Bruce Campbell's research was published in the *CCPA Monitor* (Canadian Centre for Policy Alternatives: Vol.2, No.10; April, 1996). The 1994 data on deferred corporate taxes was cited in *Unfair Shares*: *Corporations and Taxation in Canada,* produced jointly by the Ontario Coalition for Social Justice and the Ontario Federation of Labour. The Department of Finance scenario involving Martin, Nicholson and Dodge was cited in Barlow and Campbell op.cit (p.120 ff) and the role played by Marcel Massé is detailed in Greenspon and Wilson-Smith's *Double Vision*, op. cit. (pp. 207-209ff). The rift between Martin and Axworthy is described in some detail in both *Straight Through The Heart* and *Double Vision*. The quotes from the Moody's bond rating official on Wall Street and the preparation of Martin's 1995 federal budget were cited in Linda McQuaig's *Shooting The Hippo,* op.cit. (pp. 43-46). The quote from Tom Kierans was also cited in McQuaig, Ibid (p.41).

Duncan Cameron's testimony is recorded in the Canadian Centre for Policy Alternative's brief to the Parliamentary Committee on Finance, February, 1995. The Statistics Canada seminal analysis of the causes of Canada's debt problems was initially published by H. Mimoto and P. Cross, "The Growth of the Federal Debt" in *Canadian Economic Observer*, pp. 3.1 - 3.17, June, 1991. For a short but helpful discussion of various studies done on how Canada's debt grew, see John Dillon, *Turning the Tide, op.cit.* (pp. 45-49). The reference to the Dominion Bond Rating Agency comes from DBRS, *The Massive Federal Debt: How Did It Happen?* (Toronto: Dominion Bond Rating Agency, 1995). See also Lars Osberg's and Pierre Fortin's *Unecessary Debts* (Toronto: Lorimer, 1996) for a recent analysis of the causes of Canada's debt and, for a popular perspective, see Duncan Cameron's and Ed Finn's *10 Deficit Myths: The Truth About Government Debts and Why They Don't Justify Cutbacks* (Ottawa: Canadian Centre for Policy Alternatives, 1996). The 1995 examples of corporate layoffs were identified in *MacLean's Magazine* cover story on "Jobs" (March 11, 1996) as were the quotes from Chrétien and Manley. The 15 top corporate job killers between 1988 and 1994 is based on my own analysis of data provided by the *Financial Post Top 500*. The corporate tax deferral data comes from *Unfair Shares* (1996) op.cit., and the stats on foreign investment flows between 1988 and 1994 are based on an analysis of Canada-U.S. direct and portfolio investment by John Dillon of the Ecumenical Coalition on Economic Justice in Toronto. Data contained in a Revenue Canada's 1996 study showing that Canadian corporate transfers to offshore tax havens were not being fully reported were disclosed by the *Financial Post*, May 9, 1996.

The struggle over Axworthy's Green Paper on social policy reform and its replacement by the Canada Health and Social Transfer Act is described in Barlow and Campbell, op.cit (pp. 117-8, 180-9). Colleen Fuller identifies some of the key corporate players poised to move in and take over parts of Canada's public health care system in "Restructuring in Health Care: A Global Enterprise" (Council of Canadians, Discussion Paper, 1995). Stats on federal environmental deregulation and privatization measures were cited in Barlow and Campbell, op.cit. (pp. 215-6), and the quotes by McLellan were printed by the *Financial Post*, Sept. 16, 1995. The story behind the final round of NAFTA negotiations by the Chrétien government is told in Greenspon and Wilson-Smith, op.cit. (37-42, 46-8, 89-92). Data on the Team Canada contracts is based on my analysis of documents acquired from the Prime Minister's Office related to each of the trade missions. The quote from Joan Speers is taken from official testimony before a U.S. Congress Committee hearing and originally cited in reports issued by Public Citizen in Washington, D.C. Data on Canada's import-export ratios was cited in a column by David Crane in the *Toronto Star.*

4. Corporate Rule

There are no single, overview background books or documents that can be identified for this chapter. Indeed, this is somewhat experimental in its attempt to define the new political realities of corporate rule. Nevertheless, there are a number of important resources that contributed to this chapter. John Ralston Saul's quotes are taken from his Massey Lecture series on *The Unconscious Civilization* (Concord: House of Anansi Press, 1995), the chapter on "From Corporatism to Democracy," especially pp.85-96. Richard Grossman's and Frank Adams's analysis of how corporations hijacked the courts and judicial system in the U.S. is summarized in their article on "Exercising Power over Corporations Through State Charters" published in Jerry Manders's and Edward Goldsmith's *The Case Against the Global Economy,* op.cit. pp. 374-389. See also their booklet on *Taking Care of Business* (Cambridge, Mass: Charter Inc., 1993). Michael Mandel's reflections on how Canadian corporations are using the Charter of Rights and Freedoms to secure their "rights" as "citizens" in this country can be found in his article on "Rights, Freedoms, and Market Power: Canada's Charter of Rights and the New Era of Global Competition," Daniel Drache and Meric S. Gertler (eds.), *The New Era of Global Competition: State Policy and Market Power* (Montreal & Kingston: McGill-Queen's University Press, 1991). David Boyd of the Sierra Legal Defense Fund is currently doing further research into how corporations have taken on the status of citizens in Canadian law and how they have used the legal system in Canada to advance their agenda. William Greider's comments here on corporate citizenship come from his article, "'Citizen' G.E.," in Mander and Goldsmith, op.cit., pp. 323-335. The data on the leading corporate revenues in 1995 were from the annual report of the *Globe & Mail Business Report Magazine,* July, 1996, and the reference to Ottawa's paid corporate lobbying firms in Washington was cited in Korten, op.cit.

Robert Cox's views on the role of the state in the new global economy are outlined in *Production, Power and World Order* (New York, 1987), and Leo Panitch's incisive critique is presented in his "Globalization and the State," *Between Globalism and*

Nationalism (London: Merlin Press, 1994), edited by Ralph Miliband and Leo Panitch. David Osborne's and Ted Gaebler's handbook for marketizing the public service is titled *Reinventing Government: How the Entrepreneurial Spirit is Transforming the Public Sector* (New York: Plume, 1993). Details on the Internal Trade Agreement are found in Barlow and Campbell, op.cit., pp.221-223. For an analysis of the corporate takeover of the Harris government in Ontario, see Diana Ralph, André Régimbald and Nérée St-Amand 's (eds.) *Open for Business: Closed to People* (Halifax: Fernwood Publishing, 1997). While it has not been possible here to include much analysis of what is happening in the provinces, this book on Ontario contains several relevant articles including my "The Transnational Corporate Agenda Behind the Harris Regime." The chronology of federal government cutbacks between 1985 and 1995 is traced by Marjorie Griffin-Cohen in the *CCPA Monitor* (CCPA: Vol. 2, No.7; November, 1995). Stats depicting the substantial decline in overall federal government economic activity were cited in Larry Brown's analysis of these trends in the *CCPA Monitor* (CCPA: Vol.3, No.6, December-January, 1997). The analysis of wealth transfers between governments and banks was cited in campaign material prepared by Canadian Auto Workers' economist Jim Stanford (June, 1996).

Michael Lind's reflections on economic oligarchy and class realities is found in his article "To Have and Have Not: Notes on the Progress of the American Class War," published in *Harper's* magazine (June, 1995). Ed Finn's commentary is available in his *Under Corporate Rule* (Ottawa: CCPA, 1996) pp.24-26. The list of Canada's billionaires is published in *Unfair Shares,* op.cit (1997). The stats here on wealth transfers are taken from a study published in the *CCPA Monitor*, Vol.1, No.9, March, 1995. The comparisons between CEO compensation packages and workers wages was cited in the *CCPA Monitor*, Vol.3, No.3. July-August, 1996. Appendix III contains the latest stats on CEO compensation packages. On the media and manufacturing consent, see James Winter's *Democracy's Oxygen: How Corporations Control the News* (Montreal: Black Rose Books, 1997) for an excellent overview analysis (also contains charts identifying media ownership and interlocking corporate boards). The data and quotes in this section are taken from a summary article of Winter's book in the *CCPA Monitor*, Vol.3, No.6, November, 1996. The 1994 study of Canadian values and attitudes cited here is available from Ekos Research.

Regarding the corporate takeover of education, the classic work in Canada is Maude Barlow's and Heather-jane Robertson's *Class Warfare* (Toronto: Key Porter, 1994). For regular reports on what is happening in terms of corporation and technology issues in our public school system, see the *CCPA Education Monitor*, published quarterly by the Canadian Centre for Policy Alternatives.

The quotes by George Soros cited here are taken from his article on "The Capitalist Threat" in *The Atlantic Monthly*, February, 1997. Ed Finn's reflections on the topic of plutocracy are outlined in his article, "Bread and Circuses," published in *Under Corporate Rule,* op.cit. pp. 16-18. Benjamin Barber's philosophical reflections on the theme of corporate tyranny and democracy can be found in his book, *Jihad vs. McWorld: How the Planet is Both Falling Apart and Coming Together and What This Means for Democracy* (New York: Times Books, 1995) p. 220.

5. Citizens' Agenda

In terms of the general theme of this chapter, the Canadian Auto Workers' document "Recapturing the Agenda" and the Council of Canadians' "A Citizens' Agenda" provide some initial attempts to re-establish the foundations for the democratic rights of workers and citizens in general in relation to corporate rule. The quotes from popular uprisings in 1837 were cited in the work of historian Stanley B. Ryerson, *Unequal Union: Confederation and the Roots of Conflict in the Canadas, 1815-1873* (Toronto: Progress Books, 1975). See especially Chapters 3, 4, and 5 (and Chapter 20 for the Riel rebellion for self-government). Information on the Fraser Institute's plans was taken from "Towards the New Millenium: A Five-Year Plan for the Fraser Institute." The data on investment plans in health and education were cited in Lehman Brothers, "Investment Opportunity in the Education Industry," February 9, 1996.

There are several resources worth mentioning here that could be useful for citizens' movements in developing strategic priorities around the theme of corporate rule: Jed Greer and Kavaljit's *TNCs and India: An Activists' Guide to Research and Campaigns on Transnational Corporations* (New Dehli: Public Interest Research Group, 1975) provides a valuable introduction in an international context; Dan La Botz, *A Troublemaker's Handbook* (Detroit: Labor Notes Book, 1991) contains some useful case studies and tips on corporate campaigns for both labour and community organizing; David Langille (ed.), *Exposing the Facts of Corporate Rule* (Toronto: Jesuit Centre for Social Faith, 1997) contains an up-to-date list of resources; Ed Finn's (ed.) monthly publication, *CCPA Monitor* (Ottawa: Canadian Centre for Policy Alternatives) features regular articles on issues of corporate power and campaign work; and *The Emergence of Corporate Rule: And What Can Be Done About It* (San Francisco: IFG Publication, 1996), which I prepared as a work-book for social movements in collaboration with colleagues involved in the International Forum on Globalization.

In addition to the research and campaign tools outlined in Appendix I and II, various groups have begun to develop resources and tools for campaigns on several fronts. In Battlefield #1, for example, the Action Canada Network has developed a resource kit for corporate campaign activists around *jobs! jobs! jobs!*; the Ontario Coalition for Social Justice has produced tools like *Unfair Shares* for campaigns around corporate taxation; the Canadian Auto Workers and the Ecumenical Coalition for Economic Justice have produced resources that could be used for corporate campaign work focused on the banks and their role in financial speculation. In Battlefield #2, for example, the Canadian Health Coalition has begun to target certain for-profit health care corporations as targets for potential campaign work (which will be reinforced by Colleen Fuller's forthcoming book on this topic); the CCPA's *Education Monitor* is becoming a key resource for corporate campaign work emerging in the public school system; the Campaign for Public Broadcasting is producing resources and tools for campaigns aimed at the major corporate media moguls; and Low Income Families Together (LIFT) in Toronto has prepared a comic book on the corporate agenda and its impacts on social policies and poor people in this country. In Battlefield #3, groups like Greenpeace and the Rainforest Network have mounted major campaigns in the forestry sector, while the Sierra Legal Defense Fund has been developing some important legal challenges. Other groups like the Sierra Club of Canada, the Canadian Environmental Law Association, and the Communications, Energy and Paperworkers' Union are focusing more attention on issues of corporate power in their campaign work.

6. Democratic Control

Several important background sources were used in the development of this chapter. Sam Gindin's and David Robertson's
monograph on *Democracy and Productive Capacity: Notes Towards an Alternative to Competitiveness* (Ottawa: CCPA publication, 1991) helped in developing a basic framework for an alternative political platform. For a somewhat similar approach,
see also Colin Hines' and Tim Lang's "The New Protectionism"
in J. Mander's and E. Goldsmith's *The Case Against Global
Economy,* op.cit. pp. 485-94. The comments by Leo Panitch and
Greg Albo on democratizing the state were cited in *A Different
Kind of State? Popular Power and Democratic Administration*
(Toronto: Oxford University Press, 1993), edited by Gregory
Albo, David Langille and Leo Panitch. The book in part is based
on a three-day conference on "Democratic Administration in the
1990s" at York University in 1991. Panitch's article is "A Different Kind of State" while Albo's is called "Democratic Citizenship and the Future of Public Management." See also in this volume Hilary Wainwright's "A New Kind of Knowledge for a New
Kind of State" and David Langilles's "Putting Democratic Administration on the Political Agenda." The *Alternative Federal
Budget Papers 1997,* published by the Canadian Centre for Policy
Alternatives and CHO!CES: A Coalition for Social Justice, outlines a number of alternative policy tools that could be incorporated in a platform designed to dismantle mechanisms of corporate rule and develop new mechanisms of democratic control.
The book contains the 1997 Alternative Budget, the framework
document used in developing the budget, discussions from an
economists' round table, and a series of background papers. John
Dillon's *Turning the Tide* op.cit was also useful in thinking
through alternative financial strategies, and Paul Leduc Browne's
Love in a Cold World? (Ottawa: CCPA publication, 1996), as
well as some of his unpublished papers, were helpful in identifying potential connections between a revitalized public sector and
the social economy. And, for a much more detailed and graphic
view of the contradictions and vulnerabilities of the global
economy today, see William Greider's *One World, Ready or Not,*
op.cit

The *Alternative Federal Budget Papers* contain more detailed
proposals of policy tools that are related to the components outlined in our alternative platform. In terms of **public finance**, see

the sections dealing with "macro-economic and fiscal policy" in both the budget proposals (pp.7-12) and the framework document (pp.56-62), the revenue proposals (pp. 34-8), plus the sections dealing with taxation (pp. 341-368). In terms of **economic production**, see the sections on job creation in the budget proposals (pp.13-16) and the framework document (pp.63-72), plus the background paper by Andrew Jackson (pp.293-311) and the proposals for community economic development (pp.124-9). In terms of **social security**, see the various social policy components (e.g., the national funds for income support, heath care, child care, post-secondary education, unemployment insurance, retirement income, etc.) in the budget proposals (pp.17-28) and the framework document (pp.107-140), plus the background paper on public pensions by Monica Townsend and Bob Baldwin (pp. 313-340). In terms of **sustainable development**, see the sections on the environment (pp. 148-52) and taxation (pp.360-1). In applying any of these or other policy tools here, it is important to consider how and in what way they can be designed and implemented to diminish corporate rule and enhance democratic control.

For references to the NDP, two recent works worth noting are James Laxer's *In Search of a New Left* (Toronto: Viking, 1996) and Ian McLeod's *Under Siege: The Federal NDP in the Nineties* (Toronto: James Lorimer & Co., 1994.) For an excellent perspective on what an alternative, pro-democracy trade policy would look like, see Ian Robinson's *North American Trade As If Democracy Mattered* (Ottawa: CCPA publication, 1993).

Postscript

Ursula Franklin's reflections on the concept of "military occupation" were outlined in a presentation she made on "Global Justice—Chez Nous" to a Ten Days for Global Justice seminar, February 1, 1997.

Corporate Research Tools

Appendix I

IN CHAPTER 5, THE NEED for citizens' groups and individuals to develop new tools for challenging corporations as political machines was discussed. Obviously, one of the principal tools than needs to be developed is how to research and investigate the operations of corporations as targets for citizen action and democratic social change.

While there are many ways of doing research on corporations, the task here is to briefly outline a method for researching corporations as political machines—a method that can be used by community-based citizens' groups, as well as national or provincial organizations. The following is a research method—together with some tools and resources designed for this purpose. (**Note:** *Several sources were used to prepare this guide, including Who's Cashing In? published by the Canadian Union of Public Employees*).

Getting Started

The main starting points for any kind of corporate research related to struggles for social change are the issues and policies that concern our communities and daily lives. In Chapter 5, for example, we discussed three battlefields where major struggles over public policy were likely to be waged over the next few years and where corporations will be big players in determining government priorities and direction. Whether our prime concern is job creation or health care, government deficits or public education, farm markets or waste management, social assistance or workfare, forest preservation or fishery conservation, food security or social housing, trade policies or international development, community development or military armaments—corporations, both domestic and foreign-based, will be playing a decisive role in shaping what happens on these policy fronts.

Whichever battlefield we find ourselves on, it is important to begin by choosing one or two of the key corporate players as targets for action.

In doing corporate research, it makes a difference whether the targets we choose are "publicly-held" or "privately-held" corporations. The distinction lies in whether or not a corporation sells shares on the open stock market. Publicly-held companies do, privately-held companies do not. The distinction is important for finding out further information. Publicly-held companies, for example, are obligated by law to make certain information (e.g., annual reports, balance sheets, etc.) available to the public on request, whereas privately-held corporations are not.

Similarly, it is important to know whether the corporate targets are Canadian-based companies or subsidiaries of foreign-based corporations. The reason for making these distinctions at the outset is that different tools may be required for obtaining information on different types of corporations. However, whether a corporation is considered public or private, domestic or foreign, what's important for our purposes is how these corporations act as political machines in this country.

Once you know the exact name of your corporate target(s), the location of the company's headquarters and where it primarily operates, you are in a position to gather information. You could begin by talking with people in the workplace or the community about what they know about the corporation. If the corporate target you have chosen has a public presence in the business community, then the business pages of newspapers may be a useful source of information. Or, if your target is a transnational corporation, then it would be worthwhile to contact other national and international groups in your network to see what information they have on the company.

Before you can go much further, however, it is important to develop a research method and strategy that relates to your priorities for organizing a corporate campaign.

Setting Priorities

As noted in Chapter 5, there are different types of campaign styles that can be adopted to challenge corporations. Our priority here, however, has been on tackling corporations as political machines. This calls for a research method that makes use of a variety of tools. The following is a six-step research strategy that may be useful to pursue in gathering information on your particular corporate target.

1. Organizational Profile: It is usually helpful to get a handle on how the corporation is structured and its basic operations. This might include: the company's history, management structure, CEO salaries, board members, and corporate ownership (if a subsidiary, who is the parent; if a publicly-held parent firm, who are its main investors; of a privately-held company, if it is owned by a single individual or family). This profile could also include information on the company's divisional breakdown, including the number, location, and activities of its facilities, including foreign subsidiaries. In addition, the corporation's particular rank in the industry (by production or market share), its main distribution channels, as well as any mergers or acquisitions, would be useful data.

2. Policy Profile: Depending on what set of policy issues are to be the focal point of your corporate campaign—e.g., jobs, health care, food security, public education, forestry conservation, poverty, wealth transfers, other environmental concerns, child care, or workfare—it would be important to develop a profile of the corporation on the particular policy issues. This would include an analysis of the position taken by the company on issues of public policy concern, the level of government (federal, provincial, municipal) responsible for this policy development, and the track record of the company in promoting its agenda with governmental authorities.

3. Political Profile: Once you have a clear picture of the corporation's public policy agenda, the next step is to get a handle on the political apparatus used to promote this agenda. This includes identifying and gathering information on what law firm and/or public relations firm are employed by the company, what political connections the corporation's officers have with cabinet ministers and/or senior bureaucrats, and what membership the company holds in government advisory committees, as well as in trade and business associations (e.g., the BCNI, Chamber of Commerce, etc.). A special feature of this profile is whether the corporation has done any kind of political advertising and what contributions it has made to a political party, or parties (which ones, how much, when?) and to the party's election campaigns.

4. Business Profile: In order to identify potential points of leverage, a profile of the corporation's business operations and practices is essential. This should include the company's creditors and sources of financing (e.g., banks, trust companies, insurance firms), as well as its major investors or stockholders. A picture of the company's domestic and foreign sales, its profits and assets, its indebtedness, new stock issues and foreign exchange would be useful here. A profile of the corporation's major markets, customers, suppliers, and competitors is also strategically important.

5. Community Profile: You would also need to develop a profile of the corporation's relations and impacts on the community at large. In addition to information on the corporation's relations with its workers and the community(ies) in which it operates, it would be useful to have some basic information about the company's track record in labour relations (e.g., unions, collective bargaining practices, employee benefit programs, occupational health and safety, etc.), environmental performance (e.g., pollution record), consumer protection (e.g., record on product safety, marketing practices and pricing), and human rights (especially in countries which have oppressive political regimes).

6. Legal Profile: Finally, to complete the profile of a corporation or group of corporations, it is important to clarify the company's legal status. In order to operate legally in Canada, corporations must be granted a charter or a certificate by either the federal or a provincial government. By contacting the headquarters of the company(s) in Canada, you should be able to find out where the corporation is registered (i.e., at the federal level or in a particular province). Once you have this information, you can request a copy of the charter or certificate from the relevant federal or provincial ministry (see list of provincial government sources below). At the same time, it is worth inquiring whether there is a law or procedure that the government can use to revoke the charter or certificate of a corporation which has been shown to have violated its legal status, reponsibilities or conditions. In the U.S., the legal procedure for revoking corporate charters is called a "quo warranto" statute.

Doing Research

Obviously, each of these profiles could be expanded to include useful data on a range of other items as well. But, for now, the question is: how do citizens' groups get access to this kind of information? Well, believe it or not, the place to start could well be your local library or resource centre. Most medium-sized libraries do have a section on corporate directories and other information on companies. Your local librarian should be able to identify what documentation they have available on hand. If they do not have the documents you require, then they should be able to do a search of other library facilities on their computers. In any case, here is a basic list of sources for corporate research:

a) Corporate Directories: Some of the general information on companies for these profiles can be found through various corporate directories. For example, the *Canadian Key Business Directory* publishes data on all the major Canadian-based corporations every year. Similar corporate directories are produced each year in Ontario, Quebec, British Columbia, Alberta, Saskatchewan, Manitoba, and one for the Atlantic provinces combined. While these directories provide basic data on corporate sales, number of employees, company officers, etc., other directories like *Who Owns Whom* can provide more information on things like inter-corporate ownership links; and the *Financial Post Directory of Directors* gives the names of all the people who are on the boards of directors of corporations.

b) Annual Reports: These can be useful for compiling basic information, particularly related to organizational and business profiles. If your corporate target is a publicly-held company, then it is obligated to publish an annual report which can be sent to you free by phoning the company's investor relations department. If your corporate target is a privately-held company, some basic information can be found by contacting the "corporate registration" or "consumers' affairs" department of the provincial government in which the company's headquarters are located. A listing of these provincial ministries, including phone numbers, can be found below. In making these inquiries, be sure to also ask for copies of the speeches made by the CEO and other officers of the corporation, which may contain information on recent company views relevant for developing your policy and political profiles.

c) Newspapers/Magazines: Articles which have been published in newspapers or magazines can be another useful source of information on your corporate target. The *Canadian Index*, a quarterly publication which indexes articles from Canadian newspapers and magazines, can be used to track down articles that may have been written on your company, its CEO or its board of directors. Other publications like the *Canadian Press Index* and the *Alternative Press Index* can also be used for these purposes. If your library happens to be equipped with CD-ROM technology, it may be able to hook you up with the computer data base called "Canadian Business and Current Affairs" (CBCA). Each of these indexes should be useful in identifying and locating articles that can be found in magazines or newspapers available through your library system.

d) Court Records: If your corporate target has been involved in some form of litigation, then this could be a valuable source of information on the company and its track record. Court records represent the results of someone else's serious investigation. Documents filed by opposing parties in court can sometimes provide valuable information on a corporation's operations, its policies, attitudes and related matters that may not easily be acquired elsewhere. Gaining access to such court records may not be easy, but by consulting with a friendly lawyer, steps can be taken to do a search and identify ways of securing this information, if it is available.

e) Human Sources: In the end, there may be no substitute for the information that individuals and groups may have on your corporate target. Speaking or corresponding with different people who have worked in or investigated your particular company, could provide additional information or lead you to other sources. They may include: journalists who have done stories on the company; former employees who have stories to tell and are willing to talk; trade association representatives who may be open to answering specific questions; lawyers who have been involved in court cases against the corporation; industry consultants or investment analysts who may be willing to share some information on the company's operations; professors or students in business schools who have done case studies on your corporate target; other business players (e.g., competitors, suppliers, etc.) who may or may not be willing to talk; and, of course, citizens of the local community(ies) where the corporation's main operations are located.

f) Securities Exchange Commission: If your corporate target is a U.S.-based company and a publicly-held one, then extensive information is available through the U.S. Securities Exchange Commission. The most useful of these company reports through the SEC is known as the 10-K report, which provides a comprehensive review of corporations' business operations. By phoning your company's investor relations department, you should be able to get a free copy of the SEC's 10-K report. Or you can search for SEC reports on the World Wide Web of the Internet (SEC address is: http://www.sec.gov—choose "Edgar database"; then choose "search Edgar database"; then choose "quick forms lookup"; then select the form you want and enter the name of the company). If you only want an annual report of a U.S. publicly-held corporation, then you can request it from the company's investor relations department or contact the Public Register's Annual Report Service at 1-800-426-6825.

In conclusion, it should be noted that corporate research is not always easy. Like any other research project, it requires patience, persistence, politeness (generally), and being open-minded about any leads and sources that might be useful. Above all, it is essential to keep your focus on the strategic profiles that you are trying to develop for your particular corporate campaign.

In doing your research, it should always be kept in mind that corporations rarely welcome close scrutiny of their operations. They may well refuse to cooperate, and may even try to throw you off track. Whatever you do, don't satisfy them. In planning direct contacts with the company, you may want to make use of a variety of approaches. Like any good researcher, you should also document your sources of information, keeping track of dates and names of people with whom you have had conversations (using discretion, of course, in cases where conversations were confidential and "off the record").

Finally, this kind of research can be carried out on an individual or group basis. The team approach can be more effective, provided that the group members are committed and disciplined. The following is a more extensive resource list of corporate directories and related tools for gathering information about your corporate targets.

RESOURCE LIST

(NOTE: The following list of sources is largely drawn from *Who's Cashing In?*, a guide to corporate research prepared by the Canadian Union of Public Employees).

1. Canadian Sources:

Blue Book of Canadian Business - **1996:** Provides profiles of around 4,000 major Canadian corporations with revenues of over $10 million and 500 or more employees. Edited by Canadian Newspaper Services Ltd.

Canadian Key Business Directory: An annual directory of over 20,000 companies (see reference above), published by Dun & Bradstreet Canada.

Financial Post Directory of Directors 1997: An alphabetical listing of individual directors (or corporate officers) and all the directorships they hold.

Financial Post Survey of Industrials: An annual directory with investment information on 2,700 large manufacturing and industrial companies published by the Financial Post Datagroup.

National Services Directory: An annual directory containing information on 15,000 service companies, published by Dun & Bradstreet Canada. Similar information as in above-mentioned directories, but with focus on service industries.

Report on Business Canada Company Handbook: Provides detailed financial information, industry summaries, current company news, and stock information on the 520 largest Canadian corporations. Published by the Globe Information Services *(Globe & Mail).*

Who Owns Whom 1997: Volume 2 on North America includes complete listings for the U.S. and Canada. Good for tracking corporate ownership links. Published by Dun & Bradstreet International.

* Also, the July edition of the Globe & Mail's *Report on Business Magazine* usually contains a ranking of the top 1,000 corporations in Canada, including a section called "The Power Book" which contains some useful charts.

2. United States Sources:

Hoover's Handbook of American Business: A basic directory covering the 755 largest U.S.-based corporations. Includes lists of the largest corporations, largest employers, industry profiles, stock indexes, and corporate profiles. Published annually: 2 volumes.

Standard & Poor's Register of Corporations, Directors and Executives: A three-volume publication listing some 55,000 public and private U.S.-based corporations.

Ward's Business Directory of U.S. Private and Public Companies: A seven-volume directory listing some 120,000 companies, 90% of which are privately-held companies. Provides basic data on these corporations.

* See also the Fortune Global 500 Report published by *Fortune Magazine* every year, usually in early August. Contains a global ranking of the world's largest transnational corporations by industry, performance, revenues, profits, assets, employees, and other factors.

3. Computer Services:

Some libraries offer access to the following computer services. Ask your librarian for assistance.

Dialog - On-Line Service: Contains over 450 data bases on a wide range of topics, including corporate news and finance, government and public affairs. Operated by Southam News and Knight-Rider, likely on a fee-for-service basis.

Lexis-Nexus - On-Line Service: Probably the largest database available for full text searches. Holds files on thousands of newspapers, journals, trade periodicals, corporate reports, and court proceedings. Some libraries subscribe. Fee-for-service. Can be expensive.

Multinational Monitor On-Line: A comprehensive database of articles and other information on select transnational corporations. Analysis from labour, environmental, social and human rights perspectives. (http.//www.essential.org/monitor/monitor.html)

Corporate Watch: An on-line service providing access to documentation produced by citizens' movements involved in corporate campaign work in the U.S. and elsewhere in the world.

4. Provincial Government Sources:

All provincial governments have ministries or offices which require that privately-owned corporations operating in the province be officially registered. The following is a list of provincial offices and telephone numbers:

- British Columbia—Ministry of Finance and Private Property Registration: Tel: (604) 775-1041.
- Alberta—Corporate Registration Office: Tel.(403) 427-2311.
- Saskatchewan—Corporations Branch: Tel. (306) 787-2962.
- Manitoba—Companies Branch: Tel. (204) 945-2500.
- Ontario—Ministry of Consumer & Commercial Affairs: Tel. (1-800-268-1142).
- Quebec—L'inspecteur general des institutions Financières: Tel. (514) 873-5324.
- New Brunswick—Department of Justice - Corporate Affairs: Tel. (506) 453-2703.
- Nova Scotia—Business & Consumer Services: Tel. (902) 424-7579.
- Prince Edward Island—Provincial Affairs & Attorney General - Corporate Division: Tel. (902) 368-4550.
- Newfoundland—Registry of Deeds & Companies - Commercial Registration Division: Tel. (709) 729-3317.

Corporate Campaign Tools

Appendix II

MAKING USE OF THE METHODS and tools for corporate research outlined in Appendix I will set the stage for organizing a corporate campaign. As noted in Chapter 5, there are many ways of designing citizen-based campaigns for challenging corporations. Our concern, however, is the need to design a new style of corporate campaign that challenges the nature and power of corporations as political machines which are redefining and redirecting economic, social and environmental policy-making in this country.

The basic characteristics of corporations as political machines are outlined in Chapter 4. The intention here is to take a look at what it means to redesign some basic campaign tools for citizens' movements to tackle these corporate political machines. The following are some steps, along with tools and resources, that may be helpful for these purposes.

Setting Goals:

As discussed in Chapter 5, it is important for citizens' movements to launch a series of corporate campaigns over the next five years. The strategic goal here is to begin creating a political climate for dismantling the mechanisms of corporate rule. Over the past 20 years or so, big business and its allies have been successful in making governments Public Enemy No.1. The short-term objective here is to turn this perception around by making the corporations which are the driving forces behind government decision-making the prime targets for social change.

Our campaigns, in other words, need to demonstrate that the country is, in fact, being run by large corporations rather than by democratically-elected governments. In turn, this calls for campaigns designed to expose the operations of corporations as political machines on the three major battlefields identified in Chapter 5. The name of the game is to confront the key corporate players that are driving the public policy-making agenda on economic, social and environmental fronts.

Each of these campaigns will, of course, be primarily focused on major policy struggles— e.g., jobs, health care, education, the media, pensions, farms, fishery, forests, housing, trade, culture, or public finances. What needs to be done in each of these struggles is to unmask and expose the corporate faces that lie behind government policy-making on these fronts.

Campaigns need to be organized in such a way as to target and delegitimize the political power wielded by these corporations. This means, for example, casting a public spotlight on corporations which have become "super-citizens" on the public dole, which now run the country by hiring their own big gun lobbyists and by buying their own governments and policies. Whichever policy struggles are the focal points of our citizen-based campaigns, it is important that they be organized in such a way as to unmask and discredit the system of corporate rule that is now in place. In turn, this will require a considerable amount of creative cultural activity, if our campaign strategies are to be effective.

At the same time, these corporate campaigns should be designed to build and mobilize popular resistance. This is not only a matter of organizing campaigns in such a way as to attract more widespread citizen participation. Through these campaigns, people need to develop a strong sense of popular sovereignty as the base from which they can fight to reclaim their democratic rights which have been hijacked by corporations. That's why it is important to expose these corporations as political machines that have taken control of the policy-making apparatus of governments.

In doing so, steps need to be taken to target the individual players, the power and influence they wield, and the kind of money being used. These campaigns also need to restore public confidence by demonstrating that citizens can mobilize sufficient clout to effectively challenge these corporate political machines. This means not only choosing the right tactics, but also dissecting each corporate target to identify strategic options.

Choosing Tactics:

A variety of tactical tools have been devised for use in corporate campaigns. The choice of tactical tools, of course, depends a great deal on what the purpose of the campaign is, and on the capacity of the organization to make effective use of them. While most conventional tactics may be applied to campaigns designed to challenge corporate political machines, they would have to be refined for this kind of strategic purpose.

When it comes to organizational capacities, for example, it is likely that only a labour union can make effective use of strike action as a form of economic leverage on a corporation, whereas other citizens' movements may be able to make use of consumer boycotts or litigation through the courts as tactical tools. In any case, experience has shown that the most effective corporate campaigns have often been waged by choosing the most appropriate tactical tools to achieve the intended purpose.

For our campaign purposes, there are at least three major tactical tools that could used which could, in turn, be supplemented by several others.

1) Charter Challenges: Although litigation through the courts has been and continues to be an important tactical tool for citizens' movements, a new approach is needed to tackle the nature of corporations as political machines. Challenging corporate charters through the courts provides a means for getting at the actual mandate and authority of individual corporations, not just its specific abuses. By doing research on the specific charter or certificate granted to a corporation by the federal or provincial authorities, the performance of a targeted corporation can be evaluated and proceedings launched to have the charter revoked or revamped.

The performance evaluation could be done in terms of the company's track record on both the policy issues being raised and the ways in which the corporation has operated as a political machine to affect government decisions. While a clear legal and legislative base exists in the U.S. for citizens' movements to launch charter challenges, more work needs to be done to clarify what base citizens' groups would have here in Canada for using this tactical tool.

2) Political Lobbying: Demands for government action are likely to be a key component of any campaign strategy aimed at disrupting and dismantling mechanisms of corporate rule. If for nothing else, it is imperative that a counterweight to the political machinery of the corporation be established and mobilized. As a tactic, political lobbying would be used not only to generate government support for the policy demands of the campaign, but also to expose the political machinery of the corporation and its linkages with government structures.

The strategic objective here would be to force a split and a conflict in the corporate-government linkage. Lobbying tactics would have to be used in such a way as to expose the key corporate and political players involved, and demands for government intervention need to be crafted with an awareness of the limitations of the corporate state. To be effective, however, political lobbying should be used as one of several tactics in a campaign, especially if citizens' movements are to avoid being caught in the trap of government fixation in developing strategies for social change.

3) *Direct Action:* An important tactical tool for building popular resistance in corporate campaigns is the use of non-violent forms of direct action. This can take the form of sit-ins, occupations, blockades, and other forms of civil disobedience. Direct action campaigns, for example, were mobilized in the early 1990s by farmers and peasants in India against the expoitative operations of the grain giant Cargill corporation, and by the "Janitors for Justice" movement in the U.S.

In Canada, environmentalists used non-violent direct action in Clayquot Sound off Vancouver Island in their campaign to stop MacMillan Bloedel's massive clearcut logging of old growth forests. Direct action tactics would certainly be useful for building popular resistance against corporate political machines, provided that a clear moral principle was at stake: the hijacking of citizens' rights and the violation of democracy by the exercise of corporate power.

The use of direct action also requires well-trained and disciplined troops, as well as effective media and public relations tools.

Although these three tactics may be useful in organizing campaigns to challenge corporations as political machines, they could be supplemented by other tactics designed to generate leverage at key points. For example:

• *Legal Action:* Litigation would be a useful back-up tool to obtain court injunctions and restraining orders against continued corporate abuses related to the particular policy struggles being addressed. It could also be used to establish new laws regulating (or outlawing) the operations of corporations as political machines. Class action suits can provide further opportunities for citizen-based action through the courts (e.g., the class action suit against Texaco for health and environmental damages in the Amazon region of Ecuador, and the case that was brought here in Canada by the COC and the CEP against Conrad Black's Hollinger Inc.).

• *Consumer Boycotts:* It is conceivable that a well-organized consumer boycott could be used as a tactic in citizen-based campaigns against corporate political machines. But emphasis would have to be placed on action as "citizens," not simply as "consumers." The company's products would also have to have sufficient brand name recognition if this kind of consumer action were to affect the corporation's market sales and profit margin. Moreover, if the target is a transnational corporation, then the capacity to organize internationally would be essential.

• *Shareholder Action:* Filing resolutions at the corporation's AGM and mobilizing other shareholders (individual and institutional) to support these resolutions (through proxy votes) can be a useful tactic for raising major policy issues and struggles within the operations of corporations. It can also be a tool for mounting pressure on the corporation's financiers, suppliers and major customers. A corporation's AGM can also provide an occasion for publicly challenging its image. But this is largely a reformist tool that should be used to supplement other tactics, with emphasis once again being put on action as "citizens," not simply as "investors."

Whatever tactical tools are chosen for your corporate campaign, they will likely need to be further sharpened and refined if they are going to measure up as effective instruments in tackling the political challenges we face in an age of corporate rule.

Engaging Culture:

Whatever tactical choices are made, it will be important to organize in such a way as to build a "culture of resistance" for the long haul. Greater use should be made of the tools of popular culture to communicate the message of the struggle to a wider public, and to deepen the commitment of citizens to the struggle in the long run. In part, this means rooting our campaigns in our political culture by drawing upon some of the heroes, legends and values of popular resistance in the past.

It also means making more creative use of tools for popular education, such as posters, games, and entertainment in reaching out to people. But, as Michael Moore has shown, a mix of humour, satire and ridicule is also essential for corporate campaigns. Through films like *Roger and Me* and books like *Downsize This!*, Moore helps people to think, laugh, and get angry at the same time about what big business and its CEOs are doing to people in everyday life.

The following are a few examples of how tools of popular culture could be utilized in corporate campaigns:

• *Posters 'n' Stickers:* Posters like "Exposing the Face of Corporate Rule" by the Jesuit Centre for Social Faith and Justice, which features pictures of Canada's top CEOs, or "Mediasauras" by the Campaign for Press and Broadcasting Freedom, caricaturing media moguls like Conrad Black, and stamps issued by the Canadian Union of Postal Workers on themes like "Stop the Greed" and "Job Killers".

• *Election Capers:* A take-off on Michael Moore's suggestion that, instead of voting for political candidates in an election, why not organize a write-in campaign naming the CEOs who have the real power to control governments and decide policy? A Corporate Canada slate could be drawn up and promoted by citizens' movements as a means for debunking federal and provincial elections where corporate money and power determine the only real winners.

• *Trading Cards:* Like hockey or baseball cards, a series of trading cards could be produced featuring pictures and stats on the country's leading corporate players. The Canadian Union of Public Employees, for example, has issued a series of trading cards under the theme "Who's Cashing In" with information on the corporations which are moving in on health care, education, and municipal services.

• *Public Displays:* Another take-off on a Michael Moore spoof is the idea of planting posters of "Corporate Welfare Mammas" on telephone poles and public buldings all over the city. The posters could include pictures of CEOs of major corporations that get subsidies and tax credits from governments while paying relatively little tax on rising profit margins. The stats could highlight the theme of "Aid to Dependent Corporations."

• *Comic Book:* An effective form of popular communication continues to be cartoons and comics. A popular comic book series portraying, for example, the deficit scam in terms of "The Great Canadian Bank Robbery" or the political machinery of several major corporations in terms of "The Great Canadian Hold-Up" could help to communicate these and other complex issues in more meaningful (and entertaining) ways.

• *Ad Busters:* One way of countering the political advertising of big name corporate players is to "beat them at their own game." This is what the group called Ad Busters specializes in when they produce "uncommercials" on television, "subvertisements" in magazines, and "anti-ads" opposing the ads placed by corporations in publications and on billboards. Drawing upon a global network of artists, activists and educators, these "culture jammers" strive to "uncool" the billion-dollar business images promoted by corporate advertising.

• *Street Theatre:* There is probably no substitute for popular theatre as a medium for communicating political humour, satire and ridicule. The status of some of Canada's leading CEOs as super-citizens and their corporate political machines would make colourful subjects for the kind of circus enterainment that can be provided through street theatre.

These are just a few of the tools that could be used to root your corporate campaign in popular culture. Wherever possible, these strategies should be developed in collaboration with local artists and entertainers. It should also be kept in mind that a major task of these corporate campaigns is to change the values and attitudes of Canadians, which means changing our political culture. Making effective use of popular culture is essential.

Leveraging Power:

Our campaigns must also be organized in such a way as to demonstrate that citizens' movements can have economic and political clout over corporations. This is what the veteran labour organizer Ray Rogers, founder of Corporate Campaign Inc. in the U.S., emphasizes. Before starting any campaign, Rogers insists on doing a "power analysis" of the corporate target. Doing homework on the CEO, board of directors and top management, he says, "I research them thoroughly so that I understand how much influence they really wield in terms of the other institutions they're tied into, their political connections, etc. Then I lay everything out on a chart. And I begin to get a picture of who really wields power."

According to Rogers' power analysis and strategy, the corporation you are targeting is often supported by other corporations and institutions which can, in turn, become targets in an overall campaign. These can be identified in terms of the following components: a) *the company's financing*—identifying the banks, trust companies or insurance firms which provide credit financing to the target corporation (which may also have representation on the company's board of directors); b) *the company's customers*—identifying two or three major customers who could, in turn, be potential targets for boycott action; c) *the company's suppliers*—identifying those key firms that supply the targeted corporation with resources, materials and services (noting points of vulnerability as well as their competition); d) *the company's investors*—identifying the major institutional shareholders (if the target is a public corporation). Add to this, of course, the company's *political connections*, such as its lobbying and public relations firms, plus links with cabinet ministers and senior bureaucrats.

Several of these institutions (and individuals associated with them) could provide strategic opportunities for leveraging power and generating countervailing pressures on the targeted corporation and its political machinery. As Rogers puts it: "The next step is to identify the power that can carry out the plan. This power is based on people and money. Who can be mobilized?" Are there allied unions and community groups who have significant bank accounts and insurance policies which can be called upon to withdraw and/or reinvest their money? Are there allied organizations who do business with the targeted corporation's suppliers or customers that can, in turn, exert pressure?

What steps can be taken to organize citizens' groups who are concerned about the policy struggle that lies at the heart of your campaign to become actively engaged in putting pressure on financiers, suppliers and customers? What needs to be done to publicly expose the corporation's political machinery and connections in such a way as to make it sufficiently uncomfortable for them to maintain their association?

In short, citizens' movements can develop a capacity for leveraging countervailling power by dissecting the operations of their corporate targets and developing divide-and-conquer manoeuvres. While exerting this kind of power is important for the kind of corporate campaigns we are talking about in the short run, special care must be taken to ensure that this does not become the be-all and end-all of the campaign. Leveraging power must be made subordinate to the overall goals and principles of these campaign strategies, whose ultimate goal is to create a public climate for eventually dismantling the system of corporate rule. Furthermore, developing effective strategies to leverage countervailling pressures on most targeted corporations these days will require building international links with citizens' movements and allied institutions in other countries as well.

Utilizing Media:

A well organized media strategy is a key component of any corporate campaign. After all, most corporations are very sensitive about their public image, so a negative campaign against them can do considerable damage. More than this, however, a good media strategy is important for building the kind of public climate and political will necessary to achieve the eventual dismantling of corporate rule.

In organizing your campaign, therefore, special attention should be given to seeking out potentially interested or sympathetic journalists, drawing up a good media list of newspaper, radio and television reporters, and then cultivating them for your campaign activities. Someone from your campaign team who knows the issues well should be designated to work with the media on an ongoing basis. This, of course, involves such tasks as briefing reporters, alerting them to planned events, preparing short and clear press releases, providing press information packets for certain occasions, and tracking and analyzing the coverage after events.

Even the most well-designed media strategy, however, may not be enough to achieve our campaign objectives. While it is quite possible to find and cultivate interested or sympathetic journalists (although even this task has become increasingly difficult in some cities), their work can be easily trashed by publishers and senior editors who control the newsrooms and editorial policies. The more the ownership of the news media in this country becomes concentrated in the hands of fewer and fewer corporations, the more difficult it is to spread the word about any citizen-based campaigns, particularly those aimed at corporations. All the more so when some of the country's major media outlets are owned and controlled by right-wing ideologues like Conrad Black.

As we discussed in Chapter 5, a concerted plan needs to be developed by the democratic left to gain control over strategic media and communication instruments in this country. This could be done, for example, by designating and pooling a percentage (say 5 %) of worker pension funds (estimated to be nearly $400 billion) for social capital investments. A priority could then be put on re-investing this money (e.g., $20 billion) in purchasing a series of strategically located newspapers, radio and television stations. Since these would be money-making operations, there is no reason why there would not be an adequate return on these investments for the pension funds of workers in general.

In order to move in this direction, the labour movement would need first to do a feasibility study on how the pension funds of workers could be leveraged for these purposes, as well as a study of strategically located media options across the country. A strong case would have to be made to rank-and-file workers showing how their pension funds could be re-invested for socially productive instead of socially destructive purposes, while still providing an adequate return.

At first glance, this may seem like a tall order. But the fact remains that the corporate campaigns that need to be waged on the three battlefields over the next five years will be extemely difficult to accomplish if concerted moves are not being taken at the same time to gain greater access to, if not control over, some strategically located media and communication instruments. Even if several significant corporate campaigns are fought on these battlefields in the coming years, there is little chance of generating the kind of public climate and political will necessary to dismantle corporate rule and restore true democracy in Canada (as discussed in Chapter 6) unless we have the means of reaching the majority of Canadians with our message.

This plan of action does not have to fall on the shoulders of the labour movement alone. Other progressive institutions, inclding professional and religious organizations, also have sizeable pension funds that could, in part, be designated for social investment purposes along these lines.

RESOURCE LIST

The following is a short list of documents, along with some Canadian and U.S.-based organizations that may be helpful in developing corporate campaigns.

1. DOCUMENTS

The Emergence of Corporate Rule and What to Do about It: A set of working instruments for social movements by Tony Clarke and associates at the International Forum on Globalization in San Francisco. Provides a framework for developing campaigns on issues of corporate rule in a global context. Available at cost from the Council of Canadians, 904 - 251 Laurier Avenue West, Ottawa, K1P-5J6.

CCPA Monitor: A monthly publication of the Canadian Centre for Policy Alternatives edited by Ed Finn. Contains valuable up-to-date information and statistics on corporate rule issues that are useful for campaign purposes. Available at cost from the CCPA, 804 - 251 Laurier Avenue West, Ottawa, K1P-5J6.

Under Corporate Rule: A 35,000-word collection of columns, editorials and essays by the CCPA's Ed Finn, which expose the nature and scope of the corporate agenda and suggest ways that Canadians can fight back. Available at cost from the CCPA, 804 - 251 Laurier Avenue West, Ottawa, K1P 5J6.

Exposing The Facts of Corporate Rule: A set of resources for promoting awareness and action produced by the Jesuit Centre for Social Faith and Justice. Includes pieces like "Getting Started on Corporate Rule in Canada," "How Business Leaders See The World," and "Banking 'n' Justice," as well as a variety of practical tools and resources. Contact David Langille, Jesuit Centre for Social Faith and Justice, 947 Queen Street, Toronto, Ontario, M4M 1J9.

Unfair Shares - Corporations and Taxation in Canada: Contains the latest data on corporate tax payments and tax deferrals, the best-paid CEOs, the wealthiest Canadians, and the corporate share of federal tax revenues. Excellent stats for corporate research and campaign purposes. Published annually by the Ontario Coalition for Social Justice and the Ontario Federation of Labour c/o 15 Gervais Drive, Don Mills, Ontario, M3C 1Y8.

Corporate Power and the American Dream: A set of workshop instruments prepared by the Labour Institute in New York. While the material is all based on U.S. data, the instruments could be useful for workshop training of workers and citizens' groups in general. Available at cost through The Labour Institute, 853 Broadway, Room 2014, New York, NY 10003, USA.

A Troublemaker's Handbook: A Labor Notes book written by Dan La Botz. Contains case studies of various corporate campaigns organized by the labour movement in the U.S. Available at cost from Labor Notes, 7435 Michigan Ave. Detoit, Michigan 48210, USA.

TNCs and India: An Activists' Guide to Research and Campaign on Transnational Corporations: Prepared by Jed Greer and Kavaljit Singh for the Public Interest Research Group. A very useful tool for campaign strategies, especially in relation to transnational corporations. Available at cost from the Public Interest Research Group, 142, Maitri Apartments, Plot No. 28, I.P. Extension, Delhi - 110 092, India.

Multinational Monitor: A monthly publication containing articles, interviews and case studies of corporate power issues and campaigns in the U.S. and elsewhere in the world. Good material for campaign purposes. Available at cost from Multinational Monitor, 1530 P Street, Washington, D.C. 20005, USA.

Boycott Quarterly: Monitors ongoing boycotts against corporations and the products they sell. Features reports on campaigns ranging from the boycott against Shell in Nigeria to Daioshawa in Alberta. Available from the Center for Economic Democracy, P.O. Box 30727, Seattle, WA 98103-0727, USA.

2. CANADIAN ORGANIZATIONS

(A short list of citizens' movements that have launched corporate campaign activities)

- **Action Canada Network** (on jobs and corporate taxation), contact Mandy Rocks, ACN, 804-251 Laurier Ave. W., Ottawa, Ontario, K1P 5J6 (tel. 613-563-1341)
- **Canadian Auto Workers** (on the banks as well as the auto sector), contact Jim Stanford, CAW, 205 Placer Court, Willowdale, Ontario, M2H 3H9 (tel. 416-497-4110)
- **Canadian Union of Public Employees** (on corporate takeover of health care and public services), contact Jim Turk, CUPE, 21 Florence St. Ottawa, K2P 0W6 (tel. 613-237-1590)
- **Council of Canadians** (on corporations and democracy, especially media corporations), contact David Robinson, COC, 904-251 Laurier Ave. W., Ottawa, K1P-5J6 (tel. 613-233-2773)
- **CODEV** (focus on mining corporations), contact Jim Raider, CODEV, Suite 205, 2929 Commercial Drive, Vancouver, B.C. V5N 4C8 (tel. 604-708-1495)
- **Greenpeace** (focus on forest corporations and others threatening the environment), 185 Spadina Avenue, Suite 600, Toronto, Ont. M5T 2C6. (tel 416-597-8408)
- **Polaris Institute** (focus on enhancing the capacities of citizens' movements to challenge corporate rule), 4 Jeffrey Avenue, Ottawa, Ont. K1K 0E2. (tel 613-746-8374)
- **Sierra Legal Defence Fund** (focus on legal actions against corporations that are environmentally destructive, including Charter challenges). Contact David Boyd, SLDF, Suite 214, 131 Water Street, Vancouver, B.C. V6B 4M3 (tel 604-685-6518). Toronto Office: 106 Front Street East, Suite 300, Toronto, Ont. M5A 1E1. (tel 416-368-7533)
- **Task Force on Churches and Corporate Responsibility** (focus on shareholder campaigns), 129 St. Clair Avenue West, Toronto, Ont. M4J 4Z2. (tel 416-923-1758)

3. U.S. ORGANIZATIONS

(Some U.S. contacts with information and experience on corporate campaign activities)

- **Corporate Campaigns Inc.** (focus on designing labour and community strategies for corporate campaigns). Contact Ray Rogers, 51 East 12th Street, 10th Floor, New York, N.Y., 10003, USA. (tel 212-979-8320)
- **Friends of the Earth** (focus on education tools as well as monitoring corporate impacts on the environment). 1025 Vermont Avenue, Suite 300, Washington, DC 20005, USA. (tel 202-783-7400)
- **Labor Institute** (focus on training programs for labour and community activists). 853 Broadway, Suite 2014, New York, N.Y. 10003, USA. (tel 212-674-3322)
- **National Labor Committee** (focus on monitoring overseas operations of U.S. corporations in relation to their performance on human and workers' rights). 15 Union Square, Suite 524, New York, N.Y. 10003, USA. (tel 212-242-0700)
- **Program on Corporate Law and Democracy**, focus on "Rethinking Corporations and Democracy" events, including corporate charter actions). Contact Richard Grossman, POCLAD, 211.5 Bradford Street, Provincetown, MA 02657, USA. (tel 508-487-3151) or Ward Morehouse, POCLAD, Suite 3C, 777 United Nations Plaza, New York, N.Y. 10017, USA. (tel 212-972-9877)
- **Interfaith Center for Corporate Responsibility** (focus on organizing shareholder campaigns among the churches). 487 Riverside Drive, Suite 566, New York, N.Y. ✪

Corporate Players' Guide

Appendix III

Business Organizations and their Support Groups

FOLLOWING IS A PROFILE of some major business associations, think tanks, and citizens' front groups, based on objective descriptions initially prepared by David Langille and Asad Ismi of the Jesuit Centre for Social Faith and Justice.

Alliance of Manufacturers and Exporters of Canada (AMEC)

The Canadian Manufacturers' Association recently merged with the Canadian Exporter's Association to form the Alliance. AMEC now represents 3,000 manufacturers, service companies and exporters of every size and kind. President Stephen Van Houten presents their views to the general public and governments, with the aid of a $6.5 million operating budget.

For over 100 years the CMA had been the leading advocate of Canada's National Policy which offered tariff protection to the manufacturers of Central Canada. Gradual continentalization and trade liberalization caused them to change their line in the early 1980s. Now avid free traders, they favour policies to increase the competitiveness of their products on world markets, i.e., paying lower wages and reduced social benefits to Canadian workers.

Business Council on National Issues (BCNI)

The BCNI was formed in 1976 by corporate leaders anxious to exert more influence over a state that they felt had grown too large and interventionist. They organized 150 chief executive officers from the major transnational corporations so as to be able "to contribute personally to the development of public policy and the shaping of national priorities." The fact that these companies have assets of $1.5 trillion, earn annual revenues of $400 billion, and employ about 1.3 million Canadians helps explain why they have become the most powerful and influential interest group in the country. Their chief spokesperson, President Tom d'Aquino, manages a 14-person staff in their Ottawa headquarters.

The Council now claims to be the senior voice of Canadian business on public policy issues in Canada and abroad, with a focus on helping to build a strong economy, "progressive" social policies, and "healthy" political institutions. In fact, guided by their primary objective of curbing the role and size of the state, the BCNI has helped maintain the fight against inflation, cut back public spending, and bolster corporate profits.

Canadian Bankers Association (CBA)

The CBA was established in 1891 to serve the chartered banks of Canada. Typical of most industry associations, it provides information, research, advocacy, education and operational support services to its members. The current president of the CBA is Raymond Protti.

Canadian Chamber of Commerce (CCC)

Established in 1925, the Canadian Chamber of Commerce is the country's largest business association with 170,000 members, including 500 local chambers of commerce or boards of trade, over 95 trade and professional associations, and several thousand corporations that are directly represented at the national level. The current president of the CCC is Tim Reid.

The Chamber's size and the diversity of its membership enhances its claim to represent the Canadian business community, but it also makes it more difficult for the organization to reach a consensus on current issues. Trying to balance all of these competing interests often means the Chamber generates fairly predictable, lowest-common-denominator positions. Nonetheless, when its positions coincide with those of the BCNI and AMEC, the policy demands of this "Gang of Three" dictate the corporate agenda in this country.

Investment Dealers Association of Canada (IDA)

As the Canadian investment industry's national trade association, the IDA represents approximately 118 member firms employing more than 24,000 people. It is also responsible for regulating the industry and policing the activities of its member firms. The IDA's stated mission is to foster efficient capital markets by encouraging participation in the savings and investment process, and by ensuring the integrity of the marketplace.

Think Tanks

C. D. Howe Institute (CDHI)

The Institute is named after the prominent Canadian industrialist who became "Minister of Everything" in post-war Ottawa, and was most noted for using American investment to develop Canadian industry. Although it claims to be an independent think tank, the Institute consistently represents the views of the business élite. It is funded almost exclusively from Bay Street and its board is drawn from Canada's biggest corporations, including Sun Life Assurance, Noranda and Alcan.

CDHI's main focus is on economic issues, but it has recently helped lead the attack on Canada's social programs. The Institute played a major role in generating the "hysteria" over the deficit by insisting that the problem is government spending rather than high interest rates. The Howe's current president and CEO, Tom Kierans, commands an annual budget of nearly $2 million and a great deal of respect at the *Globe and Mail.*

The Fraser Institute

For many years after the Fraser Institute was established in Vancouver in 1974, it was considered to be a radically right-wing think tank on the fringes of the policy community. However, since the political terrain has shifted to the right, the Institute has opened a Toronto office, and the organization has become far more central in public policy debates. According to its founder and prominent spokesperson, Michael Walker, the Fraser Institute is devoted to "researching the use of markets, how markets work, and how markets fail."

The institute is involved in economic and social research, publishes books and newsletters, monitors television news to ensure "balanced" reporting, and is particularly effective in involving high school and university students in its market economics programs. Besides its own staff of 22, it can hire academics from around the world to develop right-wing positions on free trade, taxation, government spending, health care and Aboriginal rights.

The Institute is supported by tax-deductible donations from more than 2,500 individuals, corporations, and charitable foundations, giving it an annual budget of $2.35 million.

'Citizen' Front Groups
The National Citizens' Coalition (NCC)

The NCC claims to have more than 40,000 supporters but has no fixed membership. It advocates individual freedom and responsibility under limited government and a strong defence, but has no democratic structures. Independent of all political parties, the NCC neither seeks nor accepts government handouts, but gets its funding from wealthy business people.

The NCC promotes privatization and contracting-out, citizen-initiated referendums, the reform of pensions for MPs and federal civil servants, free trade, government spending cuts, Senate reform, and the use of market forces in health, education and welfare. It opposes "forced" unionism and pay equity as violations of civil liberties.

Canadian Taxpayers' Federation (CTF)

The CTF claims to promote the responsible and efficient use of tax dollars by acting as a watchdog over government and providing taxpayers with information about "wasteful spending and high taxation." The federation identifies "special interests" as being responsible for "runaway spending" which leads to "continuous annual deficits" and "job-killing public debt" that hurt the "silent majority" (taxpayers). The CTF's solution is to control government spending through legislation ensuring balanced budgets and taxpayer protection.

The Federation counts among its achievements 20 "Tax Alert Rallies" across Canada, exposure of "lucrative pension plans" for provincial politicians, and balanced budget and taxpayer protection laws passed in Alberta and Manitoba.

Forums
Public Policy Forum (PPF)

This Ottawa-based body was formed in 1987 to promote private sector participation in public policy development, an "efficient" public service, and mutual understanding among leaders from government, business, labour and the academic community. The current chair is Jodi White, and the president is David Zusman.

When the Forum talks about increasing cooperation and greater consensus in public service reform, it means infusing government with the values, needs and priorities of the major corporations. About 70% of its funding comes from business, which it uses to organize conferences, seminars and an annual awards dinner where it gives recognition to the journalists, bureaucrats and labour leaders who have most faithfully advocated corporate priorities.

Corporate Data Charts

Appendix IV

THE FOLLOWING IS A SELECTION of charts which provide a picture of some of the key corporate players, along with some data referred to in previous chapters.

TOP 25 MOST POWERFUL CEOs in CANADA — 1996

Chief Executive Officer	Corporation	1995 Revenues
1. Maureen Kempston Darkes	General Motors Canada **	$ 30.9 billion
2. Lynton R. Wilson	BCE Inc.**	$ 24.9 billion
3. Mark Hutchins	Ford Motor Co. of Canada	$ 19.1 billion
4. John Cleghorn	Royal Bank of Canada **	$ 15.3 billion
5. G. Yves Landry	Chrysler Canada Ltd.	$ 13.7 billion
6. Al Flood	C.I.B.C.**	$ 13.2 billion
7. Galen Weston	George Weston Ltd.	$ 12.9 billion
8. Peter Godsoe	Bank of Nova Scotia	$ 12.1 billion
9. Matthew Barrett	Bank of Montreal **	$ 12.1 billion
10. Jean Monty	Northern Telecom Ltd.**	$ 10.8 billion
11. John D. McNeil	Sun Life Assurance Ltd.**	$ 10.6 billion
12. Khalil Barsoum	IBM Canada Ltd.	$ 10.3 billion
13. Richard Currie	Loblaws Cos. Ltd.	$ 9.9 billion
14. Edgar Bronfman Jr.	Seagram Co. Ltd.	$ 9.9 billion
15. Robert B. Peterson	Imperial Oil Ltd. **	$ 9.4 billion
16. Jacques Bougle	Alcan Aluminum Co.**	$ 9.4 billion
17. Dominic D'Alessandro	Manulife Financial	$ 8.9 billion
18. Allan Kupcis	Ontario Hydro	$ 8.7 billion
19. Richard Thomson	Toronto Dominion Bank	$ 8.7 billion
20. Brian Levitt	Imasco Ltd. **	$ 8.7 billion
21. David Kerr	Noranda Inc.**	$ 8.7 billion
22. John T. McLennan	Bell Canada	$ 8.2 billion
23. David O'Brian	Canadian Pacific **	$ 8.1 billion
24. Yvon Martineau	Hydro Quebec	$ 7.7 billion
25. Michael Brown	Thomson Corp.	$ 7.6 billion

Source: Globe & Mail's Report on Business Magazine,, July, 1996.
** Members of the BCNI's Policy Council.

50 BEST PAID CEOS in CANADA — 1996

CEO	Corporation	Compensation* Package — 1996	% Change in Pay
1. Laurent Beaudoin	Bombardier Inc.	$19,100,317.	+ 1335
2. Michael Brown	Thomson Corp.	$11,389,268.	+ 155
3. Francesco Bellini	BioChem Pharma	$ 9,993,104.	+ 2042
4. William Holland	United Dominion Ind.	$ 8,925,640.	+ 192
5. Gerald Schwartz	Onex Corp.	$ 8,375,505.	+ 166
6. William Stinson	Canadian Pacific	$ 8,301,983.	+ 648
7. Charles Childers	Potash Corp (Sask.)	$ 7,729,256.	+ 124
8. Pierre Lessard	Metro-Richelieu Inc.	$ 7,345,600.	+ 57
9. Jean Monty	Northern Telecom	$ 6,437,804.	+ 188
10. Edward Newall	Nova Corp. (Alberta)	$ 6,350,750.	+ 283
11. Wayne McLeod	CCL Industries Inc.	$ 5,312,369.	+ 779
12. L. Bloomberg	First Marathon Inc.	$ 5,060,000.	+ 56
13. John Hunkin	CIBC Wood Gundy	$ 4,903,991.	+ 507
14. Anthony Fell	RBC Dominion Sec.	$ 4,802,000.	+ 139
15. Frank Hasenfratz	Linamar Corp.	$ 4,607,737.	+ 1
16. Rich'd Harrington	Thomson Newspaper	$ 4,480,434.	+ 182
17. Robert Shultz	Midland Walwyn Inc.	$ 4,438,783.	+ 390
18. Matthew Barrett	Bank of Montreal	$ 3,876,074.	+ 54
19. William Ardell	Southam Inc.	$ 3,844,032.	+ 405
20. William Casey	Coca-Cola Beverages	$ 3,048,630.	+ 168
21. Donald Walker	Magna International	$ 3,024,650.	- 16
22. Brian Steck	Nesbitt Burns Corp.	$ 2,964,583.	+ 17
23. Al Flood	Can.Imp.Bank-CIBC	$ 2,932,075.	+ 54
24. Stephen Hudson	Newcourt Credit Grp	$ 2,908,644.	- 31
25. Peter Godsoe	Bank of Nova Scotia	$ 2,856,004.	+ 45
26. Rainer Paduch	Instar Internet Inc.	$ 2,855,686.	
27. Richard Thomson	Toronto Dom. Bank	$ 2,793,191.	- 17
28. Colin Macaulay	Rio Algom	$ 2,636,420.	+ 232
29. Norman Keevil	Teck Corp.	$ 2,580,600.	+ 225
30. John Cleghorn	Royal Bank	$ 2,570,775.	+ 13
31. Stephen Bachand	Canadian Tire Corp.	$ 2,493,586.	0
32. Michael Sopko	Inco Ltd.	$ 2,471,798.	- 33
33. Richard Currie	Loblaw Cos. Ltd.	$ 2,400,000.	0
34. Edgar Bronfman	Seagram Co. Ltd.	$ 2,381,762.	- 6
35. Bernard Michel	Cameco Corp.	$ 2,334,861.	+ 76
36. Hollis Harris	Air Canada	$ 2,247,193.	+ 68
37. Lynton Wilson	BCE Inc.	$ 2,021,483.	+ 31

38. G. Cheesbrough	Scotia McLeod	$ 1,981,600.	
39. Gerald Pencer	Cott Corp.	$ 1,969,699.	- 85
40. Hank Swartout	Precision Drilling Co.	$ 1,966,328.	+ 287
41. Galen Weston	George Weston Ltd	$ 1,900,000.	+ 92
42. Elias Vamvakas	TLC Laser Center	$ 1,894,198.	+ 780
43. Douglas Hotby	West Int'l Com(WIC)	$ 1,854,827.	+ 87
44. Gordon Arnell	Brookfield Properties	$ 1,792,007.	+ 189
45. Brian Levitt	Imasco Ltd.	$ 1,780,198.	- 3
46. James Bryan	Gulf Can. Resources	$ 1,768,853.	+ 65
47. Peter Munk	TrizecHahn Corp.	$ 1,722,550.	+ 35
48. Israel Asper	Canwest Global	$ 1,664,660.	+ 24
49. Ken McCready	TransAlta Corp.	$ 1,576,457.	+ 240
50. Reto Braun	Moore Corp. Ltd	$ 1,558,606.	+ 4

Source: Globe & Mail, Report on Business, April 12, 1997.

* Total compensation package of CEOs includes: (a) basic salary + (b) an annual bonus or longer term incentive pay or both + (c) the difference between the cost of shares acqired by the CEO and the market price at the time + (d) anything from severance pay to club dues (but is not always the whole story since corporations are allowed to omit certain perquisites worth up to $50,000.)

NOTE:

a) This chart omits some of Canada's leading corporate figures including: Frank Stronach, chairman of Magna Corporation who, in 1995, broke all records with a total compensation package of $47,226,100 (his 1996 take is reported to have been $20.6 million) and Conrad Black, chairman of Hollinger Inc. whose 1995 compensation package was reported to have been $18,399,875.
b) The chart also does not include the compensation packages paid to the CEOs of several major US subsidiary corporations in Canada, including: Maureen Kempston Darkes, CEO of General Motors Canada; Mark Hutchins, former CEO of Ford Motor Co., Yves Landry, CEO of Chrysler Canada, and Khailil Barsoum, CEO of IBM Canada.
c) Peter Munk is not only CEO of TrizecHahn but also Barrick Gold, thereby giving him a combined compensation package for 1996 of $3,176,308, which would place him in 20th position in the top 50.

CANADA'S LEADING CORPORATE JOB KILLERS
1988-1994

Corporation	Job Cuts 1988-1994	Revenues Sales Rank
1. Canadian Pacific	49,000	14
2. Imasco	26,553	10
3. K-Mart	20,510	106
4. Ford Motor	13,200	3
5. Noranda	13,000	16
6. Sears Canada	10,690	30
7. Ontario Hydro	10,147	7
8. Abitibi-Price	9,919	67
9. Stone Container	9,061	122
10 General Motors	7,230	1
11. Domtar	6,891	65
12. Alcan Aluminum	6,500	6
13. Dofasco	6,202	61
14. Provingo	5,700	17
15. Cineplex Odeon	4,800	184

Source: The Financial Post 500, 1995

CANADA'S TOP CORPORATE TAX DEFEREES

Corporation	Deferred Taxes Owed *	As of
1.Seagram Company	$ 2,163,000,000.	$US 1996
2.Bell Canada	2,039,400,000.	1995
3.BCE Inc.	1,889,000,000.	1995
4.Canadian Pacific	1,287,200,000.	1995
5.Imperial Oil	1,150,000,000.	1995
6.Alcan Aluminum	979,000,000.	$US 1995
7.Pan Canadian Petroleum	933,700,000.	1995
8.Chrysler Canada	896,000,000.	1995
9.Shell Canada	852,000,000.	1995
10.Petro Canada	621,000,000.	1995
11.Noranda Inc.	613,000,000.	1995
12.Norcen Energy Resources	467,200,000.	1995
13.Anderson Exploration	462,942,000.	1995
14.Home Oil Co.	438,500,000.	1994
15.Alberta Energy Co.	423,900,000.	1995
16.Westcoast Energy	396,000,000.	1995
17.Suncor	381,000,000.	1995
18.IPL Energy	373,100,000.	1995
19.Thomson Corporation	357,000,000.	$US 1995
20.Dofasco	353,900,000.	1995
21.Quebecor	349,047,000.	1995
22.MacMillan Bloedel	339,000,000.	1995
23.Anglo-Canadian Tel.	334,100,000.	1995
24.H.J. Heinz Co.(Canada)	319,936,000.	1995
25.Cominco	312,587,000.	1995

Source: InfoGlobe's Report on Business Database as of January 10, 1997. For a more complete list of all corporations owing more than $5 million, see Unfair Shares: Corporations and Taxation in Canada, 1997.

LEADING 1994 CORPORATE DONORS
to the FEDERAL LIBERAL PARTY

Corporation and 1994 Donation to the Liberal Party

Corporation	Donation
SNC - Lavelin	$ 81, 414.
Scotia Mcleod	$ 66, 310.
Wood Gundy	$ 65, 897.
Rogers Group	$ 61, 560.
Bombardier Inc.	$ 61, 074.
Richardson Greenshield	$ 55, 432.
John Labatt Ltd.	$ 50, 000.
C.I.B.C.	$ 49, 340.
Bank of Montral	$ 45, 744.
RBC Dominion Securities	$ 44, 825.
Bank of Nova Scotia	$ 44, 512.
Royal Bank of Canada	$ 44, 466.
Imasco	$ 42, 654.
Toronto Dominion Bank	$ 42, 180.
Toronto Dominion Sec'ties	$ 40, 000.
B.C.E. Inc.	$ 39, 636.
Coopers & Lybrand	$ 38, 337.
KPMG Peat/Marwick/Thorne	$ 37, 733.
Power Corp.	$ 37, 379.
Unitel	$ 36, 133.
Ernst & Young	$ 34, 400.
Glaxo Canada Inc.	$ 33, 997.
Nova Corp. of Alberta	$ 33, 664.
Molsons Cos. Ltd.	$ 32, 890.
Imperial Oil	$ 30, 000.
R.J. R. Macdonald Inc.	$ 30, 000.
Canadian Pacific	$ 29, 337.
Spar Aerospace	$ 27, 654.
Dofasco Inc.	$ 25, 016.
National Bank	$ 25, 000.

Source: Figures obtained from the Chief Electoral Officer by CCPA Monitor (April, 1996)

Note: In 1995, financial investment companies continued to be major supporters of the Federal Liberal Party. Leading the 1995 list was Nesbitt Burns with a donation of $88,424 followed by Midland Walwyn at $81,537. Wood Gundy gave $66,777, KPMG Peat Marwick Thorne $66,087, Scotia McLeod $64,777, Richardson Greenshields $63,450, RBC Dominion Securities $62,851, and Toronto Dominion Securities $40,000. Other major corporate donors to the Liberal Party in 1995 included: the Rogers Group of Companies, $69,921; Bombardier Inc., $62,884; Labatt Brewing Co., $59,235; Northern Telecom Ltd., $56,839; SNC-Lavalin Inc., $53,705: Canadian Pacific Ltd., $48,159; and Imasco Ltd., $43,423.

World's Top 100 Economies, 1995

plain text: COUNTRIES
bold/italic: CORPORATIONS

Country/Corporations	GDP/Sales (US $MIL)	Country/Corporations	GDP/Sales (US $MIL)
1.United States	6,648,013	*51.Daimler-Benz*	*72,253*
2.Japan	4,590,971	*52.IBM*	*71,940*
3.Germany	2,045,991	53.Malaysia	70,626
4.France	1,330,381	*54.Matsushita Electric*	*70,454*
5.Italy	1,024,634	*55.General Electric*	*70,028*
6.United Kingdom	1,017,306	56.Singapore	68,949
7.Brazil	554,587	*57.Tomen*	*67,809*
8.Canada	542,954	58.Colombia	67,266
9.China	522,172	*59.Mobil*	*64,767*
10.Spain	482,841	60.Philippines	64,162
11.Mexico	377,115	61.Iran	63,716
12.Russian Federation	376,555	*62.Nissan Motor*	*62,618*
13.Korea, Rep.	376,505	*63.Volkswagen Group*	*61,487*
14.Australia	331,990	*64.Siemens Group*	*60,673*
15.Netherlands	329,768	65.Venezuela	58,257
16.India	293,606	*66.British Petroleum*	*56,992*
17.Argentina	281,992	*67.Bank of Tokyo-Mitsubishi*	*55,243*
18.Switzerland	260,352	*68.Chrysler*	*53,195*
19.Belgium	227,550	*69.Phillip Morris*	*53,089*
20.Austria	196,546	*70.Toshiba*	*53,089*
21.Sweden	196,441	71.Ireland	52,060
22.Mitsubishi	*184,510*	72.Pakistan	52,001
23.Mitsui and Co.	*181,661*	73.Chile	51,957
24.Indonesia	174,640	*74.Nichimen*	*50,882*
25.Itochu	*169,300*	75.New Zealand	50,777
26.General Motors	*168,829*	*76.Tokyo Electric Power*	*50,343*
27.Sumitomo	*167,662*	77.Peru	50,077
28.Marubeni	*161,184*	*78.Kanematsu*	*49,878*
29.Denmark	146,076	*79.Unilever*	*49,638*
30.Thailand	143,209	*80.Nestlé*	*47,767*
31.Ford Motor	*137,137*	*81.Sony*	*47,619*
32.Hong Kong	131,881	*82.Fiat Group*	*46,638*
33.Turkey	131,014	*83.VEBA Group*	*46,278*
34.South Africa	121,888	*84.NEC*	*45,593*
35.Saudi Arabia	117,236	*85.Honda Motor*	*44,090*
36.Toyota Motor	*111,139*	86.UAP-Union des Assurances	43,929
37.Royal Dutch/Shell	*109,853*	*87.Allianz Worldwide*	*43,486*
38.Norway	109,568	88.Egypt	42,923
39.Exxon	*107,893*	89.Algeria	41,941
40.Nissho Iwai	*97,963*	*90.Elf Aquitaine Group*	*41,729*
41.Finland	97,961	91.Hungary	41,374
42.Wal-Mart	*93,627*	*92.Philips Group*	*40,146*
43.Poland	92,580	*93.Fujitsu*	*39,007*
44.Ukraine	91,307	*94.Indust. Bank of Japan*	*38,694*
45.Portugal	87,257	*95.Deutsche Bank Group*	*38,418*
46.Hitachi	*84,233*	*96.Renault Group*	*36,876*
47.Nippon Tel and Tel	*82,002*	*97.Mitsubishi Motors*	*36,674*
48.AT & T	*79,609*	*98.du Pont de Nemours*	*36,508*
49.Israel	77,777	*99.Mitsubishi Electric*	*36,408*
50.Greece	77,721	*100.Hoescht Group*	*36,407*

Source: Calculated by Sarah Anderson and John Cavanagh of the Institute for Policy Studies from data in Forbes magazine and World Bank, World Development Report 1996.
Note: company sales figures are for 1995; country GDP figures are for 1994.

Corporate Rule Treaty

Appendix V

The Multilateral Agreement on Investments seeks to consolidate GLOBAL CORPORATE RULE

[THIS IS AN EXCERPT from a preliminary analysis of the MAI official draft text prepared by the author and published in April 1997 by the Canadian Centre for Policy Alternatives under the title "The Corporate Rule Treaty."]

In January of 1997, a confidential draft text titled *Multilateral Agreement on Investment: Consolidated Texts and Commentary* was circulated among government and corporate officials in the member countries of the Organization for Economic Cooperation and Development (OECD). Behind closed doors, secret consultations and negotiations have been taking place at the OECD headquarters in Paris. The original plan was to have the draft text ready for approval at the OECD ministers' meeting scheduled for May 1997, but OECD officials subsequently decided that at least another four to five months—perhaps as long as eight to ten months—will be needed to complete the negotiations.

If this draft MAI is adopted by the OECD countries, the cornerstones of a new global economic constitution will be cemented in place. Even though the MAI will initially apply only to OECD signatory countries, an accession clause built into the proposed treaty allows non-OECD countries to sign into the pact, provided that certain conditions are met. This gives the United States the tools it needs to ensure that a "high standard" investment treaty is established on a global basis without risking a watered-down version through prolonged negotiations through the World Trade Organization.

The MAI is designed to establish a whole new set of global rules for investment that will grant transnational corporations (TNCs) the unrestricted "right" and "freedom" to buy, sell, and move their operations whenever and wherever they want around the world, unfettered by government intervention or regulation.

It can be argued that this MAI was originally pioneered by NAFTA. Many of the terms and conditions originally laid down in the investment code of NAFTA have been transplanted into the draft MAI. Even some provisions that were rejected in the final negotiations of NAFTA reappear in the OECD investment treaty. **Now a NAFTA-plus investment code is about to be adopted by the 29 countries of the OECD, thereby setting the stage for a world-wide investment treaty in the 21st century.**

This new global constitution, however, is certainly not designed to ensure that the rights and freedoms of the world's people are upheld by democratically elected governments. On the contrary, **it is a charter of rights and freedoms for corporations only—a charter to be guaranteed by national governments in the interests of profitable transnational investment and competition. It is meant to protect and benefit corporations, not citizens.** Indeed, through this new global constitution, the rights of citizens and the powers of governments themselves will be largely superseded by those of the transnational corporations.

It is no mistake that the United States, with strong support from the Canadian Liberal government, chose the OECD as the venue for establishing a "high standard" global investment treaty for the TNCs. *After all, a total of 477 out of the Global Fortune 500 corporations have their home base in the 29 OECD countries. In other words, 95.4% of the largest TNCs in the world today are headquartered in member countries of the OECD.*

In effect, **the MAI amounts to a declaration of global corporate rule.** As such, it is designed to enhance the *political rights*, the *political power*, and the *political security* of the TNCs on a world-wide scale.

The following is an analysis of the MAI in terms of these three dimensions of corporate rule, based on the draft text (dated January 13, 1997, for distribution). This is only a preliminary analysis. A more detailed study of the text by trade experts is required to get an in-depth understanding of the MAI and its implications for different sectors. Nevertheless, what follows provides a glimpse of the big picture. (**Note: italics and bold face added for emphasis only**).

Political Rights

There is nothing new about corporations having political rights. Throughout the 20th century, corporations have acquired a wide range of political rights under international law, as well as corporate law within countries. Indeed, corporations were given rights to "personhood" and "citizenship" in most countries before women and Aboriginal peoples were. Today, a vast body of corporate law and legal doctrine is now in place which serves to recognize and protect the property rights and operations of corporations.

This legal apparatus, in turn, has been reinforced by the new free trade regimes (e.g., the FTA, NAFTA, WTO) which provide constitutional protection for the rights and freedoms of the TNCs. If enacted, the proposed MAI will further consolidate and enhance the political rights of corporations in the following ways:

1. The MAI seeks to codify a special set of rights for corporations as investors. Throughout the official draft text, corporations are seen as investors having a legal status equal to that of the contracting parties which are the nation states of the OECD. The implication here is that TNCs shall be treated as having a legal status with political rights equal to those of nation states. Some delegations go so far as to propose *that investors (i.e., corporations) and the "contracting parties" (i.e., governments) be given the same definition in the MAI* (p. 90, II, 5). Moreover, the provisions calling for "temporary entry and stay of investors and key personnel" investing "a substantial amount of capital" serves to establish corporations as having a **superior** class of citizenship rights (p. 12 - A).

2. The MAI attempts to expand the scope of investor rights of corporations by advancing a much broader definition of investment. By investment, the MAI means "every kind of asset owned or controlled ... by an investor ..." (p. 7). It extends to "an enterprise ... whether or not for profit," to "rights under contracts" and to "intellectual property rights," and to "rights conferred pursuant to law or contract" (e.g., concessions, licences, authorizations, and permits). (p. 8). It even covers "real estate or other property, tangible or intangible ... acquired in the expectation or used for the purpose of economic benefit or other business purposes." (p. 9). In other words, *the investor rights of speculators are also to be enshrined in this treaty.* Moreover, it includes "portfolio investment" (i.e., equity and debt shares and bonds of, and

loans to, enterprises) which is precisely the type of investment that contributed to the Mexican peso crisis.

3. Under the "national treatment" and "most favoured nation" clauses of the MAI, foreign-based corporations or investors are to be accorded special rights and privileges. Not only will governments be required to provide corporations from other countries treatment that is "no less favourable" than that given to companies within their own countries, but that treatment must include "equality of competitive opportunity." (p. 139). Since the standard of "no less favourably" is being applied, countries *may treat foreign-based corporations better than they do domestic companies.* What's more, national governments will be forbidden from imposing performance requirements on the investments of foreign-based corporations (e.g., job content, export quotas, import quotas, technology transfers, local purchasing, etc.). **Even if a national government imposes these performance requirements on domestic companies, it cannot apply them to foreign-based corporations.**

4. In addition to codifying property rights ranging from the rights of petroleum corporations to hydro-carbon resources (p. 95, sec. 35), to all forms of intellectual property rights (e.g., patents, copyrights, industrial design, trade secrets, etc.), the MAI emphasizes the right to the free flow of capital. "All delegations agreed," the text says, "that the free transfers of returns was a critical element of the protection of the investors." (p. 117). No government, therefore, would be allowed to impose restrictions on the return of profits made on production in the host country to the parent corporation. It is also agreed that the MAI "should provide *an absolute guarantee that an investor will be compensated for an expropriated investment.*" (p. 122). This could include investments that consist of intellectual property rights (p. 114). *Even non-conforming tax measures on corporations may be designated as "creeping expropriation"* **for which they could demand compensation.**

5. These investor rights of corporations would be applied in all political jurisdictions by all levels of government in those countries that are party to the MAI. While the precise details of how the MAI is to apply to sub-national levels of government are not spelled out, it is clear throughout the text that important aspects of *the investment rules are to be followed by all levels of government (i.e., provincial and municipal, as well as federal governments).* Moreover, the MAI grants to corporations the right to

sue governments or states and provides *a binding investor-state dispute settlement mechanism* (pp. 53-64) for these purposes (see below). While governments can also challenge other governments under the state-to-state dispute settlement procedure (pp. 44-52), *governments are not granted reciprocal rights to sue corporations for damages on behalf of their people*. Hence, the political rights of corporations are greatly enhanced by the inclusion of this investor-state dispute mechanism.

In effect, the draft MAI points to *a massive transfer of "rights" from citizens to investors* in the new global economy. At a time when peoples all over the world feel that their fundamental democratic rights as citizens (e.g., the Universal Declaration of Human Rights) and the ecological rights of the planet (e.g., the Earth Charter from the Rio Summit on the Environment) are not protected by governments, **the rights and freedoms of transnational corporations are being guaranteed through trade and investment treaties (like the MAI) that have become the new global economic constitutions.** This transfer of rights, in turn, is reinforced by radical shifts in the balance of power between governments and corporations.

Political Power

Once again, there is nothing new about the fact that transnational corporations wield tremendous political power when it comes to determining the economic, social and environmental policies of nation states. Armed with their own corporate think tanks and machinery for political lobbying and advertising, corporations can virtually call the shots when it comes to key policy issues. The formation of big business coalitions (e.g., the Business Round Table in the U.S. and the Business Council on National Issues here in Canada) has resulted in a much more systemic and coordinated approach to influencing political decisions in the capitals of nation states around the world.

Through these and related measures, such as privatization and deregulation, the balance of power between the public and private sectors has been drastically altered, with corporations increasingly gaining the upper hand over governments. The MAI includes a number of measures which serve to strengthen the political power of corporations:

1. Although the MAI does not require governments to privatize state-owned enterprises, it will certainly lay down new constraints

on the conditions imposed when the ownership and control of public assets are privatized. The agreement will require, for example, that the *"national treatment" and "most favoured nation" clauses apply to the initial stages of privatization, as well as to subsequent stages*. This means in effect that, when a government decides to privatize a public enterprise, it must allow foreign-owned corporations as well as domestic companies to bid on the assets. While the commentary to the text indicates that there is still some dispute, the MAI could prevent governments from utilizing "special share arrangements" to encourage local workers and communities to buy the company or to distribute shares to the general public. It is also understood that these new obligations will apply to provincial and municipal governments, as well as the federal government.

2. At the same time, the MAI will impose constraints on governments in the operation of their state enterprises and monopolies. In the future, these public enterprises and monopolies will have to adhere to "national treatment" provisions in their regulatory functions and market activities. All purchases and sales of goods and services will have to be "non-discriminatory." Cross-subsidization and "anti-competitive" practices will be prohibited (p. 27). As in the case of NAFTA, state enterprises and monopolies will also be required to act "solely in accordance with commercial considerations." (p. 27). Hydro power and water utilities, for example, that provide discounted services to rural communities could be prevented from doing so under these provisions. The draft MAI even includes a proposal *that even state monopolies based on "national standards" be prohibited*. (p. 26, notes). Once again, these constraints and obligations are expected to be applied to state enterprises and monopolies in provincial and municipal jurisdictions, as well as those of national governments.

3. Under the MAI, all foreign-based corporations are to be assured of "fair and equitable treatment and full and constant security." "In no case" shall foreign investors be treated "less favourably than required by international law." Obviously, the rules on expropriation identified above apply here. *No government will be allowed, by its regulatory measures, to "impair ... the operation, management, maintenance, use, enjoyment or disposal of investments in its territory" by corporations based in another country*. (p. 40). The role of governments, in other words, is not only to ensure that the properties of foreign-based corporations

are protected, but also to provide a safe haven for profitable transnational investment and competition. All of this serves to entrench not only the economic but the political power base of foreign-owned corporations, in terms of the pressure they can exert on their host governments.

4. Governments would also be obligated to follow certain rules with respect to "investment incentives." This involves direct financial contributions such as grants, loans, equity infusions, and loan guarantees, as well as tax credits and foregone revenue. (p. 33). While there are differing views on how explicit this should be in the text, it has been agreed that the "national treatment" and "most favoured nation" requirements would be applied to all these "investment incentives." A more rigorous set of rules regarding the application of government investment incentives may be developed after further negotiations under the MAI. (p. 132). *The most dramatic development here is the indication that tax measures may be included. (p. 132-3), including even payroll taxes such as social security provisions.* This means that governments would be obligated under the MAI to follow the national treatment rules in applying tax measures and tax credits to all foreign-based corporations.

5. Perhaps the most powerful new weapon which the MAI gives the TNCs is the mechanism for investor-state dispute settlements. Unlike NAFTA, which grants corporations a much more limited scope for litigation, this mechanism provides corporations with the power to directly sue governments *over any breach of MAI provisions "which causes [or is likely to cause] loss of damage to the investor or his investment."* (p. 53). It is also understood that *even "a lost opportunity to profit from a planned investment would be a type of loss sufficient to give an investor standing to bring an establishment dispute" under this section.* (p. 53 footnote). If challenged by a corporation, governments are obligated ("unconditional consent") to go before the tribunal. The tribunal members are to make their judgments based not on the laws of the host country, but on the rules of the investment treaty itself (i.e., the MAI). (p. 60). All awards (which may provide for "compensatory monetary damages," restitution, or "any other form of relief") are "binding" and shall be enforced "as if it were a final judgment of its courts." (p. 63). According to a footnote, this is designed to ensure that no government denies enforcement of an award based on the claim that it would be "contrary to its public policy."

In these clauses, the MAI further expands the power of transnational corporations over that of nation states and national governments. This does not mean that national governments are to be rendered powerless, but rather that, in the new global economy, their power is to be used mainly to provide a favourable climate for profitable investment and competition. **Political power is to be harnessed to serve the "rights" of investors, not the rights of citizens.** The MAI will reinforce this selective use of government power.

Political Security

One of the essential conditions for transnational corporations in developing their investment strategies is the assurance of political stability and security. Measures must be taken to provide favourable conditions and a safe haven for profitable transnational investment and competition. From the standpoint of the TNCs, it is the responsibility of the state to provide this kind of political security if corporations are going to be free to exercise their political rights and power in the new system of corporate rule.

For these reasons, it is important for a global investment treaty like the MAI to include built-in measures designed to provide political security for the investments of transnational corporations. While some of the components identified above (e.g., the *Political Power* section, item 3) serve this function, the MAI contains other features which perform this task as well. The following are some examples:

1. The MAI includes a set of *"rollback clauses"* designed to ensure that transnational corporations will have ongoing favourable conditions for investment. *Any regulatory measures of nation states which do not conform with the principles and conditions of the MAI are to be reduced and eventually eliminated.* The rollback provisions are designed to facilitate this process of liberalization. The contracting governments would agree to liberalize certain areas of their regulatory regimes when the MAI comes into force. Although each participating country has the right to exempt certain laws, policies and programs from the Agreement, the MAI will include restricted use of these exemptions to ensure that they do not apply to all the obligations under the MAI (p. 122), or that they are not used to avoid the main obligations of the MAI (p. 65). Unlike other international agreements, failure by a contracting government to list any reserva-

tions in the annex of the Agreement would result in all of that
country's laws being subject to the MAI (p. 126). It is likely that
only certain types of reservations will be acceptable and that contracting governments may be expected to set "sunset" dates for
the termination of "non-conforming" laws, policies or programs.
2. These "rollback" provisions, in turn, are reinforced by what is
known as the *"standstill"* measures in the Agreement. Under the
"standstill" clauses, the contracting government would agree not
to introduce any new non-conforming laws, policies or programs
in the future. What this means, in effect, is that, if any future
government wanted to take public ownership and control over a
sector of the economy that had been previously privatized or re-
introduce regulations that had been scrapped in the past, it would
be forbidden to do so under the MAI. And *when the "standstill"
clauses are combined with the "rollback" clauses in the Agreement, they produce a "ratchet effect."* (p. 127). "Any new liberalization measures," the draft Agreement states, "would be
'locked in' so they could not be rescinded or nullified over time."
(p. 127). Through these measures, the MAI is designed to facilitate the continuous expansion of investor rights for corporations.
3. In addition to the obligations of governments to protect the
future investments of corporations (see *Political Power* section
above, item 3), the MAI could include provisions designed to
protect **existing** investments. It is proposed that investments made
before the MAI is signed will be protected under the Agreement.
Disputes arising before the Agreement comes into force, however, may not be allowed access to the MAI's dispute settlement
mechanism. Nevertheless, *transnational corporations can use the
MAI to enforce investor rights that derive from other investment
agreements,* including *"a contract granting rights with respect
to natural resources or other assets or economic activities controlled by the national authority."* In effect, the MAI could be
used to enforce contracts that have no binding arbitration channels in the first place. What's more, the MAI *secures the rights
and powers of absentee landlords* by allowing, for example, a
British corporation to lay a claim in Canada on behalf of its Canadian subsidiary. (p. 86).
4. **The draft of the MAI also contains clauses protecting corporations from being targeted by governments for operations
in other countries where they are seen to be violating labour,
environmental and human rights standards.** Application of the
"most favoured nation" clauses would prevent any government

from distinguishing between TNCs based on these standards. Similarly, existing bans, sanctions or embargoes that restrict investment in certain countries because of repressive human rights or labour practices could be challenged as a violation of the MAI rules and therefore revoked. For example, the U.S. and Canadian restrictions on investment in South Africa, which were instrumental in helping to dismantle apartheid, would be prohibited under the MAI rules if these countries were signatories to the Agreement. *The sections dealing with "secondary investment boycotts" and "conflicting requirements" are designed to secure the rights and freedoms of corporations to operate in other countries, regardless of their labour, environmental and human rights records,* unless there is a direct violation of international law.

5. Perhaps the most extraordinary measure proposed in the MAI draft to ensure political security for investors is the clause dealing with "withdrawal." Contracting governments will not be able to withdraw from the MAI until five years after it has come into force. On top of that, it is proposed that the MAI rules continue to cover existing investments in that country for an additional 15 years. (p. 71). In other words, once a country has ratified the Agreement, it is virtually locked-in for a 20-year period. *Under this provision, all corporations based in the contracting countries will have an ironclad guarantee that the MAI's investment rules will remain in force for at least 20 years.* Moreover, the accession clause will outline the terms and conditions for expanding the MAI to include non-OECD countries. One of the key terms, of course, will be unconditional acceptance of the investment rules ratified by the original OECD contracting governments. Any amendments to the MAI would have to be ratified by all the parties.

*   *   *

Viewed in terms of these three basic dimensions—political rights, political power, and political security—the MAI would consolidate and entrench the system of **corporate rule** that is emerging in the new global economy. If the MAI is ratified by the OECD countries, it will greatly strengthen the power of the transnational corporations, while correspondingly weakening the power of nation states. Increasingly, the role of democratically elected governments will be confined to developing and implementing economic, social and environmental policies that serve the interests of transnational corporations, rather than the broader interests of their own citizens.

So what does this mean for Canada? It is true that we have already been burdened with the equivalent of many of the MAI provisions under the FTA and NAFTA. But the MAI will include several additional measures that will tighten the stranglehold corporations already have gained over public policy-making in this country. What's more, the new MAI regime will establish investment rules favouring corporations not only in the U.S. and Mexico, but in 26 other OECD countries as well. And this is only the beginning. **The MAI is meant to set the stage for the establishment of a world-wide investment treaty under the WTO.**

There has been talk in Washington circles that the U.S. might consider the addition of side-bar aggreements to the MAI on labour and the environment. But the main big business lobby coalition behind the MAI, the U.S. Council for International Business, has issued a stern warning to the Clinton Administration against such a move.

"The MAI is an agreement by governments to protect international investors and their investments and to liberalize investment regimes," said the USCIB President in a letter to senior U.S. officials on March 21, 1997. **"We will oppose any and all measures to create or even imply binding obligations for governments or business related to environment or labor."**

For Canadians, the real danger is that the MAI, like the WTO, will be swept under the rug and ratified without anyone being aware of its harmful implications and consequences. If any semblance of democracy is to be salvaged in Canada, concerted steps must be taken to challenge this latest and most lethal surrender to corporate rule.

Canadian Flash-Points

There are at least a dozen major sets of public policy issues that will be directly affected by the MAI in Canada. While it is not possible to cover them all, five policy "flash-points: can be briefly examined here.*

---

*   **Note:** Other policy issues directly affected include: taxation policies, agriculture, public services, regional development, native lands, and human rights (re the operations of Canadian corporations overseas).

1. JOB CREATION

The MAI will further tie the hands of existing and future governments in Ottawa and the provinces when it comes to developing a comprehensive job creation strategy:

• Forbidden to apply performance requirements on the operations of foreign-based corporations, governments are prohibited from levering employment and other economic benefits from investors.

• The commentary states that "the MAI should prevent the application of national employment quotas or labour market (economic needs) tests." (p. 105)

• Even if the Bank Act were to be amended to ensure that the big five national banks invest more in loans for local economic development, this could be struck down under the MAI.

• What remains of Ottawa's policy tools for redirecting investment to impoverished regions will likely be eliminated (p. 34).

• The technology transfer restrictions in the MAI place severe limitations on Ottawa's ability to ensure adequate R&D is done to advance Canada's economic development. While we have seen some of these restrictions before through NAFTA, the expansion of these investment rules to include the other industrialized countries will multiply the constraints on Ottawa's future options.

2. CULTURAL PROTECTION

The MAI could have more serious consequences for the protection of Canadian culture than NAFTA, the WTO, or any other instrument of globalization seen so far.

• The intellectual property rights provisions (e.g., copyright laws) are bound to have implications for the cultural sector (even though we have this restriction with NAFTA, we are talking here about all the industrialized countries) (p. 94-5).

• Under MAI, Ottawa would not be able to use tax credits to promote Canadian cultural industries (p. 33, 1.1).

• France (perhaps supported by Canada) has proposed that "literary and artistic works" be exempted from the MAI obligations (which is not likely to be acceptable to the U.S.)

• If there is no cultural exemption, then Canadian "educational products" cannot be protected. (p. 16).

• Under the "rollback" provisions, Canada may attempt to reserve laws that restrict foreign investment in Canadian magazines but may be required to lay out a time table for allowing more foreign ownership, if not removing its restrictions altogether. (re. ratchet effect).

3. PUBLIC HEALTH CARE

Under the MAI, the pressures to turn Canada's $72 billion public health care program into a two-tier system will intensify.

• The MAI could circumvent any of the very limited ("fig-leaf") reservations or exemptions for public health care that were written into the NAFTA and the GATT (the only really allowable exemption under the MAI is for "national security" purposes).

• The MAI clauses dealing with restrictions imposed on governments regarding "privatization rights" and "monopoly/ state enterprises" could have major implications in setting the stage for a two-tiered health care system in this country

• The fact that payroll taxes and social security contributions are to be included in the definition of taxation under the MAI (p. 77), in terms of investment rules in the future, could also have serious implications for health care.

4. ENVIRONMENTAL SAFEGUARDS

The current process of environmental deregulation and the weakening of environmental standards and protection that is taking place in this country will very likely accelerate under the MAI investment rules.

• The NAFTA provisions insisting that governments not apply environmental measures in an arbitrary or unjustifiable manner and not constitute a disguised restriction on trade and investment, will be expanded to include all the OECD countries under the MAI.

• Under the investment products provisions, corporate challenges to the environmental regulation of production will likely accelerate, as witnessed by the case brought by the Ethyl Corp. Canada against Ottawa over the banning of MMT (manganese fuel additive).

• The intellectual property rights provisions giving patents full protection are likely to conflict with the provisions of the bio-diversity convention.

• Under the MAI, acquiring land for preservation and conservation is not protected, whereas a logging corporation that buys up a rain-forest for commercial purposes is protected.

• Sections dealing with rights from concessions, licences, and permits have serious implications for governments which attempt to regulate corporations developing natural resources in their jurisdictions.

5. CONSTITUTIONAL POLITICS

The investment rules being laid down under the MAI have serious implications for both the sovereignist and federalist positions in the current constitutional debate, as well as First Nations and the provinces themselves.

• Sovereignists should be wary of the ways in which the MAI (which, by the way, the current Quebec government has no role to play in negotiating) will tie the hands of any future national government in developing policy for the transition towards an independent Québec.

• Federalists should be equally wary that virtually all the provisions being negotiated under the MAI will be applicable to subnational governments (which, in turn, have not been party to the negotiations that have been taking place).

• First Nations should also beware that their rights to self-government and control of their lands and resources could be threatened by corporations more than by governments under the MAI.

Finally, it should be emphasized that there are many more public policies and programs in Canada that are bound to be threatened (directly or indirectly) by the expansion of corporate rights, powers and protections under the MAI.

These include: corporate taxation; agricultural marketing boards; other public services; regional development programs; Aboriginal rights; foreign economic control; and human rights, especially in terms of being able to regulate the overseas operations of Canadian corporations. ❧

NOTES

NOTES

NOTES

NOTES

NOTES

NOTES

NOTES

NOTES

NOTES

NOTES

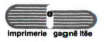

imprimerie gagné ltée